Un été tout en saveurs

Conception graphique : Bruno Paradis
Photos de la couverture : Shutterstock
Crédits photos :
Istockphoto : 9, 11, 13, 18, 21, 24, 40, 55, 65, 69, 80
Shutterstock : 15, 16, 20, 33, 34, 37, 41, 45, 49, 54, 59, 81, 83, 84, 85, 86, 94,
103, 111, 112, 114, 136, 141, 142, 143
Mise en pages : Marie Blanchard
Révision : Natacha Auclair
Correction d'épreuves : François Roberge

Imprimé au Canada

ISBN : 978-2-89666-005-6

Dépôt légal – Bibliothèque et Archives nationales du Québec, 2010

Les Éditions Caractère remercient le gouvernement du Québec – Programme de crédit
d'impôt pour l'édition de livres – Gestion SODEC
Les Éditions Caractère reconnaissent l'aide financière du gouvernement du Canada par
l'entremise du Fonds du livre du Canada pour nos activités d'édition.

# Un été tout en saveurs

## Vinaigrettes, trempettes et marinades

Anik Tia Tiong Fat

QUÉBEC
LOISIRS
Le club

# Table des matières

# Introduction

Au cœur de l'été, les étals des marchés sont garnis de légumes variés et colorés. De quoi inspirer une cuisine simple et savoureuse qui met à l'honneur les salades, les trempettes et les vinaigrettes, bref une cuisine conviviale et festive.

Une fois la belle saison passée, il est possible de prolonger ces précieux moments à l'intérieur; les salades, les trempettes et les marinades présentées ici se prêtant à toutes les saisons et à toutes les occasions. Elles concilient agréablement notre mode de vie et notre besoin de bien manger en toute convivialité sans pour autant passer des heures en cuisine lors de réunions entre amis ou en famille.

Les trempettes mettront les convives en appétit, tandis que les salades arrosées de leur vinaigrette accompagneront merveilleusement les viandes ou les poissons grillés préalablement marinés. Voilà de quoi manger équilibré et vitaminé!

Alors, cet été, osez!

# Les vinaigrettes

## :: Les huiles ::

Chaque huile a ses caractéristiques gustatives et des usages bien déterminés. Les huiles sont des liquides gras et visqueux qui ont la propriété de ne pas se mélanger à l'eau. Celles considérées dans cet ouvrage sont toutes comestibles et d'origine végétale. Elles sont extraites d'un fruit dont elles portent le nom. Chaque huile se caractérise par sa saveur et son caractère qui éveillent nos organes sensoriels. Tout comme pour le vin, pour en connaître davantage sur les différentes huiles, il ne faut pas hésiter à les goûter ; vous pourrez ainsi vous délecter de chaque parfum libéré, admirer leur couleur, percevoir leur viscosité et apprécier leur arôme.

### Huile d'argan

Cette huile produite par les femmes marocaines est peu connue et peu utilisée ici. En effet, entièrement faite à la main, sa production est limitée et son prix, élevé. De cette huile brun-roux au parfum très fort, quelques gouttes suffisent pour agrémenter une préparation. Elle se marie bien aux recettes sucrées et aux plats typiquement marocains (agneau, légumes, etc.). À la page 54, la vinaigrette inspirée d'une crème berbère, l'*amlou*, saura convaincre les plus hésitants.

## Huile de colza ou de canola

Grâce à sa composition d'acides gras insaturés, cette huile est équilibrée sur le plan nutritionnel. Meilleure lorsqu'elle est pressée à froid, elle possède des qualités diététiques intéressantes du fait de sa teneur en vitamine E et en oméga-3. Elle convient à tous les usages, mais dégage une odeur désagréable à très haute température. Il est donc préférable d'en réserver l'usage aux assaisonnements.

## Huile de noisette

Comme les amandes et les noix, les noisettes doivent tout d'abord être chauffées pour qu'on puisse en extraire l'huile. Douce et fruitée, cette huile se consomme crue, mais elle peut néanmoins remplacer le beurre dans les pâtisseries ou les biscuits sablés.

## Huile de noix

Délicate, elle se conserve au réfrigérateur. Son goût très prononcé ne demande qu'une petite cuillère à thé pour une vinaigrette qui accompagne volontiers une salade verte garnie de cerneaux de noix. Elle s'utilise de préférence crue, car ses qualités nutritives se dégradent avec la chaleur. Tout comme l'huile de noisette, elle peut cependant être ajoutée à des plats cuits au four.

## Huile d'olive

Nul n'ignore les bienfaits de l'huile d'olive. Il en existe de nombreuses, car le lieu de production et les procédés de fabrication de l'huile d'olive font que toutes les huiles ne se valent pas. Elles sont d'ailleurs réglementées par des normes commerciales internationales.

Une huile d'olive se conserve au maximum un an mais, au bout de huit mois, elle commence à pâlir et à perdre ses arômes. Il est d'ailleurs préférable de la garder à l'obscurité.

L'huile d'olive vierge résulte d'une première pression à froid d'olives fraîches. Elle n'est ni traitée ni raffinée. Un peu acide, elle est d'un beau doré tirant sur le vert.

L'huile d'olive extra vierge est l'huile la plus goûteuse et la plus fine. Elle est aussi extraite d'olives écrasées à froid qualifiées de première pression, mais se différencie de la précédente par son caractère organoleptique exceptionnel et irréprochable : cette huile peut être fruitée, douce, piquante, amère ou poivrée.

Certaines huiles peuvent résulter de plusieurs pressions, qui cependant détériorent ses arômes et lui donnent une qualité nutritive moindre.

## Huile de pépins de raisin

Ses vertus méritent d'être connues et son utilisation de devenir plus fréquente. En effet, cette huile légère n'est pas dépourvue de qualités : elle se prête bien à la cuisson et aux hautes températures, elle donne aux fritures croquant et légèreté, mais elle est aussi résistante au froid, donc parfaite pour conserver les légumes marinés (poivrons, artichauts, tomates, haricots, etc.). Ajoutée à l'huile d'olive, elle relève très agréablement une mayonnaise. En marinade, elle rehausse la saveur de la viande tout en la préservant. Enfin, son goût neutre lui donne une place de choix dans la création d'huiles aromatisées maison. Le seul hic est qu'elle s'oxyde facilement : la conserver au réfrigérateur la fera durer plus longtemps. Elle se conserve d'autant mieux au réfrigérateur qu'au froid, elle reste à l'état liquide.

## Huile de sésame

Considérée comme l'huile la plus ancienne, elle était utilisée en pharmacopée (onguent et médicament) et en cuisine par les Assyriens au VIe siècle av. J.-C. Elle est encore très utilisée dans la cuisine asiatique, et son goût prononcé de noisette grillée rehausse tous les plats. Un filet suffit ! Elle sert aussi d'huile de friture pour les tempuras, ces fameux beignets de légumes japonais.

# :: Les huiles aromatisées* ::

## Huile parfumée aux épices

| | | |
|---|---|---|
| 2 | Clous de girofle | 2 |
| 1 | Anis étoilé | 1 |
| 4 | Baies de genièvre | 4 |
| 3 | Cardamome verte | 3 |
| 1/4 c. à thé | Baies roses | 5 ml |
| | Poivre | |
| 1/2 tasse | Huile d'olive | 125 ml |

Broyer toutes les épices au moulin ou à l'aide d'un pilon. Les mettre dans un petit bocal en verre. Verser l'huile par-dessus et fermer. Pendant au moins une journée, placer le bocal dans un placard et le remuer de temps en temps.

---

\* Mise en garde : « Prenez des précautions en ce qui a trait aux aliments maison conservés dans l'huile (p.ex. les légumes, les herbes et les épices). Si ces produits ont été préparés avec des ingrédients frais, ils devraient être gardés au réfrigérateur et jetés après dix jours. » (Selon l'Agence canadienne d'inspection des aliments.) Pour en savoir plus : http://www.inspection.gc.ca/francais/fssa/concen/cause/botulismf.shtml

# Huile au persil

| | | |
|---|---|---|
| 4 branches | Persil | 4 branches |
| 2 | Gousses d'ail écrasées | 2 |
| 1 c. à soupe | Parmesan râpé | 15 ml |
| 1 tasse | Huile d'olive | 250 ml |
| | Sel, poivre | |

Fouetter tous les ingrédients. Saler et poivrer. Se conserve quatre semaines au réfrigérateur dans un bocal en verre bien fermé. L'huile d'olive se fige au froid ; ramenée à la température ambiante, elle retrouvera sa fluidité.

# Huile au poireau

| | | |
|---|---|---|
| 1 | Petit poireau | 1 |
| 1/2 tasse | Huile d'olive | 125 ml |
| | Sel, poivre | |

Blanchir le poireau préalablement coupé en rondelles dans de l'eau bouillante salée. Égoutter et sécher. Dans un mélangeur, faire une purée avec le poireau refroidi et l'huile d'olive. Saler et poivrer. Se garde trois à quatre mois au réfrigérateur dans un bocal en verre.

**Suggestion** ))) Utiliser pour une vinaigrette destinée à une salade de tomates.

## Huile au citron

| 1 | Citron non traité | 1 |
|---|---|---|
| 1/2 tasse | Huile d'olive | 125 ml |
| 2 | Petits piments | 2 |
| 2 | Gousses d'ail | 2 |
| 1 branche | Thym frais | 1 branche |

Découper le zeste du citron en lamelles et les blanchir à l'eau bouillante. Sécher. Une fois sèches, les placer dans un bocal en verre et ajouter les piments, le thym et les gousses d'ail pelées et coupées en deux. Verser l'huile d'olive. Placer le bocal au réfrigérateur quelques heures avant de l'utiliser.

**Suggestion** ))) Cette huile est toujours utile pour confectionner une bonne vinaigrette citronnée.

## Huile à l'estragon

| 1/2 tasse | Huile d'olive | 125 ml |
|---|---|---|
| 5 | Petits piments | 5 |
| 1 | Branche d'estragon frais | 1 |
| 1 | Clou de girofle | 1 |

Laver et hacher finement les piments. Verser l'huile dans un bocal en verre et y mettre les piments, l'estragon et le clou de girofle. Placer au réfrigérateur durant plusieurs mois. Une fois bien parfumée, filtrer l'huile et la conserver au frais.

**Suggestion** ))) À utiliser pour aromatiser des crudités, du poisson ou une sauce tomate.

# :: Les vinaigres ::

Depuis la nuit des temps, le « vin aigre » est un condiment utilisé en cuisine. Il est le résultat de l'oxydation du vin ou d'un autre alcool, par fermentation de l'alcool qui se transforme en acide acétique.

Essentiel dans la préparation des moutardes, de sauces froides ou de vinaigrettes, le vinaigre, parfois remplacé par du jus de citron, possède aussi un rôle important dans l'élaboration des sauces cuites. Il est indispensable pour les macérations, les marinades et les conserves.

## Les vinaigres aromatisés

Un vinaigre peut être aromatisé aux fruits, aux herbes ou aux épices. Pour cela, faire macérer le fruit (framboises, bleuets, mélange de petits fruits, zeste d'agrumes, etc.), la plante (thym, basilic, romarin, persil, origan, etc.) ou les épices (anis, cumin, coriandre, céleri, etc.) choisis, blanchis rapidement dans l'eau bouillante (sauf les épices) et séchés, dans du vinaigre de vin blanc. Laisser macérer un mois avant toute utilisation, en secouant la bouteille de temps à autre.

Ces vinaigres aromatisés agrémentent merveilleusement les salades ou les marinades.

### Vinaigre de cidre

Pour avoir un vinaigre de qualité, on recherche un produit préparé à partir de cidre brut et affiné en fût de bois. Ce vinaigre à la fine saveur de pomme est utilisé pour conserver les fruits et assaisonne bien une salade verte à laquelle ont été ajoutées des pommes ou des poires.

### Vinaigre d'érable

Pour obtenir ce vinaigre issu d'une double fermentation de sirop d'érable, il faut d'abord élaborer un vin d'érable qui sera ensuite transformé en vinaigre. Le goût de ce vinaigre ambré sera apprécié des becs sucrés !

### Vinaigre balsamique

Obtenu à partir du moût de raisin (le résidu du pressage), le vinaigre balsamique de Modène est le résultat le plus célèbre de ce procédé. Affinés durant de nombreuses années, les vinaigres de qualité peuvent atteindre des coûts exorbitants. Ceux qui sont de moindre qualité ont été élaborés dans de grands fûts et vieillis moins longtemps. Souvent, on y ajoute aussi du caramel et des ingrédients censés imiter l'authentique goût de ce vinaigre réputé, mais personne n'est dupe !

### Vinaigre de riz

Ce vinaigre asiatique est peu acide, et le plus doux vient de la Thaïlande. Préparé à partir d'alcool de riz, il est piquant et légèrement sucré. Il entre dans la préparation du riz à sushis et est excellent pour confectionner les salades aux saveurs d'Asie.

### Vinaigre de vin

Rouges, rosés ou blancs, tous les vins peuvent donner du vinaigre. Produit à partir d'un vin réputé, il pourra lui aussi bénéficier de l'appellation d'origine : vinaigre de champagne, de bordeaux, de banyuls, de xérès, etc. Choisir un bon vinaigre déterminera la saveur de la vinaigrette ou de la marinade. Le choisir rouge ou rosé donnera un goût plus affiné tout en mettant de la couleur. Pour une sauce au yogourt, préférer le vinaigre de vin blanc. Ce dernier est aussi idéal pour les salades croquantes et les marinades de viande et de poisson, ainsi que pour préparer des vinaigres aromatisés.

## :: Les fines herbes ::

Ce sont des herbes aromatiques utilisées fraîches, ciselées ou hachées : persil, cerfeuil, estragon, ciboulette, etc. Elles parfument finement les sauces, la viande ou les légumes cuisinés, aromatisent un fromage frais ou une simple omelette.

## Basilic

Il en existe de nombreuses variétés. Pour conserver un bouquet frais, le plonger dans un grand verre d'eau et le mettre au frais. Pour en faire ressortir les arômes, le déchirer avec les doigts et l'incorporer en dernier aux plats. L'erreur à ne pas commettre : ne pas l'ajouter en présence de carottes, qui neutralisent sa saveur.

## Cerfeuil

Utilisé comme le persil, il a cependant un goût plus prononcé et une saveur légèrement anisée. Il est préférable de le parsemer au dernier moment sur un plat, car il est fragile : il ne supporte guère la cuisson et s'abîme rapidement lorsqu'il est en contact avec de l'huile ou du citron. Les meilleures associations sont à faire avec le poisson, les fruits de mer, les œufs et sur les salades.

## Ciboulette

De la même famille que l'oignon, elle relève un fromage frais et décore merveilleusement, tout en donnant un goût très subtil aux salades ou aux plats chauds.

## Coriandre

Sa forte odeur en fait l'herbe préférée de la cuisine orientale. Elle parfume agréablement tous les plats. Ne pas hésiter à en parsemer un peu partout, en fin de cuisson.

## Estragon

Son goût anisé parfume à merveille la volaille et le poisson blanc. Le placer dans une bouteille de vinaigre de vin pour accommoder et parfumer vinaigrettes et marinades.

## Persil

Pour faire le plein de vitamine C, le croquer cru ou le parsemer sur les salades vertes ou de légumes. Il peut être plat ou frisé, mais préférer le premier pour son arôme et n'utiliser le dernier que pour décorer.

## Romarin

Indispensable pour le barbecue, le parsemer directement sur la viande ou dans les braises pour qu'il se fasse plus discret.

## Sarriette

Elle accompagne souvent les légumineuses, car elle a la propriété de favoriser la digestion. Si vous n'avez plus de poivre, elle prendra tout simplement sa place.

## Sauge

Une fois séchées, les feuilles de sauge s'émiettent pour agrémenter la viande de porc.

## Thym

L'arôme du thym se marie à tous les plats, de viande comme de légumes. Il existe de nombreuses variétés. Ne pas hésiter à utiliser ses petites fleurs pour cuisiner.

## Herbes de Provence

Plantes aromatiques (basilic, laurier, romarin, sarriette et thym) hachées, séchées et mélangées. Idéales pour parfumer les grillades.

# :: Les moutardes ::

La moutarde est une plante originaire du bassin méditerranéen. Le broyage des graines noires, brunes ou blanches donne un condiment jaune plus ou moins piquant. On utilisait déjà ces graines dans la Grèce et la Rome antiques pour épicer les viandes et les poissons. La moutarde existe en nombreuses variétés (aromatisées à l'estragon, aux olives, aux champignons, etc.) qui entrent dans la composition de sauces chaudes ou froides.

## Moutarde de Dijon

Cette moutarde française, connue pour être piquante et forte, est utilisée comme condiment dans la préparation des vinaigrettes, des sauces et des marinades, ou telle quelle, pour accompagner les viandes.

## Moutarde à l'ancienne

Comparable à la moutarde de Dijon, mais de saveur plus douce, elle est préparée à partir de graines brunes de moutarde, concassées ou entières, ce qui lui donne sa texture granuleuse. Son utilisation est similaire à celle de la moutarde de Dijon. La plus répandue est la moutarde de Meaux, connu pour son pot en grès scellé de cire rouge.

## Moutarde jaune

Élaborée à partir de graines blanches de moutarde et de curcuma (ce qui lui donne cette couleur si jaune), cette moutarde est très douce. Elle accompagne les hotdogs ou les sandwiches.

### Moutarde violette au moût de raisin

Élaborée à partir de graines noires de moutarde et de moût de raisin, la moutarde violette de Brive donne de la couleur aux vinaigrettes et aux mayonnaises et accompagne volontiers les viandes froides ou les poissons.

### Moutarde en poudre

Il s'agit de graines de moutarde broyées. Utilisée pour parfumer les cornichons ou les oignons marinés, elle peut aussi être directement ajoutée dans les marinades, les trempettes ou les vinaigrettes.

Les vinaigrettes donnent plus de relief à la saveur des aliments. Qu'elle soit simplement faite d'huile et de vinaigre ou qu'elle soit plus élaborée, une vinaigrette demande que les ingrédients de base soient de qualité et que les dosages des éléments qui la composent soient proportionnés.

Préparer une vinaigrette équilibrée n'a rien de sorcier, mais comprendre cet accord permet de se diriger vers un mélange qui agrémentera délicatement les salades.

La vinaigrette est une sauce froide émulsionnée et instable, car élaborée à partir d'huile ou de crème (corps gras) et de vinaigre ou de citron (acide) qui ont tendance à se séparer. Néanmoins, elle pourra être stabilisée par un émulsifiant, comme un jaune d'œuf dans une mayonnaise, ou un liant, comme la moutarde pour les vinaigrettes.

---

\* Toutes les recettes proposées dans cet ouvrage sont pour quatre personnes.

# Vinaigrette traditionnelle

| 1 c. à soupe | Vinaigre de vin rouge | 15 ml |
|---|---|---|
| 4 c. à soupe | Huile d'olive | 60 ml |
| | Sel, poivre | |

Mélanger le vinaigre, le sel et le poivre du moulin. Une fois le sel dissous, ajouter l'huile et fouetter.

Ne verser la vinaigrette sur la salade qu'à la dernière minute, juste avant de la servir.

**Suggestion**

))) Cette vinaigrette toute simple, composée seulement de vinaigre, d'huile, de sel et de poivre, requiert de préférence un vinaigre de vin vieilli, de l'huile d'olive extra vierge, du sel fin et du poivre du moulin. Les variations sont bien sûr permises. Pourquoi ne pas utiliser du vinaigre de xérès, de vin blanc, de vin rosé ou même de champagne ! Quant aux huiles, il ne faut pas hésiter à tirer parti de la si délicate huile de noix ou encore de l'huile de noisette vierge pressée à froid.

))) Cette vinaigrette de base peut accompagner toutes sortes de salades, de la simple laitue à la salade composée.

))) Une simple poignée d'amandes effilées ou de graines de sésame grillées a le pouvoir de transformer une modeste salade verte en un régal.

))) Pour une salade autrement parfumée, de l'ail simplement frotté dans le saladier ne passera pas inaperçu.

# Vinaigrette au citron

| | | |
|---|---|---|
| 2 c. à soupe | Jus de citron | 30 ml |
| 3 c. à soupe | Huile d'olive | 45 ml |
| 1 c. à soupe | Sucre | 15 ml |
| 5 brins | Ciboulette | 5 brins |
| | Sel, poivre | |

Mélanger le jus de citron, le sel et le sucre. Ajouter l'huile et poivrer. Émulsionner le tout.

Au moment de servir la salade, répandre la ciboulette finement ciselée.

**Suggestion**

》》》 Léger, son parfum subtil est idéal pour accompagner une simple laitue.

》》》 Parsemée de pignons de pin dorés quelques minutes dans le four, une salade saura vous régaler.

》》》 Aussi délicieux avec une petite gousse d'ail en purée.

》》》 Le citron peut être remplacé par une lime.

》》》 Son taux élevé en vitamine C en fait le meilleur allié de l'hiver.

》》》 Convient à toutes vos salades et permet de préserver les fruits ou les légumes qui s'oxydent rapidement à l'air libre, comme l'avocat ou la pomme.

**Variante**

## Vinaigrette citronnée
## pour carottes râpées aux raisins secs

| | | |
|---|---|---|
| 3 c. à soupe | Jus de citron | 45 ml |
| 1 c à thé | Sucre | 5 ml |
| 1 c à thé | Moutarde | 5 ml |
| 3 c. à soupe | Huile d'olive | 45 ml |
| 3 c. à soupe | Huile de canola | 45 ml |
| 2 lb | Carottes râpées | 900 g |
| 1/2 tasse | Raisins secs | 125 ml |

Mélanger le jus de citron, le sel, le sucre et le poivre du moulin. Ajouter la moutarde et les huiles en fouettant. Mélanger les carottes râpées et les raisins secs. Arroser de la moitié de la vinaigrette, mélanger, couvrir et réfrigérer pendant au moins deux heures. Remuer de nouveau avant le service et rectifier l'assaisonnement. Au besoin, ajouter de la vinaigrette.

**Suggestion**

))) Remplacer les raisins secs par des canneberges, des câpres, des figues ou des dattes sèches.

))) Cette vinaigrette se prête aussi à la salade verte ou aux légumes cuits à la vapeur.

))) Frotter le saladier avec une gousse d'ail donne un goût supplémentaire.

# Vinaigrette classique

| | | |
|---|---|---|
| 1 c. à soupe | Vinaigre de vin rouge | 15 ml |
| 4 c. à soupe | Huile d'olive | 60 ml |
| 1 c. à thé | Moutarde | 5 ml |
| | Sel, poivre | |

Mélanger le sel et le poivre du moulin au vinaigre. Ajouter l'huile et la moutarde et émulsionner.

Bien mélanger à la salade et servir.

**Suggestion**

››› Cette vinaigrette trouvera sa singularité dans le choix de la moutarde, que ce soit une moutarde de Dijon, à l'ancienne ou aromatisée.

››› Plus onctueuse que la vinaigrette traditionnelle grâce à la moutarde, elle se prête aussi à toutes sortes de salades.

››› Si elle est faite avec une simple moutarde de Dijon, de l'ail frotté dans le saladier lui donnera son unicité.

# Salade rose de radis

| | | |
|---|---|---|
| 2 bottes | Radis | 2 bottes |
| 3 | Oranges | 3 |
| 2 | Échalotes françaises | 2 |
| 1/2 | Grenade | 1/2 |

Émincer finement les échalotes françaises. Nettoyer les radis, les essuyer et les couper en rondelles. Garder les fanes les plus tendres. Réserver.

Peler deux oranges et en détacher les quartiers. Mélanger délicatement les rondelles de radis, les quartiers d'orange, les échalotes, les grains de grenade et les fanes de radis.

Dans un bol, ajouter 2 c. à soupe de jus d'orange à la vinaigrette précédente. Verser cette vinaigrette sur la salade. Goûter et, au besoin, ajouter du sel et du poivre.

**Suggestion**   ⟩⟩⟩ *Des oranges sanguines donneront à cette salade couleur et douceur.*

## Un doux parfum de pommes

| | | |
|---|---|---|
| 2 c. à soupe | Vinaigre de cidre | 30 ml |
| 1/2 tasse | Crème sure | 125 ml |
| 10 brins | Ciboulette | 10 brins |
| | Sel, poivre | |

Combiner le vinaigre, le sel et le poivre du moulin. Une fois le sel dissous, verser la crème sure et la moitié des brins de ciboulette ciselés. Battre le mélange pour qu'il soit lisse, crémeux et léger. Réserver au réfrigérateur au moins une heure, pour que la ciboulette libère sa saveur dans la crème.

Servir sur une salade verte et décorer du reste de ciboulette.

**Suggestion**

))) Pour accentuer le parfum de pommes, trancher finement une pomme acidulée, comme une Lobo, une McIntosch ou une Spartan.

))) Cette vinaigrette s'associe aussi bien avec les poires.

## Salade croquante au fenouil, à la pomme et au fromage

| | | |
|---|---|---|
| 1 | Fenouil | 1 |
| 2 | Pommes | 2 |
| 1/2 tasse | Fromage de brebis | 125 ml |
| 1/4 tasse | Vinaigre de cidre | 65 ml |
| 3 c. à soupe | Huile d'olive | 45 ml |
| 1/4 tasse | Pignons de pin | 65 ml |
| | Sel, poivre | |

Faire dorer les pignons au four à 350 °F (180 °C) et laisser refroidir.

Laver le fenouil et émincer le bulbe en petits morceaux de 1/2 po (1 cm). Laver les pommes et les couper en petits dés.

Retirer la croûte du fromage et couper ce dernier en bâtonnets. Placer le tout dans un saladier.

Arroser avec de la vinaigrette précédente. Remuer le tout.

Parsemez des pignons de pins grillés.

››› Cette salade croquante à souhait peut être faite à l'avance avec sa vinaigrette, puisque le vinaigre protégera les pommes et le fenouil de l'oxydation.

››› Garder de préférence la peau rouge ou verte des pommes pour donner de la couleur à cette salade pâlotte.

››› Accompagner cette salade d'une petite vinaigrette faite de 1 c. à soupe d'huile d'olive et de 3 c. à soupe de vinaigre de pomme. Saler et poivrer.

## Vinaigrette au vinaigre de cidre

| | | |
|---|---|---|
| 2 c. à soupe | Huile de canola | 30 ml |
| 2 c. à soupe | Vinaigre de cidre | 30 ml |
| 1 c. à soupe | Miel | 15 ml |
| 1/2 c. à thé | Cumin en poudre | 3 ml |
| | Sel, poivre | |

Mélanger le vinaigre de cidre, le sel, le poivre, le miel et l'huile d'olive. Bien émulsionner. Réserver.

# Salade de pommes de terre chaude sucrée-salée

| | | |
|---|---|---|
| 1 1/2 lb | Pommes de terre (rattes) | 675 g |
| 12 | Dattes | 12 |
| 3 | Oignons rouges | 3 |
| 1/4 tasse | Pignons de pin | 65 ml |
| | Sel, poivre | |

Émincer les oignons et les couvrir d'eau froide pendant 1 h pour les adoucir.

Laver et peler les pommes de terre, puis les cuire dans de l'eau. Couper les dattes dénoyautées en rondelles. Faire dorer les graines de sésame dans une poêle.

Égoutter les oignons et les essuyer dans un torchon.

Mélanger les pommes de terre, les oignons et les dattes. Assaisonner de vinaigrette et parsemer de pignons de pin grillés.

Couvrir le saladier d'une feuille d'aluminium, mettre au four 15 min à 350 °F (180 °C) et servir chaud.

# Vinaigrette à la tomate

| | | |
|---|---|---|
| 2 | Échalotes françaises | 2 |
| 1 | Tomate | 1 |
| 1 c. à thé | Purée de tomate concentrée | 5 ml |
| 5 c. à soupe | Vinaigre de xérès | 75 ml |
| 10 c. à soupe | Huile de canola | 150 ml |
| | Sel, poivre | |

Dans 1 c. à soupe d'huile, cuire les échalotes françaises émincées avec la tomate épépinée et en petits dés. Retirer du feu et ajouter la purée de tomate, le vinaigre de xérès et l'huile de canola. Saler et poivrer. Dans le mélangeur, réduire la préparation et la verser dans un bocal en verre.

**Suggestion**

》》 Elle se garde au frais et accompagne les salades composées de légumes d'été.

# Vinaigrette crémeuse au yogourt et au fromage persillé

| | | |
|---|---|---|
| 1 c. à thé | Vinaigre de vin blanc | 5 ml |
| 1/3 tasse | Yogourt | 85 ml |
| 1/2 | Oignon | 1/2 |
| 1/2 c. à thé | Sucre | 3 ml |
| 1/4 tasse | Fromage persillé* | 65 ml |
| | Sel, poivre | |

Mélanger le vinaigre, le sel, le poivre du moulin, l'oignon émincé et le sucre. Pour une texture lisse et crémeuse, passer la préparation initiale au mélangeur en ajoutant le fromage émietté et le yogourt.

---

\* Par exemple, le bleu d'Élizabeth, de la Fromagerie du Presbytère, le bleu bénédictin de la Fromagerie de l'abbaye Saint-Benoît, du roquefort, etc.

**Suggestion**

››› Cette vinaigrette peut être servie immédiatement ou gardée au frais dans un bocal en verre.

››› À servir sur une salade verte bien croquante, comme une romaine, ou une salade amère comme la chicorée ou les endives.

››› Ne pas hésiter à la parsemer de cerneaux de noix.

## Vinaigrette au yogourt

| | | |
|---|---|---|
| 2 c. à soupe | Yogourt | 30 ml |
| 3 c. à soupe | Huile d'olive | 45 ml |
| 1/2 | Citron | 1/2 |
| 1 bouquet | Basilic | 1 bouquet |
| | Sel, poivre | |

Émulsionner le yogourt, l'huile, le jus de citron, puis ajouter le basilic. Saler et poivrer.

## Salade de petits légumes

| | | |
|---|---|---|
| 1 | Concombre | 1 |
| 2 | Courgettes | 2 |
| 20 | Petits bocconcini | 20 |
| 20 | Tomates cerises | 20 |
| 1 bouquet | Basilic | 1 bouquet |
| | Sel, poivre | |

Laver les légumes. Couper les courgettes en fines rondelles, le concombre en fines lamelles avec un économe, et les tomates cerises en deux. Égoutter les bocconcini et hacher le basilic.

Mélanger la vinaigrette à la salade et disposer sur des petites assiettes ou dans des verres.

# Vinaigrette au sirop d'érable

| | | |
|---|---|---|
| 1 c. à soupe | Vinaigre de cidre | 15 ml |
| 1 c. à thé | Jus de citron | 5 ml |
| 1 c. à soupe | Sirop d'érable | 15 ml |
| 2 c. à soupe | Huile d'olive | 30 ml |
| 1 c. à soupe | Huile de pépins de raisin | 15 ml |
| 1 | Gousse d'ail | 1 |
| | Sel, poivre | |

Mélanger le vinaigre, le jus de citron, l'ail et le poivre du moulin. Ajouter le sirop d'érable et bien fouetter. Verser peu à peu l'huile d'olive et l'huile de pépins de raisin en continuant de fouetter.

**Suggestion**   ⟩⟩⟩ Accompagne un mélange printanier et des feuilles de betterave, de roquette et d'épinard.

# Vinaigrette à l'avocat

| | | |
|---|---|---|
| **1 c. à soupe** | Vinaigre de vin rouge | **15 ml** |
| | ou jus de citron | |
| **1 c. à thé** | Moutarde | **5 ml** |
| **2 c. à soupe** | Huile de canola | **30 ml** |
| **2 c. à soupe** | Huile de pépins de raisin | **30 ml** |
| **1 c. à soupe** | Ciboulette ou persil | **15 ml** |
| **1** | Avocat bien mûr | **1** |
| | Sel, poivre | |

Mélanger le vinaigre de vin, ou le jus de citron, au sel et à la moutarde. Poivrer. Verser progressivement les huiles et fouetter. Écraser l'avocat à la fourchette et l'ajouter à l'émulsion précédemment obtenue. Parsemer de ciboulette ou de persil.

**Suggestion**

))) Pour une salade verte parsemée de tomates cerises.

))) Plus épaisse, elle est idéale pour tartiner les sandwiches.

# Vinaigrette crémeuse

| 2 c. à soupe | Vinaigre de vin | 30 ml |
| 1 c. à soupe | Miel | 15 ml |
| 7 onces | Mayonnaise | 200 g |
| 2 c. à soupe | Crème sure | 30 ml |
| 1/2 | Oignon | 1/2 |
| | Sel, poivre | |

Mélanger le vinaigre, le sel, le miel et le poivre du moulin. Ajouter l'oignon finement émincé, la mayonnaise et la crème sure. Fouetter jusqu'à l'obtention d'un mélange lisse et aéré. Rectifier l'assaisonnement.

**Suggestion**

))) À servir sur des pommes de terre ou du chou-fleur bouillis, du chou ou des carottes râpées. Réserver au réfrigérateur pendant plusieurs heures afin que les saveurs soient absorbées par le légume choisi.

))) Ne pas hésiter à utiliser du vinaigre de xérès pour cette recette.

))) Attention à la chaleur ! Conserver la vinaigrette au réfrigérateur, surtout si elle est faite avec une mayonnaise maison.

# Vinaigrette aigre-douce

| | | |
|---|---|---|
| 2 c. à soupe | Vinaigre de vin | 30 ml |
| 2 c. à soupe | Sucre | 30 ml |
| 3 c. à soupe | Huile d'olive | 45 ml |
| 3 c. à soupe | Huile de noisette | 45 ml |
| | Sel, poivre | |

Dissoudre le sucre dans le vinaigre. Saler et poivrer. Verser peu à peu les huiles et fouetter. Ajouter de l'eau si la vinaigrette est trop acide.

**Suggestion**

))) Mélanger cette vinaigrette à des légumes crus, cuits à la vapeur ou même grillés.

))) Remplacer le sucre par du miel ou du sirop d'érable.

# Vinaigrette au vinaigre de framboise

| | | |
|---|---|---|
| 2 | Gousses d'ail | 2 |
| 2 c. à soupe | Vinaigre de framboise | 30 ml |
| 1/4 tasse | Huile d'olive | 65 ml |
| 1 c. à soupe | Moutarde jaune | 15 ml |
| | Sel, poivre | |

Réduire l'ail en purée. Le mélanger à la moutarde et au vinaigre. Saler et poivrer. Ajouter l'huile d'olive et émulsionner.

# Salade de roquette aux fraises

| | | |
|---|---|---|
| 4 oz | Roquette | 120 g |
| 5 oz | Fraises | 150 g |
| 2 | Oignons nouveaux | 2 |
| 3,5 oz | Parmesan | 105 g |
| 8 tranches fines | Jambon sec | 8 tranches fines |

Couper les fraises en lamelles, émincer les oignons et faire des copeaux de parmesan. Répartir la roquette et les autres ingrédients dans des assiettes et ajouter la vinaigrette au vinaigre de framboise.

# Vinaigrette au vinaigre balsamique et à l'échalote

| | | |
|---|---|---|
| 1 c. à soupe | Vinaigre balsamique | 15 ml |
| 1 c. à soupe | Persil | 15 ml |
| 1 c. à soupe | Basilic | 15 ml |
| 1 | Échalote française | 1 |
| 1 | Petite gousse d'ail | 1 |
| 1/4 tasse | Huile d'olive | 65 ml |
| | Sel, poivre | |

Mélanger le vinaigre à une pincée de sel et poivrer. Émincer le persil, le basilic, l'échalote française et l'ail. Ajouter au vinaigre et verser peu à peu l'huile d'olive en fouettant.

**Suggestion**

>>> Accompagne particulièrement bien des tomates juteuses et une salade de roquettes dont la saveur poivrée est relevée par le vinaigre balsamique.

# Vinaigrette au vinaigre balsamique et à la moutarde

| | | |
|---|---|---|
| 3 c. à soupe | Vinaigre balsamique | 45 ml |
| 1 | Gousse d'ail | 1 |
| 1 c. à thé | Moutarde | 5 ml |
| 5 c. à soupe | Huile d'olive | 75 ml |
| | Sel, poivre | |

Dissoudre le sel dans le vinaigre balsamique. Poivrer. Ajouter la gousse d'ail écrasée et la moutarde. Mélanger. Verser peu à peu l'huile et fouetter.

**Suggestion**

››› À déguster avec une salade verte aux foies de poulet.

››› La veille, faire macérer une poignée de raisins secs dans le vinaigre balsamique et les ajouter à la salade pour donner un petit goût sucré.

# Salade de tomates, fraises et bocconcini

| | | |
|---|---|---|
| 4 | Tomates bien mûres | 4 |
| 2 tasses | Fraises | 30 ml |
| 10 | Petits bocconcini | 10 |
| 5 branches | Basilic | 5 branches |
| 2 c. à soupe | Huile d'olive | 30 ml |
| 2 c. à soupe | Vinaigre balsamique | 30 ml |
| | Sel, poivre | |

Laver et couper les tomates et les fraises en quartiers. Ciseler le basilic. Égoutter les bocconcini et les couper en deux.

Dans un saladier, placer les ingrédients et arroser de la vinaigrette au vinaigre balsamique. Saler et poivrer.

## Vinaigrette à la grecque

| | | |
|---|---|---|
| 1/2 | Citron | 1/2 |
| 4 c. à soupe | Huile d'olive | 60 ml |
| 3 branches | Menthe | 3 branches |
| 3 | Concombres libanais | 3 |
| 2 onces | Féta émiettée | 60 g |
| | Sel, poivre | |

Dans un mélangeur, émulsionner le jus du demi-citron, le sel, les concombres et l'huile d'olive. Ajouter au mélange obtenu les feuilles de menthe ciselées et le féta émietté. Poivrer.

**Suggestion**

››› Délicieuse sur une salade grecque composée de tomates, de rondelles d'oignon rouge, d'olives noires, d'une laitue et d'un poivron vert.

››› Convient aussi à une salade de riz agrémentée des légumes précités.

# Vinaigrette aux fines herbes

| | | |
|---|---|---|
| 2 branches | Cerfeuil | 2 branches |
| 2 branches | Basilic | 2 branches |
| 2 branches | Aneth | 2 branches |
| 1 c. à soupe | Moutarde | 15 ml |
| 1 tasse | Huile d'olive | 250 ml |
| 2 c. à soupe | Vinaigre de vin | 30 ml |
| | Sel, poivre | |

Hacher les herbes au mélangeur ou au couteau. Mélanger le vinaigre, le sel et le poivre du moulin. Ajouter l'huile et les fines herbes. Fouetter et laisser reposer.

**Suggestion**

››› Utiliser vos fines herbes préférées (ciboulette, fenouil ou marjolaine).

››› Rafraîchissante, cette vinaigrette accompagne volontiers les légumes, l'avocat, la viande (porc ou poulet grillé), le saumon ou les pâtes.

## Vinaigrette à l'huile de noix

| | | |
|---|---|---|
| 2 c. à soupe | Vinaigre de vin | 30 ml |
| 2 c. à soupe | Huile de noix | 30 ml |
| 2 c. à soupe | Huile d'olive | 30 ml |
| 1 c. à thé | Moutarde | 5 ml |
| | Sel, poivre | |

Mélanger le sel et le poivre du moulin au vinaigre de vin. Ajouter la moutarde, puis les huiles. Émulsionner et rectifier l'assaisonnement.

**Suggestion**

 ››› Pour accompagner une simple salade verte, mais aussi du poisson ou du poulet.

## Salade chaude de lentilles au saumon fumé

| | | |
|---|---|---|
| 1 lb | Lentilles vertes | 450 g |
| 1 lb | Saumon fumé | 450 g |
| 1 c. à soupe | Moutarde à l'ancienne | 15 ml |
| 1 | Échalote française | 1 |
| | Sel, poivre | |

Cuire les lentilles dans trois fois leur volume d'eau. Les égoutter et les réserver au chaud.

Ajouter le saumon fumé coupé en dés et la vinaigrette à l'huile de noix agrémentée de l'échalote hachée.

Mélanger, saler et poivrer.

## Vinaigrette au miel

| | | |
|---|---|---|
| 1 c. à thé | Miel | 5 ml |
| 1 c. à soupe | Sauce soja | 15 ml |
| 3 c. à soupe | Huile d'olive | 45 ml |
| | Poivre | |

Mélanger le miel et la sauce soja. Ajouter l'huile d'olive et émulsionner. Poivrer.

**Suggestion** ))) Pour agrémenter une salade verte parsemée de pignons de pins grillés.

## Vinaigrette au soja

| | | |
|---|---|---|
| 1 | Citron | 1 |
| 3 c. à soupe | Sauce soja | 45 ml |
| 1 c. à soupe | Huile de sésame | 15 ml |
| 3 c. à soupe | Huile de canola | 45 ml |
| 1 c. à soupe | Graines de sésame | 15 ml |
| 5 brins | Ciboulette | 5 brins |

Mélanger le jus du citron avec la sauce soja et les huiles. Parsemer de graines de sésame grillées et de ciboulette finement hachée.

**Suggestion**

››› Sur du tofu mou frais, comme entrée ou en accompagnement rafraîchissant.

››› Additionnée de 1 c. à thé de gingembre râpé, le tofu ne manquera pas de piquant.

››› Pour les becs épicés, un petit piment émincé donnera le piquant recherché.

## Salade santé

| | | |
|---|---|---|
| 2 | Tomates | 2 |
| 1 | Petit concombre | 1 |
| 1/2 tasse | Tofu | 125 ml |
| 2 | Avocats | 2 |
| 1/2 tasse | Quinoa | 125 ml |
| Quelques | Noix de Grenoble | Quelques |
| 1 tasse | Germes de luzerne | 250 ml |
| 1 | Citron | 1 |
| | Poivre | |

Cuire le quinoa selon les instructions inscrites sur le paquet.

Couper grossièrement les noix de Grenoble et les ajouter à la vinaigrette au soja.

Couper le tofu, les tomates, le concombre et les avocats en cubes.

Mélanger le quinoa aux dés de légumes et de tofu. Verser la vinaigrette. Comme ils sont fragiles, les germes de luzerne ne doivent être ajoutés qu'au moment de servir.

# Vinaigrette au soja et vinaigre de framboise

| | | |
|---|---|---|
| 1 c. à thé | Sauce soja | 5 ml |
| 4 c. à soupe | Vinaigre de framboise | 60 ml |
| 5 c. à soupe | Huile d'olive | 75 ml |
| 2 c. à soupe | Huile de canola | 30 ml |
| 2 branches | Thym ou romarin | 2 branches |
| 1 | Gousse d'ail | 1 |
| | Poivre | |

Mélanger la sauce soja au vinaigre de framboise. Ajouter l'huile d'olive et l'huile de canola. Fouetter, puis ajouter le thym ou le romarin et la gousse d'ail écrasée. Réserver au réfrigérateur.

**Suggestion**

))) Pour rehausser une salade verte au poulet.

))) Ne pas hésiter à parsemer de graines de sésame grillées.

## Vinaigrette thaïe

| | | |
|---|---|---|
| 1 c. à soupe | Vinaigre de riz | 15 ml |
| 1 c. à soupe | Sauce soja claire | 15 ml |
| 1/2 c. à soupe | Sauce nuoc-mâm | 8 ml |
| 4 gouttes | Tabasco | 4 gouttes |
| 1 c. à soupe | Huile de sésame | 15 ml |
| 1 c. à thé | Sucre | 5 ml |
| | Sel, poivre | |

Ajouter le sucre, le sel et le poivre du moulin au vinaigre de riz. Verser la sauce soja, la sauce nuoc-mâm, l'huile de sésame et le Tabasco. Bien mélanger.

**Suggestion**

))) Pour accompagner une salade de germes de soja, un filet de poisson à chair blanche, des pois gourmands ou des crevettes.

))) Pour une vinaigrette plus épicée, remplacer le Tabasco par 1/2 c. à thé de sauce chili.

))) Si le goût de l'huile de sésame est trop prononcé, ajouter 1 c. à soupe d'huile de canola ou de pépin de raisin.

# Salade thaïe de nouilles de riz aux crevettes et pamplemousse

| | | |
|---|---|---|
| 1/2 lb | Nouilles de riz | 225 g |
| 1 | Pamplemousse | 1 |
| 2 c. à soupe | Graines de sésame | 30 ml |
| 4 brins | Ciboulette | 4 brins |
| 5 branches | Coriandre | 5 branches |
| 5 branches | Menthe | 5 branches |
| 1 | Petit piment | 1 |
| 1 | Gousse d'ail | 1 |
| 1 c. à thé | Sucre | 5 ml |
| 3 | Limes | 3 |
| 1 c. à soupe | Huile de canola | 15 ml |
| 2 c. à soupe | Sauce nuoc-mâm | 30 ml |
| 20 | Crevettes | 20 |
| | Sel, poivre | |

Peler le pamplemousse et le défaire en quartiers. Hacher les feuilles de ciboulette, de coriandre et de menthe. Mélanger. Éplucher et hacher l'ail. Émincer le piment.

Dans un bol, mélanger la sauce nuoc-mâm, le jus des limes, l'ail et le piment. Réserver.

Cuire les nouilles selon les indications du fabricant. Une fois cuites, les rincer à l'eau froide et les mélanger avec les quartiers de pamplemousse et les herbes hachées.

Dans une poêle, faire revenir les crevettes dans 1 c. à soupe d'huile. Saler et poivrer. Une fois refroidies, les ajouter aux nouilles et verser le mélange réservé. Parsemer des graines de sésame grillées.

**Suggestion**

⟫⟫ Remplacer les graines de sésame par des arachides grillées et hachées grossièrement ou des noix de cajou salées.

## Salade de papaye verte aux crevettes

| | | |
|---|---|---|
| 1 lb | Crevettes épluchées cuites | 450 g |
| 1/2 | Ananas | 1/2 |
| 1 | Papaye verte | 200 g |
| 1 | Lime | 1 |
| 6 c. à soupe | Huile d'olive | 90 ml |
| 3 c. à soupe | Sauce nuoc-mâm | 45 ml |
| 1 c. à soupe | Sauce soja | 15 ml |
| | Poivre | |

Râper la papaye verte. Émincer des tranches d'ananas.

Dans un saladier, mélanger les crevettes, la papaye, l'ananas, le jus de la lime, l'huile d'olive, la sauce soja et la sauce nuoc-mâm. Poivrer et saler au besoin.

## Vinaigrette aux épices

| | | |
|---|---|---|
| 1 c. à soupe | Vinaigre de xérès | 15 ml |
| 1 | Gousse d'ail | 1 |
| 1/4 | Cumin moulu | 5 ml |
| 1/4 | Coriandre moulue | 5 ml |
| 4 c. à soupe | Huile d'olive | 60 ml |
| | Sel, poivre | |

Dans le mélangeur, mettre le vinaigre, le sel, l'ail, le cumin, la coriandre et du poivre du moulin. Ajouter l'huile peu à peu, jusqu'à ce que le mélange soit onctueux. Au besoin, rectifier l'assaisonnement.

**Suggestion**
》 Pour accompagner des pâtes, mais aussi des crevettes, des calmars ou du poulet grillé sur un lit de mâche ou de romaine.

# Vinaigrette marocaine

| | | |
|---|---|---|
| 1/2 tasse | Amandes | 125 ml |
| 1/2 tasse | Miel | 125 ml |
| 1/2 | Citron | 1/2 |
| 1 pincée | Cannelle en poudre | 1 pincée |
| 1/3 tasse | Huile d'argan | 85 ml |
| | Sel, poivre | |

Faire griller les amandes pendant 5 min au four. Les placer dans un mélangeur, avec le miel, le jus du demi-citron et la cannelle jusqu'à obtention d'une pâte lisse et homogène. Verser peu à peu l'huile d'argan. Saler et poivrer.

**Suggestion**

))) Pour accompagner des fruits ou des légumes crus, du poisson ou du saumon fumé.

))) Cette variante de l'amlou est aussi à découvrir simplement tartinée sur du pain.

# Vinaigrette aux bleuets

| | | |
|---|---|---|
| 1 c. à soupe | Jus de citron | 15 ml |
| 1 c. à thé | Sucre | 5 ml |
| 4 c. à soupe | Huile d'olive | 60 ml |
| 1/2 tasse | Bleuets frais | 125 ml |
| | Sel, poivre | |

Passer tous les ingrédients au mélangeur. Saler et poivrer au goût.

**Suggestion**

))) Accompagne les avocats, les asperges ou un mélange printanier.

))) Remplacer le sucre et les bleuets par 1 c. à soupe de confiture de bleuets.

))) Décorer l'assiette de cette vinaigrette colorée.

## Vinaigrette au thym

| | | |
|---|---|---|
| 1 | Citron non traité | 1 |
| 1 tasse | Huile d'olive | 250 ml |
| 1 c. à thé | Thym frais | 5 ml |
| 1/2 | Échalote française | 1/2 |
| 1 | Gousse d'ail | 1 |
| | Sel, poivre | |

Mélanger le jus et le zeste du citron, l'huile d'olive, le thym l'échalote émincée et la gousse d'ail écrasée. Saler et poivrer.

**Suggestion**

))) Pour accompagner des pâtes, des tomates ou des artichauts, mais aussi une simple salade verte.

))) À essayer avec des côtes d'agneau poêlées et des pommes de terre sautées.

## Vinaigrette au cari

| | | |
|---|---|---|
| 1 c. à soupe | Cari | 15 ml |
| 2 c. à soupe | Eau chaude | 30 ml |
| 10 c. à soupe | Vinaigre de vin | 150 ml |
| 4 c. à soupe | Huile de canola | 60 ml |
| | Sel, poivre | |

Dissoudre le cari dans l'eau très chaude. Ajouter le vinaigre de vin et l'huile de canola. Saler et poivrer. Pour accompagner une salade composée de poissons.

**Suggestion**

))) Pour une saveur plus épicée, ajouter quelques
gouttes de Tabasco ou de sauce chili.

## Vinaigrette vanillée

| | | |
|---|---|---|
| 1/8 tasse | Sucre | 35 ml |
| 1/2 tasse | Eau | 125 ml |
| 1/2 gousse | Vanille | 1/2 gousse |
| 4 c. à soupe | Vinaigre de vin | 60 ml |
| 10 c. à soupe | Huile de canola | 150 ml |
| | Sel, poivre | |

À feu doux, dans une petite casserole, faire un sirop avec l'eau, le sucre et la demi-gousse de vanille fendue et grattée. Retirer du feu et verser le vinaigre de vin et l'huile de canola dans le mélange. Saler et poivrer. Émulsionner. Conserver au réfrigérateur dans un bocal en verre, avec la demi-gousse de vanille.

**Suggestion**

))) Découvrir cette saveur raffinée en
accompagnement d'une salade de homard ou
d'avocat est un plaisir inaccoutumé.

## Vinaigrette à la mangue pimentée

| | | |
|---|---|---|
| 1 | Grosse mangue mûre | 1 |
| 1 c. à soupe | Moutarde | 15 ml |
| 1 c. à soupe | Eau | 15 ml |
| 2 c. à soupe | Huile d'olive | 30 ml |
| 1 | Petit piment | 1 |
| 4 gouttes | Tabasco | 4 gouttes |
| | Sel, poivre | |

Coupez la mangue en deux. Enlever la peau et le noyau, puis passer la chair au mélangeur pour en faire une purée. Ajouter le petit piment coupé en deux. Continuer à émulsionner et verser 1 c. à soupe d'eau dans le mélange. Passer à la passoire pour ne récupérer que le jus de mangue pimenté. Dans un bol, mélanger ce jus avec la moutarde et l'huile d'olive. Saler, poivrer et ajouter le Tabasco.

**Suggestion**

))) Pour donner du piquant aux asperges.

))) Sur une salade de mangue verte, ne pas hésiter à sucrer. Le sucré-salé pimenté saura vous plaire.

# Vinaigrette pimentée

| | | |
|---|---|---|
| 1 c. à thé | Gingembre | 5 ml |
| 1 tasse | Huile d'olive | 250 ml |
| 1/4 tasse | Sauce chili | 65 ml |
| 4 | Tiges de persil | 4 |
| | ou de coriandre hachées | |
| | Sel, poivre | |

Mélanger le gingembre haché, l'huile d'olive et la sauce chili. Saler et poivrer.

**Suggestion**

))) Pour accompagner du poisson grillé ou du poulet garni d'une salade de mangue verte assaisonnée de cette même vinaigrette pimentée.

## Sauce mousseline

| | | |
|---|---|---|
| 1 | Œuf | 1 |
| 1 c. à thé | Moutarde | 5 ml |
| 1/2 tasse | Huile d'olive | 125 ml |
| 2 c. à thé | Jus de citron | 10 ml |
| | Sel, poivre | |

Séparer le blanc d'œuf du jaune. Avec le jaune, la moutarde et l'huile, monter une mayonnaise. Saler et poivrer.

Battre le blanc en neige et l'incorporer délicatement à la mayonnaise, puis y verser le jus de citron.

Garder au frais jusqu'au moment de servir.

**Suggestion** ››› Pour accompagner du saumon poché.

››› L'ajout de fines herbes donnera couleur et volupté.

## Vinaigrette à l'œuf

| | | |
|---|---|---|
| 2 c. à soupe | Vinaigre de vin | 30 ml |
| 1 c. à soupe | Moutarde | 15 ml |
| 1/3 tasse | Huile d'olive | 75 ml |
| 1 c. à thé | Persil | 5 ml |
| 1 c. à thé | Cerfeuil | 5 ml |
| 1 c. à thé | Ciboulette | 5 ml |
| 1 | Œuf dur | 1 |
| | Sel, poivre | |

Mélanger le vinaigre, le sel et le poivre du moulin. Ajouter la moutarde et, peu à peu, l'huile d'olive en continuant de fouetter.

Émietter l'œuf dur et le mélanger aux fines herbes.

**Suggestion**
))) Pour un classique délicieux, verser simplement sur des asperges parées ou une salade verte, puis parsemer du mélange œuf et fines herbes.

## Vinaigrette au fromage de chèvre

| | | |
|---|---|---|
| 1 c. à soupe | Vinaigre de xérès | 15 ml |
| 1 c. à thé | Moutarde | 5 ml |
| 1 | Petite échalote | 1 |
| 1 c. à soupe | Cerfeuil ciselé | 15 ml |
| 1/3 tasse | Huile d'olive | 85 ml |
| 1/2 tasse | Fromage de chèvre frais | 125 ml |
| | Sel, poivre | |

Mélanger le vinaigre, la moutarde, le sel et le poivre du moulin. Verser peu à peu l'huile, l'échalote émincée et un peu de cerfeuil. Fouetter énergiquement. Parsemer le fromage de chèvre frais sur la salade assaisonnée.

**Suggestion**
))) Sur une salade verte ou des asperges printanières.

## Vinaigrette aux graines de pavot

| | | |
|---|---|---|
| 1 | Citron | 1 |
| 1 c. à soupe | Miel | 15 ml |
| 1 c. à soupe | Graines de pavot | 15 ml |
| 4 c. à soupe | Huile d'olive | 60 ml |
| | Sel, poivre | |

Mélanger le jus du citron au miel. Verser peu à peu l'huile. Saler et poivrer. Ajouter les graines de pavot.

**Suggestion**

))) Accompagne agréablement l'avocat, mais aussi une simple salade verte.

))) Les petites graines de pavot qui craquent sous la dent séduiront vos convives.

## Vinaigrette aux noix et au yogourt

| | | |
|---|---|---|
| 1 c. à soupe | Jus de citron | 15 ml |
| 1/2 c. à thé | Moutarde | 3 ml |
| 1 c. à soupe | Huile de noix | 15 ml |
| 1 c. à soupe | Huile de pépins de raisin | 15 ml |
| 2 c. à soupe | Huile de canola | 30 ml |
| 1 tasse | Yogourt | 250 ml |
| 1/2 tasse | Crème liquide | 125 ml |
| 1/3 tasse | Noix concassées | 85 ml |
| | Sel, poivre | |

Fouetter le yogourt et la crème liquide. Ajouter le jus de citron, la moutarde, les huiles et les noix. Saler et poivrer.

**Suggestion**

))) Le goût des noix s'harmonise avec celui des tomates juteuses, de la salade verte, de l'endive ou du céleri.

))) Plus épaisse avec de la crème sure au lieu de la crème liquide, cette vinaigrette se transforme en trempette pour accompagner des branches de céleri.

))) Parsemer l'un ou l'autre de gorgonzola émietté, personne ne pourra résister...

## Vinaigrette crémeuse à l'aneth

| | | |
|---|---|---|
| 1/2 | Citron | 1/2 |
| 1 c. à soupe | Sucre | 15 ml |
| 1 c. à soupe | Huile de pépins de raisin | 15 ml |
| 1/2 tasse | Crème liquide | 125 ml |
| 2 c. à soupe | Aneth ciselé | 30 ml |
| | Sel, poivre | |

Mélanger le jus du demi-citron, le sel et le sucre. Ajouter l'huile, la crème, l'aneth et le poivre. Battre énergiquement.

**Suggestion**

))) À servir sur une salade verte, avec des lanières de saumon gravlax ou fumé.

## Vinaigrette au pamplemousse

| | | |
|---|---|---|
| 1/2 | Pamplemousse | 45 ml |
| 1 c. à soupe | Vinaigre de vin | 15 ml |
| 5 c. à soupe | Huile d'olive | 75 ml |
| 1 c. à thé | Moutarde | 5 ml |
| | Sel, poivre | |

Mélanger le jus du demi-pamplemousse, le vinaigre, le sel et le poivre. Remuer et ajouter la moutarde et l'huile d'olive sans cesser de fouetter.

**Suggestion**  ))) Pour une salade d'agrumes (pamplemousse et orange) accompagnée de tranches d'avocat.

## Vinaigrette au thé vert

| | | |
|---|---|---|
| 1/4 tasse | Vinaigre de riz | 65 ml |
| 1/4 tasse | Vinaigre de vin blanc | 65 ml |
| 1 c. à thé | Moutarde | 5 ml |
| 1/2 tasse | Huile de pépins de raisin | 125 ml |
| 1/2 tasse | Huile de canola | 125 ml |
| 1 c. à thé | Huile de sésame | 5 ml |
| 1 c. à soupe | Matcha (thé vert en poudre) | 15 ml |
| | Sel, poivre | |

Mélanger le vinaigre de riz, le vinaigre de vin, le sel et le poivre. Ajouter la moutarde en continuant de fouetter. Verser peu à peu la poudre de thé vert, puis incorporer les huiles doucement.

## Vinaigrette aux olives noires

| | | |
|---|---|---|
| 2 c. à soupe | Vinaigre de vin | 30 ml |
| 1 c. à soupe | Purée d'olives noires | 15 ml |
| 1/4 tasse | Huile d'olive | 65 ml |
| | Sel, poivre | |

Mélanger le vinaigre, la purée d'olives et l'huile. Saler et poivrer.

## Vinaigrette aux olives et au yogourt

| | | |
|---|---|---|
| 1 | Citron non traité | 1 |
| 1/2 c. à soupe | Moutarde | 8 ml |
| 1/2 tasse | Olives noires | 125 ml |
| 1 c. à soupe | Câpres | 15 ml |
| 6 | Filets d'anchois | 6 |
| 1/4 tasse | Huile d'olive | 65 ml |
| 1 tasse | Yogourt | 250 ml |
| 1/4 tasse | Crème liquide | 65 ml |
| | Poivre | |

Dans le mélangeur, placer le jus du citron et son zeste, les olives noires, les anchois, les câpres, la moutarde et l'huile d'olive. À la pâte obtenue, incorporer délicatement le yogourt et la crème liquide.

**Suggestion**

))) Une autre façon d'agrémenter une salade de pâtes.

))) Avec des tomates cerises, c'est un délice !

## Vinaigrette à l'huile de noisette

| | | |
|---|---|---|
| 1 c. à soupe | Vinaigre de banyuls | 15 ml |
| 3 c. à soupe | Huile de noisette | 45 ml |
| 2 | Gousses d'ail | 2 |
| | Sel, poivre | |

Dissoudre le sel dans le vinaigre. Poivrer et ajouter peu à peu l'huile de noisette. Fouetter énergiquement.

**Suggestion**

))) Utiliser du vinaigre de xérès.

))) Pour agrémenter une salade verte au poulet ou au fromage de chèvre.

))) Le fromage de chèvre peut être grillé sur des croûtons de pain.

## Vinaigrette pour salade César

| | | |
|---|---|---|
| 1 | Jaune d'œuf | 1 |
| 1 c. à thé | Moutarde | 5 ml |
| 1 | Gousse d'ail | 1 |
| 2 c. à soupe | Jus de citron ou vinaigre de vin | 30 ml |
| 3 | Filets d'anchois | 3 |
| | Parmesan râpé | 25 g |
| 1/2 tasse | Huile d'olive | 125 ml |
| | Sel, poivre | |

Dans le mélangeur, faire une pâte avec le jaune d'œuf, la moutarde, l'ail, le jus de citron, les anchois et le parmesan. Ajouter peu à peu l'huile et continuer à mélanger jusqu'à ce que ce soit homogène.

**Suggestion**

››› La salade César est composée de feuilles de romaine, de copeaux de parmesan et de tranches de bacon grillées.

››› Élément indissociable : les croûtons de pain à l'ail, de préférence maison. Pour cela, préchauffer le four à 360 °F (180 °C). Sur une plaque à biscuits, disposer les tranches de pain et les badigeonner d'huile d'olive. Enfourner jusqu'à ce qu'elles soient croustillantes et dorées, soit environ 10 min. Une fois refroidies, les frotter avec une gousse d'ail.

# Les trempettes

Et si on faisait une petite trempette ? Chez nous, cette expression prend toute sa signification à l'apéritif, à la collation ou devant la télévision. En général, des bâtonnets de légumes se laissent plonger, en toute occasion, dans des sauces crémeuses et savoureuses pour être croqués en libérant leur fraîcheur printanière. Et en plus, c'est santé !

Utilisée comme condiment dans lequel on trempe des légumes, du pain, des croustilles ou des fruits, les trempettes agrémentent nos repas et sont incontournables lorsqu'on reçoit des amis.

Contrairement à l'utilisation commune des sauces qui sont versées sur la nourriture, les trempettes sont suffisamment onctueuses pour tenir au bâtonnet de légume ou de pain, plongé directement avec les doigts et amené sans crainte à la bouche.

Différents types de trempette existent de par le monde : qu'elles soient froides ou chaudes, on en trouve de toutes les couleurs et elles égayent l'assiette. Cette façon de manger semble d'ailleurs avoir toujours existé et amène la convivialité. Enfant, n'avons-nous pas tous aimé plonger des biscuits secs dans le petit contenant de fromage à la crème de notre collation ? Au déjeuner, les Français ne trempent-ils pas leur croissant du matin dans leur café ? Et n'oublions pas les frites, dans le ketchup !

Oui, le simple fait de tremper et d'amener la nourriture à sa bouche sans ustensiles nous rappelle de façon incontestable qu'il est agréable de manger avec les mains !

Chaudes ou froides, salées ou sucrées, les trempettes s'adaptent à toutes les envies. D'une simplicité exemplaire et rapides à réaliser, elles épateront la galerie : l'ajout d'une simple épice ou d'une herbe fine peut faire la différence, le choix de l'aliment à tremper aussi. De quoi pouvoir satisfaire tous les goûts !

# :: Les trempettes chaudes ::

Les trempettes chaudes se font dans une petite casserole, au four ou directement dans une minimijoteuse qui a l'avantage de les garder chaudes. À défaut de minimijoteuse et pour ne pas se priver, il suffit d'utiliser un chauffe-plats : il maintiendra la chaleur des trempettes.

## Trempette de brie

| | | |
|---|---|---|
| **1** | Brie double ou triple crème | **1** |
| **3 brins** | Ciboulette | **3 brins** |

Placer le brie sur du papier parchemin, puis poser le tout sur une plaque de cuisson, et couvrir d'un chapeau formé d'une feuille de papier aluminium. Cuire au four préchauffé à 400 °F (200 °C) pendant 15 à 20 min, jusqu'à ce que le brie soit mou.

Sortir le brie et, dans la croûte, inciser un X pour ouvrir la surface du fromage. Replacer le brie ouvert au four. Prolonger la cuisson jusqu'à ébullition.

Parsemer de la ciboulette ciselée.

**Suggestion**   ))) Servir avec des croûtons de pain et des cornichons.

# Trempette chaude au fromage, au bacon et aux champignons

| | | |
|---|---|---|
| 3 tranches | Bacon | 3 tranches |
| 1 tasse | Fromage à la crème | 250 ml |
| 1 tasse | Crème sure | 250 ml |
| 1/2 tasse | Cheddar | 125 ml |
| 1 tasse | Champignons | 250 ml |
| 6 brins | Ciboulette | 6 brins |
| | Poivre | |

Couper le bacon en petits morceaux et les faire revenir dans une poêle jusqu'à ce qu'ils soient croustillants. Réserver. Dans la même poêle, faire revenir les champignons émincés.

Mélanger le fromage à la crème, la crème sure, le bacon et les champignons. Ajouter le cheddar râpé.

Placer le tout dans la minimijoteuse beurrée. Couvrir et cuire 1 h. Surveiller et remuer de temps en temps.

À servir avec des croustilles ou des gressins.

**Suggestion** ››› Il est possible de réaliser cette recette dans une casserole à feu doux. Vérifier souvent en mélangeant et en prenant soin de bien racler le fond, qui aura tendance à coller.

# Trempette chaude et crémeuse aux épinards

| | | |
|---|---|---|
| 1 tasse | Fromage à la crème | 250 ml |
| 2 c. à soupe | Parmesan râpé | 30 ml |
| 1 | Oignon | 1 |
| 1 c. à thé | Thym | 5 ml |
| 2/3 tasse | Épinards | 170 ml |
| 1/4 tasse | Crème liquide | 65 ml |
| 1 | Piment | 1 |
| 1 c. à thé | Sauce Worcestershire | 5 ml |
| 1 | Gousse d'ail | 1 |
| | Sel | |

Mélanger le fromage à la crème à la crème liquide et verser dans la minimijoteuse beurrée. Couvrir et chauffer au maximum 1 h, jusqu'à ce que le fromage soit fondu. Ajouter les autres ingrédients et prolonger la cuisson 30 min.

Servir avec des croustilles, des crudités, des craquelins ou des croûtons de pain.

**Suggestion**

》 Il est possible de réaliser cette recette dans une casserole à feu doux. Vérifier souvent en mélangeant et en prenant soin de bien racler le fond, qui aura tendance à coller.

## Trempette de fromage fondu

| | | |
|---|---|---|
| 1 tasse | Fontina | 250 ml |
| 1 tasse | Lait | 250 ml |
| 1 c. à soupe | Beurre | 15 ml |
| 2 | Œufs | 2 |
| | Poivre | |

Couper le fromage en cubes et le recouvrir avec le lait. Placer au frais pendant 3 h. Transvaser dans un bain-marie. Ajouter le beurre et les œufs et laisser cuire doucement en mélangeant jusqu'à ce que cela devienne onctueux. Retirer du feu et poivrer.

**Suggestion** ⟫ Placer dans une minimijoteuse ou sur un chauffe-plats pour le garder tiède.

## Trempette chaude à l'artichaut

| | | |
|---|---|---|
| 1 tasse | Cœurs d'artichaut | 250 ml |
| 1/2 tasse | Parmesan râpé | 125 ml |
| 1/4 tasse | Crème sure | 65 ml |
| 1/4 tasse | Mayonnaise | 65 ml |
| 1 | Piment | 1 |

Mélanger la crème sure, la mayonnaise et le parmesan. Réduire les cœurs d'artichaut égouttés en purée et les ajouter au mélange. Couper le piment en rondelles et l'ajouter. Couvrir et chauffer pendant 1 h à la minimijoteuse.

**Suggestion**

||| Il est possible de réaliser cette recette dans une casserole à feu doux. Vérifier souvent en mélangeant et en prenant soin de bien racler le fond, qui aura tendance à coller.

## Trempette aux framboises

| | | |
|---|---|---|
| 1 tasse | Framboises | 250 ml |
| 2 c. à table | Vinaigre | 30 ml |
| 2 c. à table | Sucre | 30 ml |
| 1/2 c. à thé | Sambal oelek | 3 ml |
| | (pâte de piments forts) | |
| 1 1/2 c. à thé | Gingembre frais râpé | 8 ml |
| 2 gousses | Ail | 2 gousses |
| 1 c. à soupe | Jus de lime | 15 ml |
| 1 c. à soupe | Miel | 15 ml |
| 1 c. à soupe | Fécule de maïs | 15 ml |
| 1 c. à soupe | Eau | 15 ml |
| | Sel | |

Réduire les framboises en purée dans un mélangeur. Passer la purée au tamis pour obtenir un coulis.

Dans une casserole, mélanger le coulis de framboises aux autres ingrédients. Porter à ébullition en remuant constamment jusqu'à ce que la sauce s'épaississe.

Servir chaud comme trempette pour les *dumplings* ou des petits pains chauds cuits à la vapeur.

# Trempette chaude aux crevettes

| | | |
|---|---|---|
| 1/2 tasse | Fromage à la crème | 125 ml |
| 2 c. à soupe | Mayonnaise | 60 ml |
| 1 | Oignon | 1 |
| 1 gousse | Ail | 1 gousse |
| 1/2 | Citron | 1/2 |
| 2 c. à soupe | Concentré de tomate | 30 ml |
| 1 tasse | Crevettes cuites | 250 ml |
| | Sel, poivre | |

Dans un mélangeur, verser le fromage à la crème, la mayonnaise, l'oignon émincé, l'ail écrasé, le jus du demi-citron et la purée de tomate. Ajouter les crevettes et mélanger jusqu'à l'obtention d'un mélange crémeux. Verser dans la minimijoteuse, couvrir et chauffer pendant 1 h. Servir avec des légumes, du pain, des croustilles et des gressins.

**Suggestion**

≫ Il est possible de réaliser cette recette dans une casserole à feu doux. Vérifier souvent en mélangeant et en prenant soin de bien racler le fond, qui aura tendance à coller.

# :: Les trempettes froides ::

## Houmous de fèves à la coriandre

| | | |
|---|---|---|
| 1 1/2 tasse | Fèves pelées surgelées | 375 ml |
| 1 petite gousse | Ail | 1 petite gousse |
| 3 branches | Coriandre | 3 branches |
| 2 à 3 c. à soupe | Jus de citron | 30 à 45 ml |
| 3 c. à soupe | Huile d'olive | 45 ml |
| | Sel, poivre | |

Faire bouillir de l'eau dans une grande casserole. Y plonger les fèves et laisser cuire 3 min.

Égoutter les fèves et les passer sous l'eau froide. Une fois qu'elles sont refroidies, les mettre dans un bol avec l'ail haché, les feuilles de coriandre, l'huile et le jus de citron. Mixer jusqu'à l'obtention d'une texture crémeuse (ajouter un peu d'huile ou de l'eau si la préparation est trop compacte).

Assaisonner et déguster avec des craquelins, du pain grillé coupé en longueur ou des gressins.

**Suggestion**

⟩⟩⟩ Il est préférable de ne pas préparer cette recette trop à l'avance pour en conserver toutes les saveurs.

# HOUMOUS

| | | |
|---|---|---|
| 1 boîte | Pois chiches en conserve | 540 ml |
| 1 | Citron | 1 |
| 1 c. à soupe | Tahini (pâte de sésame) | 15 ml |
| 2 gousses | Ail | 2 gousses |
| 1/4 c. à thé | Cumin | 1 ml |
| 1 c. à soupe | Huile d'olive | 15 ml |
| | Sel, poivre | |

Passer les pois chiches au moulin à légumes pour obtenir une purée. Ajouter le jus du citron, le tahini, l'ail et le cumin. Mélanger et ajouter de l'eau si le mélange est trop épais. Goûter et saler. Arroser d'un filet d'huile d'olive.

**Suggestion**

))) Pour accompagner le pain pita ou lavash, des légumes en bâtonnets et des radis.

))) En farcir des tomates ou en garnir des croûtons frottés à l'ail.

# Trempette à l'avocat

| 2 | Avocats bien mûrs | 2 |
| 4 | Petits oignons nouveaux | 4 |
| 1 | Citron non traité | 1 |
| 1 | Piment rouge frais | 1 |
| | Sel | |

Couper la chair de l'avocat en cubes. Râper le zeste de citron pour en obtenir 1 c. à soupe. Presser le citron. Mélanger le tout et saler. Couper les oignons et le piment. Mixer le tout jusqu'à l'obtention d'une purée.

**Suggestion**

》 Servir avec des tortillas, du pain grillé, des légumes en bâtonnets et du poulet froid, ou, allongée d'huile, en sauce à salade.

# Guacamole à la lime

| 2 | Avocats bien mûrs | 2 |
| 2 c. à thé | Jus de lime | 10 ml |
| 1 c. à thé | Cumin | 5 ml |
| 1 c. à thé | Coriandre en poudre | 5 ml |
| 1 | Piment | 1 |
| | Sel, poivre | |

Écraser l'avocat à la fourchette. Ajouter le jus de lime, les épices et le piment émincé. Saler et poivrer.

## Avocat en crème fouettée

| 1 | Avocat bien mûr | 2 |
|---|---|---|
| 1/2 | Lime | 1/2 |
| 1 tasse | Crème liquide froide | 250 ml |
| | Sel et poivre du moulin | |

Mixer la chair de l'avocat avec le jus de la demi-lime. Saler et poivrer. Fouetter la crème et incorporer délicatement et peu à peu la purée d'avocat. Garder au frais le temps de servir.

**Suggestion** ))) Pour décorer un gaspacho froid servi en verrines.

## Crème fouettée à la moutarde violette

| 1 tasse | Crème à fouetter froide | 250 ml |
|---|---|---|
| 2 c. à thé | Moutarde violette | 5 ml |
| | Sel et poivre | |

Fouetter la crème avec la moutarde. Saler et poivrer.

**Suggestion** ))) Pour faire trempette avec des légumes et des petits radis printaniers.

# Tapenade au thon

| | | |
|---|:---:|---|
| 1/3 tasse | Thon à l'huile égoutté | 85 ml |
| 1/3 tasse | Câpres | 85 ml |
| 2 gousses | Ail | 2 gousses |
| 1 tasse | Olives vertes dénoyautées | 250 ml |
| | Sel et poivre du moulin | |
| 1 branche | Thym | 1 branche |
| 2/3 tasse | Huile d'olive | 170 ml |

Mixer le tout en ajoutant l'huile peu à peu.

**Suggestion**

))) Présenter dans de petits verres décorés de persil et d'une fine tranche de citron.

))) Préparer du pain à l'huile d'olive.

## Betterave crémeuse

| | | |
|---|---|---|
| 1 tasse | Betteraves cuites | 250 ml |
| 1 tasse | Haricots blancs (fèves) en conserve | 250 ml |
| 1 gousse | Ail | 150 ml |
| 1/2 | Citron | 1/2 |
| 2 c. à soupe | Crème épaisse | 30 ml |
| 4 c. à soupe | Huile d'olive | 60 ml |
| | Sel, poivre | |

Peler les betteraves et les couper en morceaux. Peler l'ail et le déger-mer. Peler les haricots et les mixer finement avec les morceaux de betteraves, l'ail et la crème. Saler et poivrer. Ajouter un filet de jus de citron et mélanger. Arroser d'un filet d'huile d'olive.

**Suggestion** ))) Pour y tremper des tortillas.

# Purée d'aubergine

| | | |
|---|---|---|
| 2 | Aubergines | 2 |
| 4 gousses | Ail | 4 gousses |
| 6 branches | Coriandre | 6 branches |
| 1 | Citron | 1 |
| 1 tasse | Yogourt nature | 250 ml |
| 2 c. à soupe | Huile d'olive | 30 ml |
| | Sel, poivre | |

Poser les aubergines dans une lèchefrite. Mettre au four préchauffé à 300 °F (150 °C) jusqu'à cuisson complète des aubergines. Laisser refroidir, puis couper les aubergines en deux et en racler la chair avec une cuillère. Réduire la chair en purée dans un mélangeur, ajouter le jus de citron, trois gousses d'ail et le yogourt. Saler et poivrer. Parsemer de coriandre hachée. Bien mélanger et réfrigérer.

Avant de servir, émulsionner une gousse d'ail avec l'huile d'olive. Badigeonner de cette huile parfumée des tranches de pain et les faire griller pour accompagner la purée d'aubergine.

**Suggestion** ))) Pour tremper du pain grillé et parfumé d'huile d'olive.

# Trempette crémeuse à l'aubergine

| | | |
|---|---|---|
| 1 | Grosse aubergine | 1 |
| 2 c. à soupe | Huile d'olive | 30 ml |
| 1 | Oignon | 1 |
| 2 gousses | Ail | 2 gousses |
| 1/2 bouquet | Persil | 1/2 bouquet |
| 5 c. à soupe | Crème sure | 75 ml |
| Quelques gouttes | Tabasco | Quelques gouttes |
| | Sel, poivre | |

Préchauffer le four à 300 °F (150 °C). Mettre l'aubergine sur du papier parchemin et la faire griller 20 à 30 min en la retournant. La retirer du four quand elle est molle et la laisser refroidir.

Dans une poêle, mettre l'huile et y faire revenir l'oignon et l'ail. Retirer la peau de l'aubergine et en écraser la chair à la fourchette. Ajouter l'oignon et l'ail, le persil haché et la crème sure. Saler et poivrer.

**Suggestion** ⟩⟩⟩ **Servir tiède.**

# Caviar de poivrons

| | | |
|---:|:---:|:---|
| 4 | Poivrons rouges | 4 |
| 4 c. à soupe | Huile d'olive | 60 ml |
| 1/4 tasse | Fromage frais | 65 ml |
| | Sel, poivre | |

Chauffer le four à 400 °F (200 °C). Mettre les poivrons sur la grille et les faire cuire jusqu'à ce que la peau s'en détache facilement. Les couvrir jusqu'à refroidissement et les peler. Retirer les graines. Mixer la chair tout en ajoutant l'huile d'olive et le fromage frais. Saler et poivrer.

**Suggestion**

››› Pour accompagner le pain grillé, des filets d'anchois et des olives hachées.

››› Déguster avec du poulet froid ou du poisson en papillote.

# Aïoli

| | | |
|---:|:---:|:---|
| 2 gousses | Ail | 2 gousses |
| 2 | Jaunes d'œuf | 2 |
| 2 c. à soupe | Huile d'olive | 30 ml |
| | Sel, poivre | |

Écraser les gousses d'ail en purée. Ajouter les jaunes d'œuf à température ambiante et verser peu à peu l'huile en fouettant constamment pour monter une mayonnaise. Saler et poivrer.

## Mayonnaise au cari

| | | |
|---|---|---|
| 1 | Jaune d'œuf | 1 |
| 1/2 tasse | Huile de canola | 125 ml |
| 2 c. à soupe | Vinaigre | 30 ml |
| 1 c. à soupe | Jus de citron | 15 ml |
| 1 c. à soupe | Cari en poudre | 15 ml |
| 1 gousse | Ail | 1 gousse |
| 3 branches | Persil | 3 branches |
| | Sel, poivre | |

Battre le jaune d'œuf et y verser peu à peu l'huile tout en continuant de fouetter. Ajouter les autres ingrédients. Saler et poivrer.

Réserver au frais.

## Trempette aux pignons

| | | |
|---|---|---|
| 1/2 tasse | Pignons de pin | 125 ml |
| 1 cuil. à soupe | Huile d'olive | 15 ml |
| 1 à 2 c. à thé | Jus de citron | 5 à 10 ml |
| 1/4 c. à thé | Sel | 1 ml |
| 1/4 c. à thé | Gingembre frais râpé | 1 ml |
| 1/4 c. à thé | Piment en poudre | 1 ml |
| 3 à 4 c. à soupe | Yogourt grec | 45 à 60 ml |

Mixer tous les ingrédients jusqu'à l'obtention d'une crème. Goûter et assaisonner à votre goût.

**Suggestion** ))) Servir avec des légumes crus ou en garnir des sandwiches.

## Trempette asiatique

| | | |
|---|---|---|
| 2 c. à soupe | Sauce soja | 30 ml |
| 1/2 tasse | Mayonnaise | 125 ml |
| 1 c. à soupe | Huile de sésame | 15 ml |
| 2 c. à thé | Graines de sésame | 10 ml |

Mélanger la sauce soja, la mayonnaise et l'huile de sésame. Parsemer de graine de sésame.

**Suggestion** ))) Délicieux avec des bâtonnets de concombre.

## Tzatziki

| | | |
|---|---|---|
| 1 | Concombre | 1 |
| 1 tasse | Yogourt nature | 250 ml |
| 1 gousse | Ail | 1 gousse |
| 1/2 c. à thé | Moutarde | 3 ml |
| 1 c. à soupe | Huile d'olive | 15 ml |
| 3 c. à soupe | Aneth | 45 ml |
| | Sel, poivre | |

Râper le concombre pelé. Laisser dégorger pendant 1 h avec 1 c. à thé de sel. Dans un autre bol, verser le yogourt, la gousse d'ail pressée, la moutarde et le poivre. Mélanger cette préparation au concombre et y verser peu à peu l'huile d'olive. Ajouter l'aneth ciselé et servir bien frais.

## Trempette relevée

| | | |
|---|---|---|
| 1 | Jaune d'œuf | 1 |
| 2 c. à soupe | Vinaigre de vin blanc | 30 ml |
| 3/4 tasse | Huile d'olive | 190 ml |
| 2 gousses | Ail | 2 gousses |
| 1 | Piment | 1 |
| | Sel, poivre | |

Mélanger le jaune d'œuf et le vinaigre. Verser peu à peu l'huile d'olive en continuant de battre jusqu'à épaississement. Ajouter l'ail écrasé. Saler et poivrer. Parsemer de rondelles de piment.

# Trempette satay

| | | |
|---|---|---|
| 2/3 tasse | Arachides | 170 ml |
| 3 c. à soupe | Huile de canola | 45 ml |
| 1 | Oignon | 1 |
| 2 gousses | Ail | 2 gousses |
| 1 | Piment | 1 |
| 1 po | Gingembre | 2,5 cm |
| 1 | Citron non traité | 1 |
| 1/2 c. à thé | Cumin | 3 ml |
| 4 branches | Coriandre | 4 branches |
| 1 c. à soupe | Huile de sésame | 15 ml |
| 3/4 tasse | Lait de coco | 190 ml |
| 2 c. à soupe | Sauce soja | 30 ml |
| | Sel, poivre | |

Boyer les arachides dans un mélangeur, puis y ajouter l'huile de canola. Réserver.

Dans le mélangeur, mettre l'oignon grossièrement émincé, l'ail, le piment, le gingembre, un peu de zeste de citron, le cumin et les branches de coriandre hachées. Mixer jusqu'à l'obtention d'une pâte onctueuse

Faire chauffer un peu d'huile de canola additionnée de l'huile de sésame et faire revenir le dernier mélange pendant 10 min.

Mélanger à la pâte d'arachide. Ajouter le lait de coco, la sauce soja et le jus de citron. Saler et poivrer.

**Suggestion** ))) Pour accompagner des légumes en bâtonnets, mais aussi des ailes de poulet.

# Trempette crémeuse ailée

| | | |
|---:|:---:|:---|
| 1/2 | Concombre | 1/2 |
| 2 gousses | Ail | 2 gousses |
| 6 c. à soupe | Huile d'olive | 90 ml |
| 1 | Tomate | 1 |
| 1 c. à soupe | Vinaigre de vin blanc | 15 ml |
| 3/4 tasse | Crème sure | 190 ml |
| | Sel, poivre | |

Mélanger le concombre coupé en petits dés, les gousses d'ail écrasées, l'huile d'olive, la tomate épépinée coupée en dés et le vinaigre. Laisser reposer et égoutter.

Incorporer la crème sure. Saler et poivrer.

# Purée de tomate

| | | |
|---:|:---:|:---|
| 1 | Oignon | 1 |
| 1 c. à thé | Huile d'olive | 5 ml |
| 2 | Tomates bien juteuses | 2 |
| 1 c. à soupe | Vin blanc ou rouge | 15 ml |
| | Sel, poivre | |

Faire revenir l'oignon émincé dans l'huile d'olive. Ajouter les tomates et le vin. Porter à ébullition et laisser mijoter jusqu'à évaporation du liquide. Saler et poivrer.

## Trempette à la tomate

| | | |
|---|---|---|
| 4 | Tomates | 4 |
| 1 | Oignon | 1 |
| 1/4 tasse | Purée de tomate | 65 ml |
| 2 c. à soupe | Huile d'olive | 30 ml |
| 1 c. à soupe | Sucre | 15 ml |
| 1 c. à soupe | Origan | 15 ml |
| 3 gousses | Ail | 3 gousses |
| 1 | Piment rouge | 1 |
| 1 c. à soupe | Persil | 15 ml |
| | Sel, poivre | |

Dans le mélangeur, mettre tous les ingrédients. Saler, poivrer et parsemer de persil.

## Trempette au bleu

| | | |
|---|---|---|
| 2/3 tasse | Fromage bleu persillé | 170 ml |
| 2/3 tasse | Fromage à la crème | 170 ml |
| 5 c. à soupe | Yogourt nature | 75 ml |
| | Sel, poivre | |

Émietter le bleu dans un saladier et le battre avec une cuillère de bois. Ajouter le fromage à la crème et mélanger. Ensuite, ajouter peu à peu le yogourt afin de trouver la consistance désirée pour faire trempette. Poivrer et réserver au frais.

**Suggestion**
››› *Délicieuse avec des quartiers de poires ou des bâtonnets de légumes frais, et étonnant avec des tronçons de céleri.*

# Trempette à la coriandre

| | | |
|---|---|---|
| 1/2 tasse | Yogourt nature | 125 ml |
| 1/2 tasse | Fromage frais | 125 ml |
| 1/3 tasse | Salsa* | 85 ml |
| 5 branches | Coriandre | 5 branches |
| | Sel, poivre | |

Bien mélanger les ingrédients et placer au réfrigérateur au moins 2 h. Saupoudrer du reste de coriandre ciselée.

* Salsa du commerce ou voir la recette ci-dessous.

# Salsa

| | | |
|---|---|---|
| 3 | Tomates | 3 |
| 1 | Échalote française | 1 |
| 1 gousse | Ail | 1 gousse |
| 1 | Piment | 1 |
| 1 c. à soupe | Vinaigre de vin | 15 ml |
| 2 c. à thé | Jus de citron | 10 ml |
| 2 c. à thé | Huile d'olive | 10 ml |

Ébouillanter les tomates pour en retirer la peau, puis les couper en petits dés. Hacher l'échalote, la gousse d'ail et le piment. Mélanger. Ajouter le vinaigre, le jus de citron et l'huile d'olive.

Couvrir et mettre au frais pendant au moins 2 h.

## Trempette de fruits au gingembre et au citron

| | | |
|---|---|---|
| 1/2 tasse | Yogourt nature | 125 ml |
| 1/2 tasse | Fromage frais | 125 ml |
| 1 1/2 c. à soupe | Miel | 22 ml |
| 1 c. à thé | Jus de citron | 5 ml |
| 1/2 c. à thé | Zeste de citron | 3 ml |
| 1/2 c. à thé | Gingembre frais | 3 ml |

Bien mélanger les ingrédients et placer au réfrigérateur au moins 2 h. Saupoudrer d'un peu de zeste de citron supplémentaire.

## Raïta à l'oignon rouge

| | | |
|---|---|---|
| 1 c. à thé | Cumin | 5 ml |
| 1 gousse | Ail | 1 gousse |
| 1 | Petit piment vert | 1 |
| 1 | Oignon rouge | 1 |
| 2/3 tasse | Yogourt nature | 170 ml |
| 1/4 bouquet | Coriandre | 1/4 de bouquet |
| 1/2 c. à thé | Sucre | 3 ml |
| | Sel | |

Émincer l'oignon rouge, couper le piment en fines rondelles et ciseler les feuilles de coriandre. Mélanger au yogourt et ajouter le cumin en poudre. Sucrer, saler et bien mélanger. Réserver au frais.

⟫ Pour tremper des pappadums (petits pains indiens), mais aussi des bâtonnets de carotte ou de concombre.

⟫ Les raïtas sont des préparations indiennes, avec des variantes régionales, consommées froides. Sortes de salade au yogourt, elles accompagnent un cari très épicé en apportant au palais un peu de fraîcheur et de douceur, tout en apaisant le feu du piment.

## Trempette au thon

| | | |
|---|---|---|
| 1 boîte de 6 oz | Thon | 170 g |
| 1 tasse | Yogourt nature | 250 ml |
| 1 c. à soupe | Moutarde | 15 ml |
| 1/2 c. à thé | Paprika | 3 ml |
| | Sel, poivre | |

Mettre le thon égoutté dans le mélangeur. Ajouter le paprika et réduire légèrement.

Avec une cuillère de bois et dans un petit contenant, mélanger cette préparation au yogourt et à la moutarde. Saler et poivrer. Fermer le couvercle et réserver au frais.

# Trempette aux haricots blancs

| | | |
|---|---|---|
| 1 1/2 tasse | Haricots blancs | 375 ml |
| 1 gousse | Ail | 1 gousse |
| 1 c. à soupe | Huile d'olive | 15 ml |
| 1 c. à soupe | Graines de sésame | 15 ml |
| 1 c. à thé | Huile de sésame | 5 ml |
| | Sel, poivre | |

Égoutter les haricots blancs en réservant un peu de jus et, dans un mélangeur, réduire les haricots en purée avec la gousse d'ail.

Verser dans un bol et ajouter peu à peu l'huile d'olive. Saler et poivrer. Mélanger à la cuillère de bois et, au besoin, ajouter un peu de jus des haricots.

Couvrir et mettre au réfrigérateur. Au moment de servir, arroser la préparation avec de l'huile de sésame et parsemer de graines de sésame.

# Trempette à la purée d'ail

| | | |
|---|---|---|
| 2 bulbes | Ail | 2 bulbes |
| 1 c. à soupe | Huile d'olive | 15 ml |
| 4 c. à soupe | Mayonnaise | 60 ml |
| 5 c. à soupe | Yogourt nature | 75 ml |
| 1 c. à thé | Moutarde à l'ancienne | 5 ml |
| | Sel, poivre | |

Dans un plat allant au four, verser l'huile d'olive, y placer les gousses d'ail et les cuire 5 min au four préchauffé à 400 °F (200 °C).

Une fois les têtes d'ail grillées, retirer les peaux des gousses et réduire ces dernières en purée. Mélanger avec la mayonnaise, le yogourt et la moutarde à l'ancienne.

Poivrer et mettre au frais.

**Suggestion**  ))) Pour tremper des tortillas, des gressins ou des craquelins.

## Trempette au fromage cottage et au poivron rouge

| | | |
|---|---|---|
| 1 tasse | Fromage cottage | 250 ml |
| 3 c. à soupe | Yogourt nature | 45 ml |
| 1 | Poivron rouge | 1 |
| 1 c. à soupe | Miel | 15 ml |
| 1 c. à soupe | Huile d'olive | 15 ml |
| | Sel, poivre | |

Laver le poivron rouge, en retirer les graines et le couper grossièrement. Mettre le poivron dans le mélangeur pour en réduire finement les morceaux.

Ajouter le fromage cottage, le yogourt et le miel, puis mélanger de nouveau.

Mettre la préparation dans un bol et mélanger avec de l'huile d'olive, du sel et du poivre du moulin.

Couvrir et réfrigérer.

# Tarama

| 1 tasse | Œufs de morue | 250 ml |
|---|---|---|
| 2 c. à soupe | Huile de pépins de raisin | 30 ml |
| 2 c. à soupe | Crème sure | 30 ml |
| 1 | Citron | 1 |
| | Poivre | |

Sortir les œufs de morue de leur poche et les placer dans un grand bol. À l'aide d'une fourchette, les détacher en les écrasant. Ajouter peu à peu l'huile. Mélanger jusqu'à l'obtention d'une pâte lisse. Ajouter le jus de citron et la crème sure. Poivrer.

Réserver au réfrigérateur et servir avec des lichettes de pain grillé. Se garde trois jours au réfrigérateur.

# Pesto pistaches-coriandre

| 1 bouquet | Coriandre | 1 bouquet |
|---|---|---|
| 1/2 tasse | Pistaches | 125 ml |
| 1 gousse | Ail | 1 gousse |
| 1/2 tasse | Huile d'olive | 125 ml |
| | Sel, poivre | |

Laver, sécher et effeuiller le bouquet de coriandre. Hacher finement les pistaches et les joindre à la coriandre dans un mélangeur. Ajouter la gousse d'ail, saler et poivrer. Ajouter l'huile dans le mélangeur en marche.

## Pesto de roquette et de noisettes

| | | |
|---|---|---|
| 2 tasses | Roquette | 500 ml |
| 1/2 tasse | Noisettes | 125 ml |
| 1 gousse | Ail | 1 gousse |
| 1/2 tasse | Huile d'olive | 125 ml |
| | Sel, poivre | |

Laver et sécher les feuilles de roquette. Hacher finement les noisettes et les joindre à la roquette dans un mélangeur. Ajouter la gousse d'ail, saler et poivrer. Ajouter l'huile dans le mélangeur en marche.

## Pesto de menthe, de roquette et d'amandes

| | | |
|---|---|---|
| 1 tasse | Roquette | 250 ml |
| 1/2 tasse | Menthe | 125 ml |
| 1/4 tasse | Amandes grillées | 65 ml |
| 1 gousse | Ail | 1 gousse |
| 1/2 tasse | Huile d'olive | 125 ml |
| | Sel, poivre | |

Laver et sécher les feuilles de coriandre et de menthe. Hacher finement les amandes grillées et les joindre aux feuilles dans un mélangeur. Ajouter la gousse d'ail, saler et poivrer. Ajouter l'huile dans le mélangeur en marche.

# Trempette à la mangue

| | | |
|---|---|---|
| 1 | Mangue bien mûre | 1 |
| 2 c. à soupe | Huile d'olive | 30 ml |
| 1 | Lime | 1 |
| | Sel | |

Réduire la chair de la mangue en purée, ajouter l'huile d'olive, un peu de jus de lime et le piment. Saler.

# Trempette à la courge musquée et au parmesan

| | | |
|---|---|---|
| 1 | Courge musquée (butternut) | 1 |
| 1 c. à soupe | Beurre | 15 ml |
| 4 gousses | Ail | 4 gousses |
| 2 c. à soupe | Parmesan râpé | 30 ml |
| 5 c. à soupe | Crème sure | 75 ml |
| | Sel, poivre | |

Préchauffer le four à 400 °F (200 °C). Couper la courge en deux et en retirer les graines. Avec un couteau, faire des croisillons dans la chair et la beurrer. Mettre dans un plat et placer au four pendant 20 min. Ajouter les gousses d'ail dans leur peau et continuer la cuisson 20 min.

Retirer la chair de la courge et la placer dans un mélangeur pour la réduire en purée. Y verser peu à peu le parmesan, puis la crème sure.

**Suggestion** ⟩⟩⟩ À servir de préférence avec des croustilles au fromage.

# Trempette aux carottes

| | | |
|---|---|---|
| 1 | Oignon | 1 |
| 2 c. à soupe | Huile d'olive | 30 ml |
| 4 | Carottes | 4 |
| 1 c. à soupe | Cari épicé | 15 ml |
| 1/2 tasse | Yogourt nature | 125 ml |
| 2 branches | Persil | 2 branches |
| 2 c. à soupe | Jus de citron | 30 ml |
| Quelques gouttes | Tabasco | Quelques gouttes |
| | Sel, poivre | |

Émincer l'oignon et râper les carottes. Dans une casserole, mettre l'huile et y faire revenir les oignons. Ajouter les carottes et le cari. Couvrir et cuire 10 min.

Dans le mélangeur, réduire les carottes en purée. Laisser refroidir et ajouter le yogourt. Mélanger, ajouter le jus de citron et le Tabasco. Saler et poivrer.

Réfrigérer et garnir de persil avant de servir.

**Suggestion** ››› Servir avec des craquelins au blé entier ou des tortillas.

# Trempette au thon

| | | |
|---|---|---|
| 1 boîte de 6 oz | Thon dans l'huile | 170 g |
| 3 | Œufs durs | 3 |
| 3/4 tasse | Olives vertes | 65 ml |
| 4 | Filets d'anchois | 4 |
| 3 c. à soupe | Câpres | 45 ml |
| 2 c. à soupe | Moutarde de Dijon | 30 ml |
| | Poivre | |

Égoutter le thon. Retirer le jaune des œufs et les placer dans un mélangeur. Ajouter les olives, le thon, les filets d'anchois, les câpres et la moutarde. Mettre dans un bol et verser dessus un filet d'huile d'olive.

**Suggestion** ))) Pour y tremper des gressins.

# :: Les trempettes dessert ::

Les trempettes sucrées accompagnent les morceaux de fruits entiers, les biscuits à peine sucrés, les gaufres coupées en languettes, etc.

## Trempette à la papaye

| | | |
|---|---|---|
| 2 | Papayes | 2 |
| 1 tasse | Crème fraîche | 250 ml |

Couper les papayes en deux et en retirer les graines. Les peler et en placer la chair dans un mélangeur avec la crème fraîche. Réduire en purée.

**Suggestion** ))) Faire trempette avec des biscuits sucrés.

## Trempette au chocolat noir et à la banane

| | | |
|---|---|---|
| 2 oz | Chocolat noir | 60 g |
| 2 | Bananes | 2 |

Faire fondre le chocolat au bain-marie. Mettre les bananes dans le mélangeur et les réduire en purée. Y ajouter peu à peu le chocolat fondu et refroidi.

**Suggestion** ))) Servir avec des fraises, des quartiers de kiwi, des morceaux de pêche, d'ananas ou autre.

# Trempette de caramel au beurre salé

| | | |
|---|---|---|
| 1/3 tasse | Sucre | 85 ml |
| 1/4 c. à thé | Jus de citron | 1 ml |
| 1/4 tasse | Beurre salé | 65 ml |
| 2 c. à soupe | Eau | 30 ml |

Dans une casserole, faire fondre le sucre avec le jus de citron et l'eau. Quand le sucre commence à prendre sa couleur caramel, ajouter le beurre et bien mélanger.

# Crème pâtissière à la vanille

| | | |
|---|---|---|
| 2 tasses | Lait | 500 ml |
| 1 gousse | Vanille | 1 gousse |
| 6 | Jaunes d'œuf | 6 |
| 4 c. à soupe | Sucre | 60 ml |

Inciser la gousse de vanille en deux sur la longueur. En gratter les graines et dans une petite casserole, les ajouter au lait, avec la gousse de vanille. Porter à ébullition au bain-marie.

Dans un bol, battre les jaunes d'œuf et le sucre. Ajouter lentement le lait bouilli. Remettre le tout au bain-marie et cuire sans cesser de tourner à la cuillère de bois. Dès que le mélange commence à épaissir, le retirer du feu. La sauce ne doit surtout pas bouillir.

**Suggestion**

⟩⟩⟩ Si la sauce est trop liquide, ajouter 2 ml d'agar-agar ou une feuille de gélatine préalablement trempée.

⟩⟩⟩ Si la sauce a caillé, la verser dans un mélangeur et faire tourner le moteur à la vitesse maximale. Elle retrouvera ainsi toute son onctuosité.

## Trempette au café

| | | |
|---|---|---|
| 2 c. à soupe | Beurre | 30 ml |
| 2 c. à soupe | Sucre | 30 ml |
| 1 tasse | Crème fraîche | 250 ml |
| 1 c. à soupe | Café instantané | 15 ml |
| 1 c. à thé | Rhum | 5 ml |

Faire fondre le beurre et ajouter le sucre afin de le caraméliser. Verser la crème en continuant à remuer et cuire le mélange environ 2 min. Ajouter le café instantané et le rhum. Mélanger.

**Suggestion**

⟩⟩⟩ Si la sauce est trop liquide, ajouter 2 ml d'agar-agar ou une feuille de gélatine préalablement trempée.

## Trempette de mangue

| | | |
|---|---|---|
| 1 | Mangue mûre | 1 |
| 1 c. à soupe | Miel | 15 ml |
| 1 c. à soupe | Jus de citron | 15 ml |
| 1/2 tasse | Eau | 125 ml |

Faire bouillir la mangue dans l'eau. Ajouter le miel et le jus de citron. Cuire à feu doux environ 5 min.

Une fois la trempette refroidie, la placer au réfrigérateur.

**Suggestion** ⟫ Si la sauce est trop liquide, ajouter 2 ml d'agar-agar ou une feuille de gélatine préalablement trempée.

## Trempette de mascarpone

| | | |
|---|---|---|
| 1 2/3 tasse | Mascarpone | 420 ml |
| 2 | Jaunes d'œuf | 2 |
| 1/4 tasse | Sucre en poudre | 65 ml |

Dans un bol, mélanger le mascarpone aux jaunes d'œuf et au sucre en poudre. Fouetter jusqu'à ce que le mélange soit uniforme et onctueux.

## Trempette à la crème de marrons

| | | |
|---|---|---|
| 4 | Jaunes d'œuf | 4 |
| 1/2 tasse | Sucre | 125 ml |
| 1 tasse | Crème fraîche | 250 ml |
| 5 c. à soupe | Purée de marrons | 75 ml |

Battre le sucre et les jaunes d'œuf en mousse. Continuer de battre en fouettant dans un bain-marie. Ajouter la moitié de la crème fraîche et continuer de mélanger jusqu'à l'obtention d'une crème onctueuse. Ajouter la crème de marrons et réfrigérer.

## Trempette au sirop d'érable

| | | |
|---|---|---|
| 1 tasse | Sirop d'érable | 250 ml |
| 1/2 tasse | Crème fraîche | 125 ml |

Mélanger le sirop d'érable et la crème fraîche. Porter à ébullition, puis laisser mijoter à feu doux environ 5 min. Laisser refroidir et réfrigérer.

**Suggestion**

))) Si la sauce est trop liquide, ajouter 2 ml d'agar-agar ou une feuille de gélatine préalablement trempée.

# Trempette chaude au chocolat noir

| | | |
|---|---|---|
| 1 c. à thé | Beurre | 5 ml |
| 1 tasse | Petites guimauves | 250 ml |
| 1/4 tasse | Crème liquide | 65 ml |
| 1 tablette | Chocolat noir (70 %) | 100 g |
| 2 c. à soupe | Lait | 30 ml |

Dans la minimijoteuse, mettre le chocolat en morceaux, les guimauves et le lait. Couvrir et chauffer 30 min, jusqu'à ce que le chocolat et les guimauves aient fondu et que le mélange devienne onctueux. Remuer de temps en temps, puis incorporer peu à peu la crème liquide. Couvrir et laisser chauffer encore 30 min.

Servir avec des morceaux de fruits, du gâteau coupé en cubes ou des guimauves.

**Suggestion**

⫶⫶⫶ Il est possible de réaliser cette recette dans une casserole à feu doux. Vérifier souvent en mélangeant et en prenant soin de bien racler le fond, qui aura tendance à coller.

# Trempette chaude aux petits fruits

| | | |
|---|---|---|
| 1 lb | Fraises, mûres, framboises ou bleuets | 450 g |
| 2/3 tasse | Sucre | 170 ml |
| 1 | Citron | 1 |
| | Un peu d'eau au besoin | |

Laver les fruits. Les faires mijoter environ 20 min avec le sucre, le jus de citron et l'eau.

## Trempette chaude au chocolat noir et au rhum

| | | |
|---|---|---|
| 2 tablettes | Chocolat noir | 200 g |
| 1/2 tasse | Crème liquide | 125 ml |
| 3 c. à soupe | Sucre | 45 ml |
| 1 c. à soupe | Rhum | 15 ml |

Faire fondre le chocolat au bain-marie. Ajouter la crème et le sucre, puis mélanger jusqu'à l'obtention d'une crème homogène. Arroser de rhum.

**Suggestion**

››› Parfumer le chocolat avec le zeste d'une orange non traitée.

››› Y plonger des biscuits et des morceaux de fruits.

››› Tartiner sur des crêpes chaudes.

››› Utiliser une minimijoteuse ou un chauffe-plats pour la garder au chaud.

››› Peut se déguster froide.

# Les marinades

# L'art de la marinade

Les marinades sont des mélanges de condiments où sont bai-
gnés plus ou moins longtemps (de quelques minutes à toute
une nuit) des viandes, des poissons, des légumes ou des fruits.
Qu'elles soient crues ou cuites, les marinades sont idéales pour
les cuissons rapides.

Cette pratique culinaire ancienne, qui consistait au départ
à tremper les aliments dans un mélange de vin, de vinaigre,
d'eau, de sel, d'herbes et d'épices, adoucissait non seulement
le goût prononcé du gibier, mais avait surtout pour fonction de
conserver la viande plus longtemps. Aujourd'hui, les marinades
parfument, aromatisent et attendrissent les fibres de la viande
et conservent les légumes, le poisson ou les fruits, tout en en
renforçant la saveur.

# :: Les marinades crues ::

Elles imprègnent l'aliment de ses parfums d'herbes ou d'épices de la marinade, mais « cuira » aussi par l'action du vinaigre ou du citron. La plupart des aliments préparés de cette façon pourront être mangés crus, à condition d'être frais, surtout s'il s'agit de viande ou de poisson.

La marinade crue est acide et doit être préparée dans un récipient en verre ou en porcelaine.

# :: Les marinades cuites ::

Elles concernent surtout les viandes ou les poissons. Pendant que la viande marine, l'huile la préservera en l'empêchant de se dessécher lors de la cuisson au barbecue, au four ou à la poêle, et la viande attendrie par la marinade en sera d'autant plus savoureuse. Les pièces sont souvent retournées et, une fois prêtes à la cuisson, égouttées. La marinade réservée sert souvent pour déglacer, c'est-à-dire pour dissoudre les sucs caramélisés résultant de la cuisson de la viande, pour la confection de la sauce d'accompagnement.

# :: La composition d'une marinade ::

Une marinade est composée essentiellement d'un élément gras, l'huile, et d'un élément acide, le vinaigre, le citron ou le vin, auxquels seront ajoutées des herbes ou des épices.

### Huile

Elle humidifie et protège la viande, surtout lors de la cuisson. Si la cuisson est faite au barbecue, préférer l'huile d'olive ou de pépins de raisin, qui supporteront mieux la chaleur.

### Vinaigre et citron

Les acides attendrissent la viande et atténuent les sucres contenus dans le vin, le miel, le sirop d'érable ou d'autres composantes de la marinade.

### Herbes

Pour les marinades, les herbes séchées sont préférables. En effet, elles vont se réhydrater pendant la macération et elles résisteront mieux à la chaleur du gril, tout en concentrant leur arôme dans les aliments.

### Yogourt

Il adoucit tout en épaississant la marinade. Plus enveloppante, cette dernière protégera alors d'autant plus les morceaux de viande ou de poisson.

## :: Conditions de macération d'une pièce de viande ou de poisson ::

Déposer la viande ou le poisson dans un plat en verre ou en porcelaine et la recouvrir entièrement de la marinade choisie, surtout pour une macération prolongée. Couvrir le plat de son couvercle ou d'une pellicule plastique. On recommande une macération de 4 à 12 h pour la viande et de 30 min à 1 h pour le poisson. Toutefois, la macération d'une viande ne doit jamais être supérieure à 20 h, au risque d'abîmer la texture de la chair.

# Les recettes

## Marinade crue pour une pièce de viande

| | | |
|---|---|---|
| 1 c. à soupe | Cinq épices* | 15 ml |
| 1/4 tasse | Huile de canola | 65 ml |
| 1 | Oignon | 1 |
| 3 | Carottes | 3 |
| 2 gousses | Ail | 2 gousses |
| 1 branche | Persil | 1 branche |
| 1 branche | Thym | 1 branche |
| 1 feuille | Laurier | 1 feuille |
| 2 c. à soupe | Vinaigre | 30 ml |
| 3 tasses | Vin rouge | 750 ml |
| | Sel, poivre | |

Couper le poulet en morceaux et le placer dans la marinade pimentée. Couvrir le plat et mettre au réfrigérateur pendant 4 h en remuant de temps en temps.

Faire griller en arrosant de la marinade.

Servir avec du riz.

---

* Anis étoilé, graines de fenouil, clous de girofle, poivre du Sichuan et cannelle.

## Marinade aux épices

| | | |
|---|---|---|
| 1 c. à soupe | Cannelle en poudre | 15 ml |
| 1/2 c. à soupe | Gingembre en poudre | 8 ml |
| 3 | Limes | 3 |
| 3 c. à soupe | Huile d'olive | 45 ml |
| 2 c. à soupe | Sauce soja | 30 ml |
| 2 c. à soupe | Vinaigre de vin | 30 ml |
| 2 c. à soupe | Sirop d'érable | 30 ml |
| | Sel, poivre | |

Presser le jus des limes. Mélanger dans un bol avec la sauce soja, le vinaigre, le sirop d'érable, l'huile d'olive et les épices. Saler et poivrer.

## Flancs de veau asiatiques

| | | |
|---|---|---|
| 2 lb | Flancs de veau | 1 kg |
| 1/2 tasse | Eau | 125 ml |

Couper les tendrons en gros morceaux. Verser la marinade sur les morceaux de viande, couvrir et réfrigérer toute la nuit.

Égoutter la viande et la saisir dans un chaudron. Une fois que la viande est colorée, verser l'eau dessus et baisser le feu. Mijoter 30 min en retournant les morceaux et en ajoutant de l'eau au besoin.

**Suggestion**
À servir avec du riz basmati parfumé à la cannelle.

## Marinade au vinaigre balsamique

| | | |
|---|---|---|
| 1 c. à soupe | Vinaigre balsamique | 15 ml |
| 2 c. à soupe | Huile d'olive | 30 ml |
| 1 c. à soupe | Jus de citron | 15 ml |
| | Sel, poivre | |

Mélanger le vinaigre balsamique, l'huile d'olive et le jus de citron. Saler et poivrer.

## Agneau mariné à la lavande

| | | |
|---|---|---|
| 1 | Échalote française | 1 |
| 2 c. à soupe | Fleurs de lavande (non traitées) | 30 ml |
| 4 | Carrés d'agneau | 4 |

Émincer l'échalote française et la parsemer sur les carrés d'agneau. Ajouter les fleurs de lavande, puis verser la marinade sur la viande. Faire mariner les carrés d'agneau pendant 2 heures en les retournant régulièrement.

Allumer le barbecue et cuire la viande environ 20 min, afin qu'elle soit grillée à l'extérieur et rose à l'intérieur.

## Marinade sucrée-salée

| | | |
|---|---|---|
| 1/4 tasse | Sirop d'érable | 65 ml |
| 2 gousses | Ail | 2 gousses |
| 2 | Citrons | 2 |
| 3 c. à soupe | Sauce soja | 45 ml |
| 2 c. à soupe | Sauce Worcestershire | 30 ml |
| 2 c. à soupe | Sucre roux | 30 ml |
| 2 c. à thé | Vinaigre de vin | 10 ml |
| 2 c. à soupe | Mélange de quatre épices | 30 ml |
| | (poivre, muscade, clou de girofle | |
| | et cannelle) | |

Verser tous les ingrédients dans un bol et bien mélanger.

## Côtes levées grillées

| | | |
|---|---|---|
| 4 1/2 lb | Côtes levées | 2,2 kg |

Mettre les côtes levées dans un plat creux et arroser de la marinade sucrée-salée. Couvrir et réfrigérer une nuit entière.

Enlever la marinade et éponger la viande. Cuire les côtes levées environ 1 h en les arrosant régulièrement de marinade et en les retournant.

**Suggestion** ⟫ Servir avec des pommes de terre en robe des champs.

## Marinade au soja et au poireau

| | | |
|---|---|---|
| 1 c. à soupe | Huile de sésame | 15 ml |
| 2 c. à soupe | Sauce soja | 30 ml |
| 1 | Poireau | 1 |
| 2 gousses | Ail | 2 gousses |
| 1/2 c. à thé | Gingembre haché | 3 ml |
| 1 c. à thé | Sucre | 5 ml |

Mélanger l'huile de sésame à la sauce soja. Émincer le poireau et écraser les gousses d'ail. Ajouter le gingembre haché et le sucre.

## Brochette de bœuf aux saveurs d'Asie

| | | |
|---|---|---|
| 1 lb | Bœuf | 450 g |
| 1 | Poireau | 1 |
| 1 c. à soupe | Graines de sésame | 15 ml |

Couper le bœuf en cubes de 1 po (2,5 cm). Les disposer dans un plat et les arroser de marinade. Couper des morceaux de poireau de 1 po (2,5 cm) et les ajouter à la marinade. Couvrir et réfrigérer pendant 2 h.

Si les baguettes sont en bambou, les faire tremper dans de l'eau froide pendant environ 1 h afin qu'elles ne brûlent pas. Monter les brochettes en intercalant les morceaux de viande et de poireau.

Griller les brochettes en badigeonnant régulièrement de marinade.

Parsemer de graines de sésame avant de servir.

## Marinade aux olives

| | | |
|---|---|---|
| 3 c. à soupe | Olives violettes | 45 ml |
| 1 | Ail | 1 |
| 2 | Oignons | 2 |
| 1 | Citron | 1 |
| 1/2 botte | Coriandre | 1/2 botte |
| 2 c. à soupe | Pignons | 30 ml |
| 5 c. à soupe | Huile d'olive | 75 ml |
| | Poivre | |

Dans un saladier, mélanger l'ail, l'oignon, le jus du citron, la coriandre, les pignons, l'huile d'olive, les olives vertes et le poivre du moulin.

## Veau aux olives

| | | |
|---|---|---|
| 1 lb | Veau en morceaux | 450 g |
| 1 tasse | Eau | 250 ml |

Mettre les morceaux de veau dans la marinade aux olives et laisser mariner pendant au moins 1 h.

Dans un chaudron, verser la viande et la marinade, ajouter l'eau et porter à ébullition. Couvrir, baisser le feu et laisser mijoter pendant 3 h. Surveiller et, au besoin, ajouter de l'eau.

Parsemer de feuilles de coriandre ciselées.

**Suggestion**   ))) Servir avec des pommes de terre ou d'autres légumes.

## Marinade à la coriandre et au citron

| | | |
|---|---|---|
| 1/2 bouquet | Coriandre fraîche | 1/2 bouquet |
| 1 c. à soupe | Graines de coriandre | 15 ml |
| 1 | Citron | 1 |
| 1 c. à soupe | Miel | 15 ml |
| 4 c. à soupe | Huile d'olive | 60 ml |

Dans un mélangeur, placer la coriandre fraîche, les graines de coriandre, le jus de citron, le miel et l'huile d'olive. Mixer jusqu'à l'obtention d'une pâte uniforme.

## Lapin en papillote

| | | |
|---|---|---|
| 4 | Râbles de lapin | 4 |
| 1 | Courgette | 1 |
| 1 | Carotte | 1 |
| 1 tasse | Petits pois | 250 ml |
| | Sel | |

Mettre les morceaux de lapin dans un saladier, les arroser de la marinade et les laisser reposer 2 h au réfrigérateur.

Préchauffer le four à 350 °F (180 °C). Couper la courgette et la carotte en petites baguettes. Les blanchir avec les petits pois 2 min dans de l'eau bouillante salée. Égoutter et réserver.

Essuyer les morceaux de viande et les faire dorer à feu doux.

Découper quatre morceaux (30 cm x 40 cm) de papier parchemin. Y répartir les légumes puis les morceaux de lapin. Arroser de la marinade à la coriandre et au citron et bien refermer en papillote. Mettre au four 20 min.

## Marinade à la sauce soja

| | | |
|---|---|---|
| 2 c. à soupe | Sucre | 60 ml |
| 4 c. à soupe | Miel | 60 ml |
| 4 c. à soupe | Sauce soja | 60 ml |

Mélanger le sucre, le miel et la sauce soja.

## Filet mignon caramélisé

| | | |
|---|---|---|
| 1 | Filet mignon de porc | 1 |
| 4 c. à soupe | Huile de canola | 60 ml |
| | Poivre | |

Prévoir ce plat la veille pour que la viande marine toute une nuit.

Mettre le filet mignon dans la marinade à la sauce soja et réfrigérer. Le lendemain, mettre l'huile dans un chaudron et faire chauffer. Essuyer le filet mignon et le saisir dans l'huile chaude. Bien colorer les deux côtés, puis baisser le feu. Arroser de la marinade et cuire pendant 30 min. Continuer d'arroser la viande avec sa marinade durant la cuisson afin de la caraméliser. Poivrer.

Trancher la viande en morceau d'environ 1/2 po.

Accompagner d'une purée.

# Marinade aux fines herbes

Mélanger les ingrédients de chaque marinade. Pour parfumer la viande ou le poisson, laisser mariner au moins 1 h au réfrigérateur. Essuyer chaque pièce avant la cuisson.

## À la coriandre

| | | |
|---|---|---|
| 4 c. à soupe | Huile d'olive | 60 ml |
| 1/2 | Citron | 1/2 |
| 1 branche | Coriandre | 1 branche |
| 1 pincée | Fleur de sel | 1 pincée |

## À l'origan et au cerfeuil

| | | |
|---|---|---|
| 4 c. à soupe | Huile d'olive | 60 ml |
| 1 branche | Origan | 1 branche |
| 1 branche | Cerfeuil | 1 branche |
| 1/2 tasse | Vin blanc | 125 ml |
| Quelques | Baies roses | Quelques |

## Asiatique

| | | |
|---|---|---|
| 4 c. à soupe | Huile de sésame | 60 ml |
| 2 c. à soupe | Sauce soja | 30 ml |
| 1 branche | Basilic | 1 branche |
| 1 c. à thé | Miel | 5 ml |

# :: Poisson ::

## Marinade au curcuma

| | | |
|---|---|---|
| 2 c. à thé | Curcuma en poudre | 10 ml |
| 2 c. à soupe | Huile d'olive | 30 ml |
| 1 | Gousse d'ail | 1 |
| 1 | Citron | 1 |
| 1/4 c. à thé | Piment de Cayenne | 1 ml |
| | Sel, poivre | |

Dans un contenant, mélanger le curcuma, l'huile d'olive, la gousse d'ail écrasée, le jus du citron et le piment de Cayenne. Saler et poivrer.

## Poisson mariné cuit en feuilles de banane

| | | |
|---|---|---|
| 4 | Filets de morue | 200 g chacun |
| 8 | Feuilles de banane | 8 |
| | (épicerie asiatique) | |

Badigeonner les filets de poisson de la marinade. Couvrir le contenant et mettre au réfrigérateur pendant 1 h.

Égoutter le poisson et emballer chaque filet d'une feuille de banane, puis d'une seconde. Fixer avec des cure-dents.

Cuire les filets sur une grille chaude environ 10 min en les retournant une fois.

**Suggestion** : Servir avec une salade verte et des quartiers de citron.

## Marinade à la lime

| | | |
|---|---|---|
| 2 | Limes | 2 |
| 4 c. à soupe | Huile de Canola | 60 ml |
| 6 c. à soupe | Moutarde | 90 ml |
| | Sel, poivre | |

Presser les limes. Dans un bol, mélanger la moutarde avec l'huile et le jus des limes. Saler et poivrer.

## Daurade marinée à la lime

| | | |
|---|---|---|
| 2 lb | Daurade | 1 kg |
| 2 | Oignons | 2 |
| 2 | Piments | 2 |
| 3 branches | Coriandre | 3 branches |
| 2 c. à soupe | Huile d'olive | 30 ml |
| 1 | Tomate | 1 |

Arroser le poisson de la moitié de la marinade et mettre au réfrigérateur pendant 3 h.

Émincer les oignons et les joindre au reste de marinade. Réserver au frais une quinzaine de minutes. Égoutter.

Dans un chaudron, mettre l'huile, y faire revenir les oignons marinés quelques minutes, puis ajouter la marinade. Ajouter les piments coupés en rondelles. Quand les oignons sont cuits, ajouter le poisson et sa marinade. Couvrir, laisser cuire 20 min et arroser avec le jus de cuisson. Au besoin, ajouter de l'eau.

**Suggestion** ))) Servir avec du riz et parsemer de feuilles de coriandre ciselées et de dés de tomates fraîches.

## Marinade aux agrumes

|  |  |  |
|---|---|---|
| 1 | Lime | 1 |
| 1 | Citron | 1 |
| 2 | Oranges | 2 |
| 2 c. à soupe | Huile d'olive | 30 ml |

Presser le jus des agrumes et mélanger à l'huile d'olive.

## Lotte grillée en marinade aux agrumes

|  |  |  |
|---|---|---|
| 4 | Filets de lotte | 200 g chaque |
| 1 | Citron non traité | 1 |

Couper quatre rondelles de citron et en placer deux sur un filet. Recouvrir ce dernier d'un deuxième filet et attacher solidement avec de la ficelle alimentaire. Recouvrir le poisson d'un mélange de thym et de poivre concassé. Répéter avec les deux autres filets.

Dans un plat, poser le poisson et arroser de la marinade aux agrumes. Réfrigérer pendant 1 h. Retourner les filets deux à trois fois et arroser de marinade.

Essuyer les filets, garder la marinade.

Faire griller les filets de lotte au barbecue ou au gril environ 15 min en arrosant fréquemment de marinade.

**Suggestion** ))) Accompagner d'une salade verte et de riz basmati.

## Marinade au pamplemousse

| | | |
|---|---|---|
| 2 | Pamplemousses | 2 |
| 1 c. à soupe | Sauce nuoc-mâm | 15 ml |

Presser le jus des pamplemousses et en réserver 1 c. à soupe. Mélanger le jus de pamplemousse et la sauce nuoc-mâm.

## Thon mariné au pamplemousse

| | | |
|---|---|---|
| 1 lb | Thon rouge sans peau | 450 g |
| 1 c. à soupe | Sauce nuoc-mâm | 15 ml |
| 1/2 tasse | Huile d'olive | 125 ml |
| 1/4 tasse | Huile de sésame | 65 ml |
| 1 | Piment | 1 |
| 1/2 bouquet | Coriandre | 1/2 bouquet |
| 1 branche | Menthe fraîche | 1 branche |
| 1 tasse | Soja germé | 250 ml |
| 1/8 tasse | Germes de luzerne | 35 ml |

Verser la marinade sur le thon et laisser macérer au réfrigérateur pendant 1 h.

Préparer une vinaigrette en mélangeant les huiles et la cuillère à soupe de jus de pamplemousse réservé. Ajouter le piment émincé.

Hacher les feuilles de coriandre et de menthe.

Une fois le thon mariné, l'éponger et le rouler dans le mélange d'herbes. Couper le thon en fines tranches.

Dans un saladier, mélanger le soja germé et les germes de luzerne avec le reste des herbes hachées. Arroser de vinaigrette, disposer sur quatre assiettes et poser dessus le thon mariné.

# Marinade au genièvre et au rhum

| | | |
|---|---|---|
| 8 | Baies de genièvre | 8 |
| 4 branches | Aneth | 4 branches |
| 1 | Lime non traitée | 1 |
| 3 c. à soupe | Sucre | 45 ml |
| 1 c. à soupe | Rhum blanc | 15 ml |
| | Poivre | |

Piler les baies de genièvre et les mettre dans un grand plat. Saler, parsemer d'aneth, du zeste de la lime, de poivre du moulin, du rhum et du sucre.

# Saumon gravlax mariné au genièvre

| | | |
|---|---|---|
| 1 lb | Filet de saumon | 450 g |

Étaler la marinade dans le fond d'un plat avant d'y disposer le filet de saumon. Couvrir le plat d'un film plastique et poser une assiette sur laquelle appuieront des poids ou un gros caillou. Laisser deux jours au réfrigérateur en retournant le filet de saumon environ toutes les 12 h.

Retirer le saumon de la marinade, le rincer à l'eau froide et l'essuyer. Couper en fines tranches, en biais.

**Suggestion**

))) À servir de préférence avec une sauce préparée avec 1 c. à soupe de moutarde de Dijon fouettée avec 1 c. à thé de sucre. En continuant de fouetter, incorporer peu à peu 1 tasse d'huile de canola et 2 c. à soupe de vinaigre de vin blanc. Ajouter trois branches d'aneth ciselées. Saler et poivrer.

))) Aussi délicieux avec une sauce au yogourt.

))) Accompagner ce met avec de pain de seigle.

## Marinade à la coriandre

| | | |
|---|---|---|
| 2 c. à soupe | Paprika | 30 ml |
| 1/2 botte | Coriandre fraîche ciselée | 1/2 botte |
| 2 gousses | Ail | 2 gousses |
| 2 | Citrons | 2 |
| 2 c. à soupe | Vin blanc | 30 ml |
| 5 c. à soupe | Huile de pépins de raisin | 75 ml |
| | Sel, poivre | |

Mélanger tous les ingrédients pour obtenir un mélange uniforme.

## Truite à la coriandre

| | | |
|---|---|---|
| 4 filets | Truite saumonée | 4 filets |
| 2 | Oignons nouveaux | 2 |
| 5 branches | Coriandre fraîche | 5 branches |

Faire mariner les filets une nuit entière dans la marinade à la
coriandre.

Mélanger les oignons émincés et les feuilles de coriandre
ciselées.

Égoutter les filets de poisson et les griller au barbecue, en
les arrosant régulièrement de la marinade.

Servir les filets grillés parsemés du mélange coriandre-
oignons.

## Marinade au lait de coco et au cari

| | | |
|---|---|---|
| 1 2/3 tasse | Lait de coco | 400 ml |
| 1 | Citron non traité | 1 |
| 2 c. à soupe | Persil | 30 ml |
| 1 c. à thé | Cari en poudre | 5 ml |
| 1 | Piment | 1 |
| 2 c. à soupe | Huile de canola | 30 ml |

Râper le zeste du citron et en presser le jus. Ajouter l'huile de canola, le lait de coco, le cari, le piment émincé finement et le persil haché. Mélanger.

## Poisson mariné au lait de coco

| | | |
|---|---|---|
| 2 lb | Poisson | 1 kg |

Faire mariner le poisson choisi pendant 30 min avant de le cuire.

## Marinade au safran

| | | |
|---|---|---|
| 1/4 tasse | Huile d'olive | 6 ml |
| 2 | Citrons | 2 |
| 1 | Oignon | 1 |
| 2 gousses | Ail | 2 gousses |
| 1 | Piment | 1 |
| 1 c. à soupe | Graines de coriandre | 15 ml |
| 1/2 bouquet | Menthe | 1/2 bouquet |
| 1 c. à thé | Cumin | 5 ml |
| 1 c. à thé | Paprika | 5 ml |
| 5 filaments | Safran | 5 filaments |

Préparer la marinade en mélangeant tous les ingrédients.

## Brochettes de lotte

| | | |
|---|---|---|
| 2 lb | Lotte | 1 kg |
| | Sel, poivre | |

Couper les lottes en gros cubes de 2 po (5 cm). Les mettre dans un plat et arroser de la marinade au safran. Couvrir et réfrigérer pendant 30 min.

Si les baguettes sont en bambou, les faire tremper dans de l'eau froide pendant environ 1 h afin qu'elles ne brûlent pas. Monter les morceaux de lotte sur des brochettes doubles. Saler et poivrer.

Griller à température moyenne en badigeonnant régulièrement de marinade.

**Suggestion** ))) Avec du riz basmati arrosé d'huile d'olive et de légumes grillés (voir page 137).

# :: Légumes ::

## Marinade pour légumes

| | | |
|---|---|---|
| 1/2 tasse | Vinaigre de vin blanc | 125 ml |
| 2 c. à thé | Sucre | 30 ml |
| 1 c. à thé | Graines d'aneth | 5 ml |
| 1/2 c. à thé | Graines de moutarde | 3 ml |
| 1/2 c. à thé | Thym séché | 3 ml |
| 1/2 c. à thé | Paprika | 3 ml |
| 1 tasse | Huile de pépins de raisin | 250 ml |
| | Sel, poivre | |

Mettre une pincée de sel et le sucre dans le vinaigre de vin. Ajouter les graines de moutarde et d'aneth, le thym, le paprika et l'huile de pépins de raisin.

## Légumes marinés

| | | |
|---|---|---|
| 2 tasses | Brocoli | 500 ml |
| 2 tasses | Chou-fleur | 500 ml |
| 1 tasse | Carottes | 250 ml |
| 1 | Oignon | 1 |
| 2 | Poivrons rouges | 2 |

Mettre les légumes coupés dans un contenant et arroser de la marinade. Laisser reposer au moins 4 h avant de servir.

## Marinade à l'huile d'olive

| 1/4 tasse | Huile d'olive | 65 ml |
| 3 gousses | Ail | 3 gousses |
| | Sel, poivre | |

Hacher les gousses d'ail et les mélanger à l'huile d'olive. Saler et poivrer.

## Salade de poivrons rouges marinés

| 6 | Poivrons rouges | 6 |

Cuire les poivrons au four à 350 °F (180 °C) pendant 45 min. Une fois cuits, les sortir du four et les laisser refroidir.

Passer les poivrons sous l'eau et en retirer la peau et les graines. Bien les essuyer.

Couper les poivrons en lanières et les arroser de la marinade à l'huile d'olive.

Laisser mariner au moins 2 h au frais.

**Suggestion**

》Cette salade de poivrons marinés fraîche et parfumée accompagne une simple viande grillée ou une tranche de pain.

》L'huile d'olive fige au froid; sortir la salade au moins 15 min avant de la servir.

》Pour une salade multicolore, faire aussi griller des poivrons verts et jaunes.

》À essayer avec de l'huile d'argan.

## Marinade méditerranéenne

| | | |
|---|---|---|
| 1/4 tasse | Huile d'olive | 65 ml |
| 1 | Citron | 1 |
| 4 branches | Thym | 4 branches |
| 1 c. à soupe | Herbe de Provence | 15 ml |
| 2 gousses | Ail | 2 gousses |
| | Sel, poivre | |

Mélanger tous les ingrédients de la marinade. Ajouter les gousses d'ail écrasées. Saler et poivrer.

## Légumes marinés et grillés

| | | |
|---|---|---|
| 2 | Carottes | 2 |
| 1 | Aubergine | 1 |
| 2 | Endives | 2 |
| 2 | Poivrons | 2 |
| 4 | Oignons | 4 |
| | etc. | |

Laver les légumes. N'éplucher que les carottes et les oignons. Couper les légumes en tranches de 1/2 po (1 cm).

Verser la marinade sur les légumes et laisser macérer pendant au moins 1 h.

Préchauffer le barbecue ou le four à 450 °F (230 °C).

Essuyer les légumes et les griller à haute température, puis poursuivre la cuisson à basse température environ 5 min. Retourner les légumes et prolonger la cuisson de quelques minutes.

Disposer les légumes dans un plat et les arroser de la marinade. Bien mélanger.

Parsemer de persil, de thym et de romarin.

## Marinade de légumes

| | | |
|---|---|---|
| 10 brins | Ciboulette | 10 brins |
| 1/2 botte | Persil | 1/2 botte |
| 1/4 tasse | Huile d'olive | 65 ml |
| 2 c. à soupe | Vinaigre balsamique | 30 ml |
| | Sel, poivre | |

Hacher le persil et la ciboulette. Dans un bol, mélanger tous les ingrédients de la marinade.

## Papillote de légumes

| | | |
|---|---|---|
| 3 | Carottes | 3 |
| 2 | Oignons | 2 |
| 3 | Pommes de terre | 3 |
| 1 | Brocoli | 1 |
| 1 | Chou-fleur | 1 |
| 3 oz | Haricots verts | 90 g |

Peler les carottes et les couper en deux dans le sens de la longueur. Trancher les oignons et les pommes de terre en rondelles. Détacher les fleurs du chou-fleur et du brocoli.

Sur une grande feuille de papier aluminium (40 cm de long), disposer les légumes et arroser de la marinade. Ajouter un glaçon qui donnera l'eau nécessaire à la cuisson et refermer la feuille de papier aluminium.

Cuire au barbecue 20 min.

# Marinade à l'huile d'olive et au thym citronné

| | | |
|---|---|---|
| 1 tasse | Huile d'olive | 250 ml |
| 6 branches | Thym citronné | 6 branches |
| | Sel, poivre | |

Mélanger l'huile aux branches de thym citronné. Saler et poivrer.

## Brochettes de légumes

| | | |
|---|---|---|
| 12 | Tomates cerises | 12 |
| 2 | Poivrons | 2 |
| 12 | Oignons grelots | 12 |
| 3 | Courgettes | 3 |
| 1 | Aubergine | 1 |

Couper les légumes en cubes de 1 po (2,5 cm). Les arroser de la marinade à l'huile d'olive et les enfiler sur des baguettes ou sur des branches de romarin. Si les baguettes sont en bambou, les faire tremper dans de l'eau froide pendant environ 1 h afin qu'elles ne brûlent pas.

Cuire tout doucement sur le barbecue pendant environ 10 min.

## Marinade aux agrumes et au carvi

| | | |
|---|---|---|
| 1/4 tasse | Huile d'olive | 65 ml |
| 3 c. à soupe | Jus de citron | 45 ml |
| 1 | Pamplemousse | 1 |
| 1 c. à thé | Graine de carvi | 5 ml |
| | Sel, poivre | |

Mélanger l'huile d'olive au jus de citron et au jus du pample-mousse. Ajouter les graines de carvi. Saler et poivrer.

## Salade de fenouil et pamplemousse

| | | |
|---|---|---|
| 1 | Gros bulbe de fenouil | 1 |
| 2 | Pamplemousses roses | 2 |

Laver et émincer finement le bulbe de fenouil. Garder des petites feuilles vertes pour décorer vos assiettes.

Éplucher à vif un pamplemousse et le partager en quartiers.

Verser la marinade sur le mélange de pamplemousse et de fenouil. Réfrigérer pendant 3 h et remuer la salade de temps en temps.

Avant de servir, éplucher les deux autres pamplemousses à vif et retirer la peau de chaque quartier.

Bien mélanger la salade et décorer des quartiers de pamplemousse. Parsemer des petites feuilles de fenouil.

# :: Fruits ::

## Marinade sucrée

| | | |
|---|---|---|
| 1 | Citron | 1 |
| 3 c. à soupe | Sucre | 45 ml |

Presser le citron et sucrer.

## Pêches marinées

| | | |
|---|---|---|
| 4 | Pêches fermes | 4 |
| 3 c. à soupe | Beurre | 45 ml |
| 1/2 c. à thé | Cannelle | 3 ml |

Peler et couper les pêches en deux. Les mariner dans le jus de citron sucré.

Verser le beurre fondu et parsemer de cannelle en poudre.

Placer chaque pêche dans un morceau de feuille aluminium et cuire environ 15 min sur le barbecue chaud.

## Marinade au lait de coco

| 1 2/3 tasse | Lait de coco | 400 ml |
| 1 tasse | Sucre | 250 ml |
| 1 c. à thé | Cannelle | 5 ml |

Dans une assiette creuse, verser le lait de coco et mélanger avec le sucre et la cannelle.

## Brochette d'ananas

| 1 | Ananas | 1 |

Couper l'ananas avec la peau en triangles de 1 po (2,5 cm). Tremper les morceaux dans le lait de coco sucré et parfumé à la cannelle. Laisser mariner 15 min.

Si les baguettes sont en bambou, les faire tremper dans de l'eau froide pendant environ 1 h afin qu'elles ne brûlent pas. Enfiler cinq ou six morceaux par brochette et griller 3 min de chaque côté.

**Suggestion** ⟩⟩⟩ Servir avec de la crème glacée.

## Marinade au rhum

| | | |
|---|---|---|
| 3 c. à soupe | Rhum ambré | 45 ml |
| 1 gousse | Vanille | 1 gousse |
| 1/4 tasse | Sucre | 65 ml |

Mélanger le sucre et le rhum. Couper la gousse de vanille en deux dans le sens de la longueur et en gratter les graines. Ajouter les quatre morceaux de la gousse de vanille et les graines au rhum sucré.

## Bananes grillées au rhum

| | | |
|---|---|---|
| 4 | Bananes encore vertes | 4 |

Faire une incision à l'intérieur de chaque banane et les ouvrir délicatement pour y déposer une bonne cuillère à soupe de la marinade au rhum. Y glisser aussi un morceau de gousse de vanille. Refermer les bananes avec de la ficelle.

Laisser mariner au moins 30 min.

Poser les bananes sur la grille du barbecue et cuire doucement 15 min.

**Suggestion** ⟩⟩⟩ Servir avec une crème glacée à la vanille ou au chocolat.

# GREEN, FAIR, AND PROSPEROUS

**A BUR OAK BOOK**

Holly Carver, series editor

# GREEN, FAIR, AND PROSPEROUS

## Charles E. Connerly

UNIVERSITY OF IOWA PRESS, IOWA CITY

University of Iowa Press, Iowa City 52242
Copyright © 2020 by the University of Iowa Press
www.uipress.uiowa.edu

Printed in the United States of America
Design by April Leidig
Illustration on book cover and page iii © Claudia McGehee

Printed on acid-free paper

Library of Congress Cataloging-in-Publication Data
Names: Connerly, Charles E., 1946– author.
Title: Green, Fair, and Prosperous: Paths to a Sustainable Iowa /
Charles E. Connerly.
Other titles: Bur Oak Book.
Description: Iowa City: University of Iowa Press, [2020] | Series:
Bur Oak Books | Includes bibliographical references and index. |
Identifiers: LCCN 2020006541 (print) | LCCN 2020006542 (ebook) |
ISBN 9781609387204 (paperback) | ISBN 9781609387211 (ebook)
Subjects: LCSH: Sustainable development—Iowa. |
Sustainable Agriculture—Iowa.
Classification: LCC HC79.E5 C6165 2020 (print) |
LCC HC79.E5 (ebook) | DDC 338.9777/07—dc23
LC record available at https://lccn.loc.gov/2020006541
LC ebook record available at https://lccn.loc.gov/2020006542

*This book is dedicated to Joseph Frazier Wall.*

Joe Wall taught me American history at
Grinnell College, introduced me to Iowa history,
and wrote the bicentennial history of Iowa.
He personified the ideal teacher-scholar-citizen:
a fine scholar and a great teacher, he inspired his
students to lead lives of social responsibility.

# ⟝ CONTENTS ⟝

THIS BOOK HAS ITS ORIGINS in my childhood as a resident of
what used to be known as the Prairie State — Illinois — before it
was renamed the Land of Lincoln in 1955. Growing up in the post–
World War II era in a suburb of Chicago, I had a basic understanding of what prairie meant. I knew that radio station WLS was still
known as the Prairie Farmer station, and I enjoyed listening to
the National Barn Dance on that station every Saturday night. I
knew that a vacant lot near my house, bordering a railroad track,
was called a prairie by everyone in the neighborhood — today
that parcel is a public park. Whether it actually was a remnant of
Illinois's original tallgrass prairie, I don't know. I do remember
going to that "prairie" in the ninth grade to collect insects for my
biology class. There were lots of insects, so perhaps the prairie
ecosystem had remained intact.

But the Prairie State lost its state slogan status in part, at least,
because there was little or no prairie left. It had been plowed
under long before I was born. I was very familiar, however, with
what had replaced the tallgrass prairie: the miles and miles of
corn and soybeans that I watched as I sat in the back seat of my
parents' car when we drove to visit family in the southern Illinois
town of Flora about 250 miles south of Chicago. My parents were
both born on farms outside of Flora, and while my father's family
moved to town when he was about five, my mother grew up on a
farm. As newly married young adults, they moved to Chicago in
1934 to look for opportunities they couldn't find in a small town
in the middle of the Great Depression.

As a baby boomer, I was more fortunate than my parents: I
came of age in the strong economy of the 1960s. While not affluent, my parents were able to help me attend Grinnell College, a

private college in the middle of Iowa's miles and miles of corn and soybeans, where I majored in history. Despite the fact that Iowa featured rolling hills instead of the tabletop flatlands of my home state, its similarities to rural Illinois were quite obvious — Grinnell and Flora were of similar size, and they were both surrounded by the same row crops. Unlike some of my classmates from New York City or even Chicago, I felt comfortable in this landscape, although I was very much a city (suburb, actually) kid and not a country kid.

I was vaguely aware, therefore, of the connections among Chicago, Flora, and Grinnell and the hinterland that lay between them. I knew that farm commodities, whether corn or hogs, were traded on the Chicago Board of Trade — this I learned from the farm reports that still aired from Chicago on WLS and WGN in the 1950s. I believed that in some limited way, Chicago media played the same role for rural Iowa that national media, broadcast from Los Angeles or New York City, played for the nation. After I graduated from Grinnell in the late 1960s, I pretty much left the regional triangle that had formed the first twenty-one years of my life, spending most of the ensuing years in Florida as well as Washington, D.C., Connecticut, Massachusetts, and Michigan.

What kept me connected to the prairie over this time was Garrison Keillor's Prairie Home Companion, which I started listening to on public radio around 1980. The program was similar in both content — a mixture of music and humor — and focus — the prairie — to the old WLS National Barn Dance. It was after moving to northern Florida in 1981 that I began to appreciate Prairie Home Companion not just for its entertainment value but also for its affirmation of a prairie identity that appealed to me in an unfamiliar landscape and culture.

The tallgrass prairie essentially corresponds to the prairie I knew growing up and attending college, linking Chicago, Flora, and Grinnell with parts of Indiana, Missouri, Kansas, Nebraska, the Dakotas, Minnesota, and a tiny bit of Wisconsin thrown in.

The tallgrass prairie is estimated to have covered more than 220,000 square miles before most of it was plowed under. Illinois and Iowa lie at the heart of the tallgrass prairie, and Iowa lies at its center.

Prairie is divided into three zones: tallgrass, mixed-grass, and shortgrass, with the height of the prairie grasses corresponding to the decreasing annual rainfall as one moves westward toward the rain shadow produced by the Rocky Mountains. Defined by its native ecosystem, the tallgrass prairie is a region much like the Intermountain West and the Gulf Coast. I found the tallgrass prairie a better fit as a region, as my region, than the Middle West or the Midwest, which has always seemed too encompassing.

After twenty-seven years of teaching urban planning at Florida State University, I moved to Iowa City with my family in 2008 so that I could teach urban planning and history at the University of Iowa. As I started to think about writing this book, I began to refamiliarize myself with the tallgrass prairie — to reconnect with the landscape that first imprinted itself on me as a child, then became my home as an adult. In part, I could do this by looking out our front window at the pasture across the road that runs in front of our house, imagining what the view looked like when native grasses and grazing bison dominated large swaths of Iowa.

Now that I have lived in Iowa for more than a decade, in this book I attempt to look at the state's past with a historian's eye and an urban planner's eye to the future — a sustainable future that builds on the state's rich natural heritage as well as a prosperous and equitable future in which middle-income households thrive and Iowa achieves an equality of opportunity for its increasingly diverse population.

## — ACKNOWLEDGMENTS —

IN CLEARING MY SCHEDULE to begin this project, I had secured a semester sabbatical to start in January 2015. Just prior to that, in December 2014, I became very ill. In forty-eight hours, I moved from serving as a marshal at fall commencement to having the flu to undergoing septic shock: my heart stopped, my blood pressure dropped precipitously, and my lungs and kidneys began to give out.

Fortunately, I was in the right place at the right time: the University of Iowa Hospitals and Clinics. A team of physicians and nurses, overseen by Dr. Joseph Zabner, filled me with antibiotics and vasopressors. With their care, my body came around, although with the probability that I was going to lose my feet, which had turned black and brown as the vasopressors concentrated blood flow to my organs. Again fortunately, my lower legs were not infected, and Dr. Thomas Lawrence, chief of plastic surgery, was assigned to my case. Dr. Lawrence decided that it would be safe to wait and see how much my feet would recover; consequently, I lost only my toes. I will be forever grateful to Dr. Lawrence for his patience and willingness to let my body heal and to Physician Assistant Becky Rosenberg for assisting Dr. Lawrence with my amputations and skin grafts.

The bad news was that my start on this book was delayed a year, but the good news, of course, was that I was alive and I was recovering.

I want to express my gratitude to all the University of Iowa Hospitals and Clinics medical staff who have assisted me over the last five years. Besides Drs. Zabner and Lawrence, these include the physicians and nurses in the emergency room, the cardiovascular and medical intensive care units, and Pulmonology. I also benefited greatly from the care of the physicians, therapists, and nurses of the rehabilitation clinic at Genesis Medical Center in Davenport and the home health care provided by the nurses and staff of Mercy Iowa City Home Health Care and University of Iowa Community HomeCare.

Since leaving the hospital, I've appreciated the continuing care of my physical therapist, Dick Evans, who along with fellow PTs Rhonda Barr, Rick Willenbring, Kathy Boyd, and Barbara Van Gorp literally got me back on my feet. My walking was still slow and limited until 2018, when Dick introduced me to Jason Wilken, a University of Iowa Department of Physical Therapy and Rehabilitation Science faculty member and researcher who works with the Department of Defense to develop and test the custom dynamic orthoses that enable people like myself to walk faster with less pain. Every time I put on my CDO, I thank Dick and Jason not only for helping me walk but for the psychological boost that my braces gave me to keep working and to complete this book.

Other UIHC personnel who continue to help my body deal with chronic conditions related to sepsis include Infectious Diseases staff Dr. Judy Streit and Physician Assistant Laura Stulken, Family Medicine Drs. Kyle Smoot and Brian Shian, and Podiatry staff Drs. Chester Pelsang, Mindy Trotter, and Adam Arendt, and Wound Care Nurse Valerie Vetter.

This book could not have been completed without the support of many others. My spouse, Martha Ann Crawford, told the doctors in the first days of my sepsis, "You have to save him, he has a book to write!" On the scene were our son, Robert, and our daughter, Beth, who quickly used social media to let distant friends and family know what was happening, thereby triggering many sustaining thoughts and prayers. Our three grandchildren patiently helped maintain the vigil while I was in the ICU.

In the University of Iowa's School of Urban and Regional Planning, where I teach, John Fuller ably took over directorship responsibilities while administrative assistant and close family friend Pam Butler delayed her retirement to make sure everything ran smoothly. Urban and Regional Planning staff Janet Bell and Tanya Kooi joined her in visiting me at the hospital and helping my return to the office in May 2015 go as smoothly as possible. Dean John Keller and Graduate College staff Donna Welter and Sandy Gay made sure that I could recover at home with peace of mind without worrying too much about my responsibilities at the university. Faculty colleague Lucie Laurian kindly volunteered to read my ungraded student papers, thereby enabling me to focus on healing. Another faculty member, Jim Throgmorton, marked my departure from the ICU and my induced coma by reading me a chapter from a book on the political economy of the American labor movement in the 1970s — thereby letting me know that not only did I understand what he was reading, but that my personal commitment to social justice continued to be stimulated by the injustices of which he read. Faculty colleague Pete Damiano, both a dentist and a health policy expert, came to the hospital nearly every day to check on me and to be with Martha Ann and the family, often joined by his wife, Julie. And faculty colleague Carolyn Colvin encouraged me to return to the book when I began to think about this project again; she was very clear with me that I needed to ask to defer my sabbatical to spring 2016.

After Reverend Bill Lovin announced from the pulpit on Christmas Eve that I was very ill, many members of our church, the Congregational United Church of Christ, visited me in the hospital and spent time with my family as they waited for me to recover. Among these were pulmonologist Dr. John Fieselmann, who prior to his retirement had trained and worked with many of my doctors. John helped explain to Martha Ann and my family what was being done to treat me and how I was progressing.

I had many other visitors, including students. Among these was UI colleague Diane Finnerty, who had been diagnosed with ovarian cancer a few months before I became sick. I will never forget her visit with me—giving me hope all the while facing her own uncertain future. Unfortunately, she did not live to see this book's publication.

Another visitor was Jeffery Ford, who had contracted sepsis about a year before me. He visited at a time when I was coming to grips with the possible loss of my lower legs, which he had lost. His example continues to give me courage. Jeffery and his wife, Lynette Marshall, provided continual support to Martha Ann both during and after my hospitalization. And I will never forget good friend Linda Snetselaar's visit to me as I began to come out of my coma in the ICU. I greeted her by saying, "Hi, Linda," after which physical therapist Rhonda Barr asked me if I knew Linda's last name. Fortunately, I said, "Snetselaar," thereby passing an impromptu mental ability test. Thankfully, Rhonda didn't ask me to spell Linda's last name!

I was finally able to begin this project in January 2016. The university kindly allowed me to shift my sabbatical to that semester, and the Obermann Center for Advanced Studies at the university provided me with an office where I could finally begin the deep dive into this book. My thanks go to director Teresa Mangum and assistant director Jennifer New, who supported me as a fellow-in-residence. Teresa and the other fellows, Ana Rodríguez-Rodríguez, Kathleen Diffley, Mary Trachsel, and Shanna Greene Benjamin, gave me the first feedback on this book. I also appreciate the time that several UI colleagues took to review my manuscript: Connie Mutel of IIHR—Hydroscience and Engineering, Chris Jones, also of IIHR, and David Osterberg of the College of Public Health and the Iowa Policy Project. Connie has followed this project from the very beginning and has given me support while I mixed recovery with writing.

This book began at the suggestion of Catherine Cocks, then an editor at the University of Iowa Press. I remain grateful to her for planting the seed. I also appreciate the great support I have received from the University of Iowa Press, including director Jim McCoy, Meredith Stabel, Jacob Roosa, Susan Hill Newton, and Bur Oak Books editor Holly Carver, whose supportive guidance, insightful and careful editing, and timely prodding added immeasurably to the quality of this book as well as the pleasure of completing it. The book has been ably indexed by Alisha Jeddeloh.

## IOWA COMMUNITIES AT A CROSSROADS

IN 2009, in my second year of teaching at the University of Iowa, our School of Urban and Regional Planning created the Iowa Initiative for Sustainable Communities, which has developed into a campus-wide program in which students from across the university work closely to help Iowa communities become more sustainable with regard to their environmental, economic, and social equity issues—for example, working with Sioux City on plans to encourage nonmotorized pedestrian and bicycle transportation or a green downtown to reduce the heat island effect that compounds the impacts of climate change. The Iowa Initiative was created in response to President Sally Mason's 2008 commitment to making Iowa a sustainable university, both on and off campus.

In one of our first sustainability-focused projects, students working on energy and stormwater issues in Decorah employed a slide in a spring 2010 presentation titled "Iowa Communities at a Crossroads." The students' work highlighted the key decisions and hard choices that Iowa communities face with regard to sustainability in these areas and made estimates of how household carbon emissions varied with energy sources and how alternatives such as rain gardens and rain barrels could reduce storm runoff. As our initiative developed into a permanent student-community engagement program, I found the crossroads metaphor useful for identifying the sustainability challenges faced by Iowa communities. Employing Scott Campbell's triangular conceptualization of sustainable development—which shows the contradictions among environmental protection, economic growth, and social justice issues of economic opportunity and equality—our initiative's narrative emphasized the key choices that Iowans face in each of these areas. As I began to think about this book, Campbell's definition of sustainability and the crossroads metaphor increasingly became my focus.

Campbell's triangular definition of sustainability clearly shows the conflicting nature of the most commonly employed dimensions of sustainable development: economic development, environmental protection, and social justice. For continued development to be sustainable, he says, these three dimensions must be kept in balance. If not, economic development will destroy the environment or, conversely, environmental protection will inhibit growth and thus damage the economy. If not kept in check, economic development will result in economic inequality as only the rich will get richer, and economic inequality will slow development because only a few will have buying power. Economic inequality also reflects social justice issues related to discrimination against minority groups. Furthermore, given income inequality, the poor will sacrifice environmental protection to improve their income. For development to be sustainable, therefore, society must achieve and maintain a balance among economic development, environmental protection, and social justice.

Sustainable development in Iowa requires recognition both of its tallgrass prairie ecosystem and of its historic economic system. In this way, Iowa has much that links it to Chicago. In *Nature's Metropolis: Chicago and the Great West*, William Cronon demonstrates how Chicago used its position vis-à-vis the railroads and Lake Michigan to become the center for processing and shipping grain, meat (from Illinois, Iowa, and farther west), and lumber (from Wisconsin and Michigan). Using bankruptcy maps to show the tight economic links connecting businesses within the tallgrass prairie states, Cronon tells us that Chicago represented the "intersecting geographies of nature and capital" embodied by the prairies to the west and the forests to the north combined with the capital invested in Chicago by New York financiers and turned over in the city's hinterland by farmers and business leaders. The tallgrass prairie was not only a coherent natural region, it was also a discernible economic region in which, by the nineteenth century, the economies of Chicago and Iowa were closely intertwined.

In the late nineteenth and twentieth centuries, as urban centers such as Omaha, Kansas City, and Minneapolis–St. Paul emerged in the tallgrass prairie region and nearby, Chicago's economic dominance gradually subsided. But its influence remained significant. Cronon notes that while meatpacking itself was increasingly performed in Kansas City and Omaha, the meatpacking industry remained in the hands of Chicago firms. But it was in Iowa that Chicago's influence remained strongest, even into the twenty-first century. Cronon writes that "perhaps the most telling evidence of Chicago's western shadow was nearer to home: the state of Iowa never developed a regional metropolis of its own. . . . Chicago remains the chief metropolis of Iowa to this day."

In addition to sharing a common economic history, communities within the tallgrass prairie states continue to share dependence upon a farm economy centered on the production and sale of corn, soybeans, hogs, poultry, and to a lesser degree cattle. The top five corn-producing states (as measured by bushels of corn) in 2017 were all tallgrass prairie states, with Iowa leading followed by Illinois, Nebraska, Minnesota, and Indiana. The same was true for the top soybean-producing states, with Illinois leading followed by Iowa and three other tallgrass prairie states: Minnesota, Nebraska, and Indiana. The tallgrass prairie states of Iowa, Minnesota, Illinois, and Indiana accounted for four of the top five leading states in hog numbers, with Iowa leading the nation by over twice the value of its nearest rival, North Carolina. Iowa was also the nation's leading egg-producing state. Although the state is less well known for raising cattle, Iowa's inventory ranked fourth in the nation in 2017. As a region, along with Ohio the Corn Belt states that substantially coincide with the tallgrass prairie — Iowa, Illinois, Indiana, and Missouri — have the highest farmland value in the nation. In 2018 Iowa farmland, at an average price of $8,080 per acre, was the most valuable of any of these states and included some of the most valuable farmland in the United States, topping the national average by over 2.5 times.

The tallgrass prairie states also share similar environmental challenges. Reliance on corn and soybeans accompanied by extensive employment of chemical fertilizers has resulted in significant negative effects on water quality, not only in tallgrass prairie rivers and streams but in the Mississippi and Missouri Rivers and the Gulf of Mexico as well. Researchers have found that nitrogen and phosphorus, derived in great part from the application of chemical fertilizers to corn and soybean production, have created a dead zone in the Gulf of Mexico that was 8,776 square miles in 2017, about the size of the state of New Jersey, and 6,952 square miles in 2019. According to a 2008 study Illinois, Iowa, Indiana, and Missouri, in descending order, contributed nearly 50 percent of all nitrogen originating from the thirty-one states in the Mississippi/Atchafalaya River Basin. Illinois, Missouri, and Iowa, in descending order, contributed slightly more than one-third of the phosphorus originating from the same thirty-one states. More recent research calculates that Iowa alone accounts for 29 percent of nitrate-nitrogen flowing into the Gulf of Mexico.

With regard to issues of social justice, particularly racism, ethnic bias, and segregation, the tallgrass prairie states, particularly in their rural areas, share similar histories. Historically, many of the communities in these states — as well as entire states such as Iowa, Nebraska, and the Dakotas — have been predominantly white. In recent years, as the nation has become more diverse, so have these communities and states. This is partly related to increases in the Latin American population in the United States. In the tallgrass prairie states, Hispanics have been attracted and recruited by meatpacking plants — plants that proliferated as the meatpacking industry decentralized from large cities such as Chicago, Kansas City, and Omaha to smaller communities in Iowa, Minnesota, Nebraska, Missouri, and Kansas. Similarly, as

African Americans began to leave large cities like Chicago and Detroit, some moved to smaller communities in the tallgrass prairie states to seek the economic opportunities offered by a relatively strong economy and a respected education system. Iowa City and Dubuque, for example, have seen significant increases in their African American populations—albeit against a very small base—since 2000. In recent years, both these cities have confronted racial issues that were generally unheard of in the past when they were nearly all white. Since 1975, when Governor Robert Ray invited the Tai Dam Vietnamese refugees to come to Iowa, the state has also welcomed Asian refugees, including, most recently, Asian Americans originally from Myanmar.

Please note that while Scott Campbell's conceptualization of sustainable development urges a balance among competing goals, I don't mean to imply that Iowa, any more than the rest of the world, naturally inclines toward or away from some kind of ideal equilibrium. However, in order for development to be sustainable, we as a society must attempt to achieve and maintain a balance among economic development, environmental protection, and social justice. In this book I want, first, to show how far away Iowa is from being green, fair, and prosperous and, second, to recommend how we can accomplish these goals in our state. In the following chapters, I examine Iowa as, in its crucial crossroads moment, it confronts its past and its future.

Chapter 1 summarizes historical changes in the Iowa economy, particularly those that have affected the state's working and middle classes. Meatpacking and manufacturing and their boom and bust cycles, the growth and decline of labor unions, the Farm Crisis, losses in income and population—all these have had profound effects on Iowa's communities.

Using Iowa's economy as a backdrop for my discussion of environmental protection, in chapters 2 and 3 I explain the evolution of Iowa's natural environment—how the unimpeded and sustainable tallgrass prairie that preceded Euro-American settlement has been transformed into a highly productive but unsustainable ecosystem. Additionally, climate change, resulting in increased temperatures and precipitation over the last decades, has led to an increased incidence of floods as well as periods of drought, thereby testing the resilience of Iowa's communities and eventually the health of its humans, crops, and animals.

In the fourth chapter, I again use Iowa's economy as a backdrop to focus on the tallgrass prairie states' history of diversity and social justice in the context of a predominantly white population. I pay particular attention to Iowa's transformation from a region and a territory occupied by Native Americans to a predominantly white state, which has now entered a period of growing diversity with accompanying social equity issues.

By exploring Iowa's history, chapters 1 through 4 tell us how Iowa got to where it is today. They also tell us where the state currently is with regard to social justice and the environment. In the concluding chapter, I use a Best States ranking to compare Iowa to other states and make recommendations for how Iowa communities and the state of Iowa and, by extension, the tallgrass prairie region can do a better job of balancing the three sustainable development goals of economic development, environmental protection, and social justice. This chapter asks the question, What kind of state does Iowa want to be? Iowans are at a crossroads when it comes to answering this question. Put bluntly, neither the state's environmental nor its social justice record is exemplary, and Iowa appears to be on a path in which environmental degradation is made justifiable by the health of the economy—or at least the agricultural portion of the economy.

This book is written in the faith that the ideas I present here will advance Iowa in a direction that better approaches the sweet spot of sustainable development and will provide guidance for the citizens of Iowa and other states who seek to live in healthful and equitable communities.

# GREEN, FAIR, AND PROSPEROUS

# ~ ONE ~

## AGRICULTURE, MANUFACTURING,
## AND IOWA'S MIDDLE CLASS

SINCE 1832, the story of Iowa's economy has been primarily the story of the possession, cultivation, and marketing of the fruits of the land by white settlers. Large numbers of Euro-Americans immigrated into the state between 1840 and 1900. After Iowa achieved statehood in 1846, its 1850 census population was 192,214. In the 1850s, the state's population tripled; for the rest of the nineteenth century, its ten-year increases were never less than 17 percent.

By 1900, Iowa was effectively possessed for cultivation and grazing. After that, mass immigration slowed dramatically, and the state's population increases exceeded 6 percent only once, during the 1910s, and population actually decreased by nearly 5 percent in the decade of the 1980s during the Farm Crisis. In 1900, one-third of Iowa's ninety-nine counties had reached their peak populations—from Ida County with 12,327 residents to Harrison County with 25,597. These counties would shrink in population into the twentieth and twenty-first centuries, and the population of many other counties would peak thereafter. By 2016, the population of only ten counties would be at their highest level ever, and six of these were in two urbanizing areas—Des Moines in Polk County with 474,045 residents and Cedar Rapids–Iowa City in Linn and Johnson Counties with 368,208. Rural population decline in Iowa has characterized the state since its population boom ended in 1900.

The tallgrass prairie that once dominated Iowa's landscape had largely disappeared by 1900, replaced by crops and nonnative grazing grasses on farms that covered nearly 97 percent of the state's land area. And the number of farms, which peaked at nearly 228,622 in 1900, began to decline thereafter, particularly after 1930 with the Depression but afterward as well, reaching a more level plateau of about 90,000 after the Farm Crisis ended in the late 1980s. According to the U.S. Census of Agriculture, there were 86,104 farms in Iowa in 2017. This decline was accommodated not by a decrease in agricultural activity but by an increase in the size of farms. By the second decade of the twenty-first century, farms continued to cover more than 85 percent of Iowa's land but had grown in average size from about 150 acres in 1900 to 355 acres in 2017.

Effectively, therefore, by 1900 the state of Iowa was built out. There was no further room to grow except in its metropolitan areas, none of which ever grew to the size of the tallgrass prairie's urban giants—Chicago, Minneapolis–St. Paul, Omaha, St. Louis, and Kansas City. Access for Iowa farmers to these cities, all of which were important market centers for agricultural products, was made possible by the extensive network of railroad lines whose growth coincided with the state's growth spurt in the second half of the nineteenth century. The expansion of railroads in nineteenth-century Iowa laid the foundation for the state's development as an agro-industrial center—a state whose economy has continuously been centered on agriculture and agriculture-related manufacturing. In addition to enabling immigration into the state, the railroads assisted Iowa's farmers with the sale of their grain, hogs, and cattle and furthermore with the shipment of processed meat and farm machinery and implements manufactured in the state.

Iowa's location west of Chicago made it the logical state through which railroads would reach the Pacific Ocean. Quite simply, Iowa was in the right place at the right time. Congress recognized this fact when in 1856 it granted 4 million acres of federal land to the state to be used to encourage railroad development along four east-west routes through Iowa. In the 1850s, five railroads began construction across the state's width, connecting Chicago and eastern markets with western cities and towns and the Pacific Coast. The first was the Chicago and Rock Island, which crossed the Mississippi River at Davenport and reached Iowa City on New Year's Eve of 1855, finally getting to Council Bluffs on the Missouri River in 1869. The North Western (later the Chicago and North Western) crossed the Mississippi River at Clinton and reached Council Bluffs by 1867, where it linked to the Union Pacific–Central Pacific transcontinental route in 1869. In 1870, the railroad that later became the Chicago, Burlington and Quincy completed its route from Burlington to Council Bluffs. The Illinois Central crossed the Mississippi at Dubuque before completing its westward route to Sioux City and the Missouri River in 1870. The fifth east-west railroad to cross Iowa, the Milwaukee Road, completed its route from McGregor west to the Big Sioux River and Dakota Territory in 1879.

The state's major north-south railroads — the Iowa Central (later the Minneapolis and St. Louis), the Chicago Great Western, and the Wabash — were in operation by the end of the nineteenth century and ensured that Iowa was well connected with Minneapolis–St. Paul, Kansas City, and St. Louis. By 1894, Iowa possessed 8,513 miles of railroad tracks, placing it fifth in the nation in total trackage. The historic boast that there was no place in Iowa farther than thirteen miles from a rail line is certainly consistent with the high number of tracks in the state. Without the fast pace of railroad growth in Iowa, settlement would not have happened quite as quickly or peaked quite as early as it did.

The advent of the railroad in Iowa also enabled the state, particularly after the Civil War, to become a leading if lesser-known center for agricultural manufacturing, a status that remained in place in 2016: Iowa ranked seventh that year in the percentage of gross domestic product originating in manufacturing. Many of Iowa's early manufacturing firms took quick advantage of locations close to agriculture as well as to the new railroad infrastructure. Historian Wilson Warren describes the Midwest's industrial development in the nineteenth century as centered on [agro-industrialization, chiefly flour milling, meatpacking, and the manufacture of farm machinery and implements]. Iowa's economy featured all three, and by the twenty-first century agro-industrialization was the dominant theme in the state's manufacturing sector. In 2015, 43 percent of all manufacturing jobs in Iowa were either in machinery (19 percent), including farm machinery, or food and beverages (24 percent). More specifically, the two largest manufacturing sectors were animal slaughtering and processing (27,880 employees) and farm machinery and implements (13,678). Together, they accounted for nearly 25 percent of manufacturing employment in Iowa.

Iowa is not unique in this respect. Its path to capitalist growth is shared with the rest of the Midwest—a path in which both agriculture and industry grew synergistically. This synergy was fed by the fact that since its inception, farming in the Midwest was about more than sustenance: it was also driven by the cash market for grain and meat. Consequently, farmers could afford to invest in improved technologies while purchasing manufactured goods for their homes. And because of the close connection between agriculture and manufacturing, factories were often located in small to medium-sized communities close to both their farming suppliers and their customers. Moreover, over time and into the present, farmers, men and women, have often found the opportunity and the necessity to supplement their income with jobs off the farm, including jobs in manufacturing. In Iowa and the Midwest, the relationship between agriculture and manufacturing is more than simply a relationship between buyer and seller. It is also bound up with the fact that the same people work in the factories and farm the land—triply entwined with the economy as laborers, producers, and consumers].

## The Rise of Meatpacking

In the early years of Euro-American settlement, Iowa farmers had yet to discover their destiny in corn and hogs. Instead, they grew wheat — in 1860, Iowa was the eighth-largest wheat producer in the country — and flour-milling operations consequently multiplied. Although many operations served their rural neighborhoods, a number were exclusively merchant mills, selling to a broader market. The milling centers were located in towns and cities on the Mississippi River, from which they shipped flour to St. Louis. The chief among these was Davenport, which had fifteen flour mills in 1858. By the last quarter of the nineteenth century, however, as Iowa farmers switched to corn and hogs, wheat farming shifted to the north and west and Minneapolis rose to become the nation's great milling center.

With the switch to corn and hogs came the rise of Iowa's meatpacking industry. Originally centered on the Ohio and Mississippi Rivers, with the advent of the railroad in the second half of the nineteenth century meatpacking shifted to stockyard facilities in Chicago, Kansas City, and Omaha. At the same time and well into the twentieth century, meatpacking operations, also aided by the coming of the railroad to Iowa, opened in smaller midwestern centers that had more direct access to animals, especially hogs, and that characterized farming in the Corn Belt. Beef cattle, poultry, and sheep would be added to these operations in the twentieth century.

Unlike the large meatpacking firms in turn-of-the-century Chicago that purchased livestock from the city's stockyards, these Iowa direct-buying firms purchased livestock directly from Iowa farmers. In Cedar Rapids the Sinclair Meatpacking Company, founded in 1871, located its 1872 plant near two of the railroads that ran through that city as well as the Cedar River. By 1878, it had distinguished itself as the fourth-largest meatpacking plant in the world. In 1877, Thomas Dove Foster launched the John Morrell and Company meat-processing operation in Ottumwa. Proximity to the railroad, to the Des Moines River, and to the animals them-selves drove Foster's decision to locate the British firm's plant in Ottumwa. Both the Sinclair and the Morrell plants in Iowa would grow in the 1880s to become major meatpacking centers in the Midwest, helping shape Iowa's legacy as a leader in the industry.

In the latter part of the nineteenth century and the early twen-tieth century, other Iowa meatpacking operations—Rath Packing Company in Waterloo, J. E. Decker in Mason City, Tobin Packing Company in Ft. Dodge, Iowa Packing Company in Des Moines, and Dubuque Packing Company in Dubuque—followed the pat-tern set by Sinclair and Morrell. Especially after the advent of trucking, Iowa farmers preferred shipping to these closer loca-tions because their costs were lower and their animals would lose less weight than when shipped by rail to Chicago, Kansas City, or Omaha. Packers preferred locations with the same characteristics as Morrell in Ottumwa and Sinclair in Cedar Rapids: proximity to a river, railroads, and workers, especially farmers with experience in slaughtering. Waterloo's Rath Packing Company, founded in 1891, grew from a small hog-processing facility on the Cedar River to what was said to be the world's largest multistory, multispecies meatpacking operation. Like other Iowa packers, Rath began with hog processing but later expanded to include beef processing. In Mason City, in 1899, Jacob E. Decker and his son Jay purchased a small hog-packing facility and grew it into what became by the 1930s the city's largest industry, with 1,200 employees.

By the second decade of the twentieth century, Sioux City would become the largest pork packer in Iowa. Unlike Ottumwa, Cedar Rapids, Waterloo, and Mason City, Sioux City constructed large stockyards in the same manner as Chicago and became home to three large national meatpacking companies: Cudahy, Armour, and Swift. These firms would purchase most of their livestock at auction from the city's stockyards. In contrast, in the other Iowa meatpacking towns, packers typically purchased directly from farmers or dealers.

Smaller Iowa communities sought opportunities to add meat-packing to their economy. They were aided by their proximity to corn and hogs and other animals but limited by their smaller work-forces. One community that succeeded was Storm Lake. Kingan and Company, out of Indianapolis, opened a small slaughtering operation there in 1935. After Hygrade Food Products purchased Kingan in 1952, it became the nation's fourth-largest meatpacker and grew its workforce to 650 employees by the early 1970s—a large workforce for a town of 8,500 in 1970. Columbus Junction also succeeded in attracting a hog-slaughtering plant when Rath Packing opened an operation there in 1961.

Rath, Morrell, Sinclair, Kingan, and other Iowa packinghouses and their communities thrived in the first half of the twentieth century. Iowa meatpacking employment increased by 132 percent between 1929 and 1954, helping drive large overall increases in manufacturing employment, population, and average wages during that period in the major direct-buying meatpacking cities of Cedar Rapids, Des Moines, Ft. Dodge, Dubuque, Ottumwa, Water-loo, and Mason City. The successful rise of meatpacking unions in the 1930s and 1940s, along with post–World War II prosperity, led to increased income for meatpacking workers and their communities, including significant growth in the number of homes built between 1940 and 1950.

While each of these cities prospered with meatpacking, some of their economic fortunes rested more firmly upon meatpacking than others. By 1950, meatpacking employed nearly two-thirds of Ottumwa's manufacturing workers, while the corresponding percentages for Mason City, Ft. Dodge, Waterloo, and Dubuque were 49, 36, 33, and 26 percent. In these cities, meatpacking shake-ups, whether positive or negative, would have an amplified impact. Other cities, such as Des Moines and Cedar Rapids, had more diversified economies with 6 percent and 15 percent, respectively, of their manufacturing workforce employed in meatpacking.

Beginning in the 1960s, new directions in meatpacking trans-formed Iowa and beyond, and the economies of the Iowa cities with the greatest concentrations in meatpacking came tumbling down. These years saw the birth of a new type of meatpacking firm led by Iowa Beef Packers, founded in 1961 in Denison, a member of what would become known as the Big Three, which also included two other midwestern meatpackers, ConAgra and Excel. Like their Iowa predecessors, these firms directly purchased hogs from Iowa farmers or dealers. But they reshaped hog farming by purchasing from fewer and larger hog operations, and their contracts with the producers increasingly narrowed the scope of hog rearing to tightly controlled standards dictated in part by more detailed consumer expectations. Tighter corporate control of the hog production process, along with technological changes in hog rearing, led to the rise of concentrated animal feeding operations — CAFOs — and their attendant environmental problems.

The Big Three adopted technological changes that permitted firms like Iowa Beef Packers to employ assembly-line butchering, which reduced the skill level needed in meatpacking while enabling IBP and the others to ship boxes full of precut meat, originally beef and then in the 1980s pork, unencumbered by bones sliced from the carcass. Because packers could now save on shipping costs, and grocery stores and wholesalers no longer needed to invest in specialized butchers to slice meal-sized cuts from larger carcasses, these changes were felt at both the production and the consumption ends of the meatpacking industry. The Big Three increased efficiency by moving to single-story, single-species operations that stood in contrast to multistory, multi-species operations like Rath in Waterloo. And the newer plants were less reliant on railroad connections, preferring to ship their entire product by truck. This made it possible to move operations to smaller communities closer to where livestock was raised. In Iowa in the late 1980s and 1990s, IBP, Excel (now Cargill), and ConAgra invested in small towns like Denison: Storm Lake, Columbus Junction, Marshalltown, and Perry as well as Waterloo and Ottumwa.

For beef packing, the shift to smaller communities also meant a shift westward to small towns in Nebraska and Kansas, where beef-packing employment increased much more rapidly in the 1980s and 1990s than in Iowa. Instead, Iowa became more directly focused on hog processing. The shift to smaller communities also meant a decline after the 1970s in the higher wages that had been enjoyed since the 1940s and 1950s. IBP was strongly anti-union and was able to negotiate lower wages in the 1970s, and ConAgra followed in IBP's footsteps. In the early 1980s, all the meatpacking firms succeeded in reducing union-negotiated benefits, in part by moving operations to non-union facilities. The result was a significant decline in membership in the United Food and Commercial Workers International Union. The impact on meatpacking workers was clear. By 1977, Iowa meatpacking wages had increased to a peak of 50 percent of value added in manufacturing. By 1992, Iowa meatpacking wages had declined to 31 percent of value added in manufacturing. Compared to 1977, by 1997 the buying power of Iowa meatpacking employees had declined by 51 percent with similar declines in Minnesota, South Dakota, Nebraska, and Kansas.

The overall economic effects on these communities appear at best to be mixed. In Columbus Junction, the introduction of a new IBP meatpacking plant in 1985 significantly increased average annual manufacturing wages, but only after they had dipped by more than $10,000 to a low point in 1984, probably due to the closure of the town's Rath meatpacking plant, with nearly six hundred employees, in 1983. In Perry and Storm Lake, average manufacturing wages in the 1980s and early 1990s fell when IBP acquired plants formerly operated by Oscar Meyer and Hygrade. In Storm Lake, Hygrade had closed its plant after the UFCW local refused a pay cut of $3.00 an hour in 1981. IBP purchased the plant in 1982 and converted it from a union to a non-union workplace. By the 1990s, its workers were taking home the equivalent of one-third of the wages that Hygrade's employees had earned.

In Perry, workers were also unionized, but their company, Oscar Meyer, was under pressure from IBP's Storm Lake operation to pay lower wages, to which the Perry union local agreed. This did not stop Oscar Meyer from closing the plant in 1989. Soon after, IBP announced that it was returning to Perry and would purchase the plant. Under IBP, the starting wage was reduced from $9.50 to $5.80 per hour, although former Oscar Meyer workers received $7.00 per hour. In addition, IBP increased its employees' work week to sixty hours, dropped the seniority system, and greatly increased the speed of the processing line.

By eliminating union contracts and importing labor—described more fully in chapter 4—the new-style meat-processing companies undercut the middle-class lifestyle that the unionized line meatpacking companies had supported from the 1940s through the 1970s. In the wake of the new plants in smaller communities, the older meatpacking plants in Iowa collapsed, either being replaced, as in Perry and Storm Lake, by non-union IBP-style operations or closing. The number of meatpacking jobs in the state declined from about 21,000 in 1975 to about 13,000 to 14,000 in 1982. Given the large size of some of these operations, it is not surprising that community effects were significant and long lasting. In Mason City, for example, the 1975 closing of the Armour (formerly Decker) plant, with its loss of 1,300 jobs, began what turned out to be a long-term exodus of manufacturing jobs and population from that city's north end.

In Waterloo, Rath Packing Company had not only survived the Depression but had thrived; by 1941, it had reinvested in an all-new physical plant. With nearly 4,500 employees, Rath was at that time Iowa's second-largest employer, next to Deere's Waterloo Tractor Works, each of which straddled the Cedar River. The company's net earnings and number of employees—8,851—peaked in 1956, but earnings slipped from a record $1.37 on the sales dollar in 1956 to $.50 one year later, a pattern repeated in subsequent years. In 1962, corporate restructuring forced the Rath family to abandon its operating role in the company, and two years later Rath was hit by a major strike. In the late 1970s and early 1980s, the Black Hawk Economic Development Committee helped obtain $7.6 million in low-interest federal loans so that the company could invest in new equipment, and Rath raised an additional $6 million through the creation of an employee stock ownership program, but the investment was to no avail: the company closed its doors in December 1984. The rapid decline of Rath along with the Iowa Farm Crisis led to a major shedding of 9,000 manufacturing jobs in Waterloo between 1980 and 1984.

Dubuque's story is similar to Waterloo's. The city's leading packing company, Dubuque Packing Company or the Pack, was the city's second-largest employer, behind only Dubuque's John Deere plant, whose workforce overtook the meatpacker in the 1960s. Founded in 1891, by 1980 Dubuque Packing had 2,700 employees next to Deere's 8,157. One of the largest packing operations in the country in the 1940s and 1950s, the Pack remained profitable until the late 1970s. As it faced increasing difficulties in retaining the support of its creditors, the company began to ask Local 150-A of the United Food and Commercial Workers International Union for concessions to its collective bargaining agreement. A series of wage, benefit, and workplace concessions ensued, but the company still struggled. In 1982, after the union rejected a proposed wage concession, the Pack closed the plant. The plant was sold to FDL Foods, which operated in Dubuque until 1995, when it again closed. It was operated by Farmland Foods from 1996 until 2000, at which point it closed again, shedding 1,176 jobs and never reopening.

Dubuque Packing had been vital to the city's industrialized and unionized economy, providing well-paying jobs with good benefits. In 1979, Dubuque ranked tenth in the nation in per capita consumer goods spending. Its prosperity would come crashing down as both Dubuque Packing and John Deere experienced rapidly declining employment in the 1980s—7,500 jobs disappeared from

Dubuque County between 1979 and 1982, and at the beginning of 1983, the county's unemployment rate reached a Depression-era level of 23 percent. While the city's economy has recovered significantly since the 1980s, with an overall growth in regional employment of 10,000 jobs since 1990, the loss of nearly 3,000 well-paying blue-collar jobs in meatpacking clearly represents a challenge that is difficult to overcome. As of 2018, the plant's site remains a vacant parcel near the center of the city.

Like Mason City, Waterloo, and Dubuque, meatpacking in Ottumwa was one of the top employers — in fact, in Ottumwa the John Morrell plant was the largest employer, with a peak number of 3,430 production workers in 1949. At that time, about two-thirds of Ottumwa's manufacturing workers were employed at Morrell. Morrell's workers were leaders in the Congress of Industrial Organizations' unionizing of packinghouse workers in the 1930s, earning the title of United Packinghouse Workers of America Local 1 when it became the first packinghouse local in the nation to seek a CIO charter. After World War II, Local 1 asserted a militant brand of unionism that enabled it to gain influence over workplace rules that determined the pace of work and the treatment of its members by management. As early as 1954, however, Morrell's management began to talk about the plant losing money, which eventually turned into talk about the plant closing. As in Dubuque, plant closure was preceded by union concessions to management, but the plant closed on July 14, 1973.

The impact on Ottumwa was quick and hard. The city's unemployment rate rose from 5.6 percent in 1971 to 10.3 percent in 1974. Manufacturing jobs declined from 5,000 in 1971 to 4,000 in 1980. Seeking to take advantage of the available and trained workforce, in October 1974 the Hormel meat company opened a new hog-slaughtering and hog-packing facility next to the abandoned Morrell plant. At $10.74 per hour in base pay in 1982, Hormel paid higher-than-expected wages. At the same time, however, it played the Ottumwa plant against other Hormel plants by contributing fewer benefits to its Ottumwa workers. By the mid-1980s, Hormel began to threaten the Ottumwa workers with large layoffs if their union did not accede to concessions on wages and benefits. Ottumwa's union local resisted, and Hormel laid off a total of 558 workers in spring 1984. Finally, the Ottumwa workers relented and agreed to a drop in base pay to $8.75 per hour and an end to bonuses. More concession demands followed along with the nationally known strike of Hormel's workers in Austin, Minnesota, in 1985. Although Ottumwa's workers were initially sympathetic to the Austin strike, their support began to fade in early 1986, especially after Hormel laid off 507 workers. This did not prevent Hormel from closing the plant in 1987. Excel, one of the new direct-buying plants that followed in IBP's low-wage footsteps, then leased the Hormel plant and advertised 450 openings at $5.50 to $6.50 per hour. The higher wage was for former Hormel employees, although active union members were underrepresented among those hired.

### Manufacturing Farm Machinery

Besides meatpacking, the manufacture of farm machinery and implements has also defined Iowa's agro-industrial economy. Because midwestern farmers have historically been limited in the supply of labor — typically relying on their own families — they were eager for new equipment to improve their productivity and consequently their economic advantage in a competitive market. Accordingly, between 1850 and 1900 the manufacturing of farm machinery moved westward across the nation; by the latter date, Illinois dominated the business with Iowa, Wisconsin, and Minnesota playing significant roles. In 1969, Illinois claimed 22 percent of all farm machinery manufacturing employment in the United States, placing it first in the nation, followed by Iowa with 19 percent. Iowa's role was twofold. Important farm machinery operations developed in Charles City, Dubuque, Waterloo,

Ottumwa, and Davenport. In addition, Davenport residents commuted across the Mississippi River to work in the agricultural manufacturing centers of Moline, East Moline, and Rock Island, Illinois. Iowa residents were at the center of farm machinery production in both Iowa and Illinois.

After John Deere moved his plow-manufacturing works to Moline in 1848, the small Illinois town grew to become one of the Midwest's centers of farm implement manufacturing. In addition to its Plow Works in Moline, in 1912 Deere and Company built its Harvester Works in nearby East Moline as a direct challenge to archcompetitor International Harvester, the harvesting machine conglomerate formed in 1902. International Harvester returned the favor in 1926 when it began to produce the very successful Farmall tractor at a plant it had purchased in Rock Island, Illinois, next door to Moline and East Moline. J. I. Case, another important farm implement manufacturer, was also located in Rock Island, having purchased the Rock Island Plow Company in 1937. All three manufacturers had facilities on the Mississippi River, just a short distance from the other half of the Quad Cities: Davenport and Bettendorf in Iowa. In 1980, when manufacturing was at its peak in the area, as well as more recently, Davenport's population of around 100,000 placed it at more than twice the size of the next-largest city in the Quad Cities, accounting for a little more than 25 percent of the Quad Cities' population. Consequently, while Moline and Rock Island were at the intersection of three of the largest farm machinery companies in the country, the greatest share of the population came from Davenport. In 1980, Iowa accounted for 45 percent of the population of the counties comprising the Quad Cities' planning region.

Iowans also worked in significant numbers in Iowa-based agricultural manufacturing operations. Charles City in north central Iowa played a significant role in the development of the tractor. Charles City was home to Charles Hart, who in the 1890s at the University of Wisconsin–Madison conducted research into internal combustion engines with fellow student Charles Parr. Hart

and Parr's research fed their interest in employing internal combustion engines on the farm, and the two subsequently moved
their new company to Charles City, where local investors put
up $50,000. The first traction engine, Hart-Parr Number 1, was
completed in 1902. In 1906, the new company started calling its
product "tractors," and its Charles City plant was the first in the
nation to exclusively build tractors. By 1917, the plant employed
1,800 workers, and in 1929 the company merged with other farm
implement companies into the Oliver Farm Equipment Company
and began to produce Oliver tractors in Charles City.

Although it had experimented with developing its own tractor,
John Deere elected to purchase the Waterloo Gasoline Engine
Company in 1918 and its small line of Waterloo Boy tractors. After
facing fierce competition in the still developing tractor industry,
Deere introduced the John Deere Model D tractor in 1923, moving
tractor sales upward after that. From there Deere's operations in
Waterloo expanded in the late 1920s and during the post–World
War II period; by 1980, Deere employed 16,300 workers in Waterloo. Elsewhere in Iowa, in 1911 Deere had purchased Dain Manufacturing, featuring Joseph Dain's hay-harvesting equipment, in
Ottumwa. By the late 1950s, the Deere Ottumwa Works had 1,500
employees, second in that city only to the Morrell meatpacking
plant.

[Deere came to Dubuque, Des Moines, and Davenport relatively
late—during and after World War II] Deere's Dubuque operations
began with the manufacture of 75-millimeter shells during World
War II, followed by the construction of a new $9.4 million plant
that began to manufacture Deere's Model M tractor in 1947. Deere
opened its Des Moines Works in Ankeny, which began manufacturing farm implements, soon after World War II. From there,
Deere began to build construction and forestry equipment in its
new Industrial Equipment Division in both its Dubuque Works
and its Davenport Works, which began production in 1974. By
1980, the Dubuque Works had 8,157 employees.

As with meatpacking, labor unions were at the center of the

farm machinery industry in Illinois and Iowa. Immediately after World War II, two unions affiliated with the Congress of Industrial Organizations—the United Auto Workers and the Farm Equipment Workers—competed against each other for the right to represent farm machinery workers in the Moline manufacturing plants as well as in Deere's Dubuque Works. The UAW viewed farm machinery as an extension of automobile manufacturing and therefore sought the right to represent the industry's workers. The FE was the more militant of the two unions, preferring shorter contracts and, similar to the United Packinghouse Workers of America in Ottumwa, the use of work stoppages to contest shop floor rules. The FE also favored a strong steward system that enabled workers to file grievances. In contrast, the UAW preferred longer-term contracts that focused on wages and benefits with fewer stewards to help workers file grievances.

Conflict between the two unions, which lasted until 1955, also took place over issues related to the Communist Party in community organizing, with the FE resisting the requirement under the federal Taft-Hartley Act of 1947 for its members to sign non-Communist affidavits. In turn, UAW organizers used this fact, along with a major capitulation of the FE to International Harvester in a 1952 strike, to discredit the FE and successfully convert its members to the UAW. Consequently, by 1955 farm machinery manufacturing workers were primarily represented by the United Auto Workers. Iowa's and Illinois's struggle over the nature of unionism in the farm machinery industry marks an important transition point from the democratic unionism spearheaded by the Congress of Industrial Organizations in the 1930s to the more bureaucratic and centralized unionism that characterizes the period beginning in the 1950s.

Prior to eradication of the FE, the UAW had signed a contract in 1949 with John Deere that covered seven of Deere's plants. Negotiations reopened the following year over pensions and wage adjustments. Deere had not fully accepted the idea of a union, and the company's major demand was a no-strike clause, to which the UAW responded with a strike on September 1, 1950. In Ankeny and Waterloo, Deere opened the plant up to employees who wished to return to work, thereby infuriating the UAW and leading to violence between strikers and returning workers. The UAW held out for 110 days before Deere agreed to a limited right to strike during the contract period. With the establishment of the UAW as the primary representative of Iowa labor working for John Deere in farm machinery and construction equipment manufacturing, a period of relative labor peace ensued, buoyed by the general prosperity of the thirty-five years following World War II. There were comparatively few strikes between the UAW and Deere during this period, with one of the lengthier ones, thirty-nine days in 1976, resulting in an agreement that the UAW said was the best ever in the farm machinery industry.

With the prosperity of the 1970s, farmers were encouraged to purchase new equipment, which spurred demand for the increased production of farm machinery. Accordingly, farm machinery employment in Iowa grew from 21,173 workers in 1970 to 31,668 in 1975 and 29,039 in 1980. Things began to change rapidly by 1980, however.

### The Farm Crisis

The major changes in Iowa's economy associated with the evolution of the meatpacking and farm machinery industries are, of course, only part of the story of the last half century. Another great part was the Farm Crisis of the late 1970s to the mid- to late 1980s, when farm commodity prices plummeted and many farmers went out of business. As agricultural historian Gilbert Fite has made clear, the Farm Crisis was not unique in twentieth-century agricultural history. Sharp fluctuations in food commodity prices have marked other periods of time and therefore the fortunes of U.S. agriculture. Historian Leland Sage writes that the fundamental challenge of U.S. and Iowa agriculture did not change in the twentieth century—it continued to feature a chronic problem with overproduction of food commodities, thereby resulting in lower prices combined with a lack of parity between the prices farmers received and the prices they paid for goods and services.

In the United States, farm commodity prices climbed dramatically during World War I, then fell precipitously during the early 1920s and, after rising in the latter 1920s, fell even further during the Great Depression. Iowa's farm fortunes followed the same pattern. Nationally, commodity prices grew rapidly during World War II and afterward into the early 1950s as U.S. food exports increased dramatically as part of the Marshall Plan to restore overseas economies decimated by war. Thereafter, commodity prices fell again in the 1950s and 1960s before rising sharply in 1973 and 1974 and then dropping from 1975 through 1977.

In 1973 and 1974, enhanced world demand for U.S. grain helped strengthen the market and the prices paid to Iowa farmers. U.S. exchange rate policy aided grain exports by moving to a flexible exchange rate that cheapened what had been viewed as an overvalued dollar. Suddenly, the chronic U.S. challenge of too much farm production had turned into a worldwide shortage of food. With higher prices for commodities, farmland values also increased sharply in the 1970s, as did farm income. Credit for operations, new land, and new equipment flowed easily as rising land values provided collateral and the cost of borrowing declined. Indebtedness could grow as well because the high rate of inflation in the 1970s reduced the real interest rate—the difference between the nominal rate of interest and the inflation rate—to nearly or below zero in the late 1970s. The Farm Credit System, a source of credit on which farmers have relied since its creation by the U.S. government in 1916, made loans on the basis of the average rather than the marginal cost of funds. Consequently, the interest rates on FCS loans were slow to adjust upward and trailed far behind increases in land values. The overall result was a quadrupling of farm debt between the early 1970s and the early 1980s.

Changes in U.S. agricultural policy also contributed to an increase in the production of farm commodities like corn. After decades of attempting to shore up commodity prices by limiting production, the U.S. Department of Agriculture under Earl Butz reversed course after he famously encouraged farmers to plant fencerow to fencerow as he brokered deals with the Soviet Union and others to sell surplus U.S. grain. In return for higher production, farmers would be rewarded with price supports regardless of the price at which their grain was actually sold—a clear incentive to produce more.

The result for Iowa farmers was a colossal boom in production and revenue. Iowa farmers increased harvested cropland by 20 percent between 1969 and 1974. Over the same period, the average market value of agricultural products per farm sold in Iowa increased by 44 percent (in 1974 dollars) to $50,114. Farmland values in Iowa more than doubled (in 1981 dollars) between 1970 and 1981. Suddenly, Iowa and other tallgrass prairie farmers were far wealthier than they had been. With rising values and rising prices, at least in the mid-1970s, farmers took on more debt as they bought more land and newer equipment to farm their larger holdings. By 1984, 28 percent of Iowa farmers (versus 19 percent of farmers nationally) had a debt-to-asset ratio of more than 40 percent; collectively, they were accountable for two-thirds of Iowa farm debt.

When commodity prices declined in the second half of the 1970s and on into the 1980s, farmers faced increased difficulty paying their increased debt. The decline in commodity prices was aided by a reduction in the foreign grain sales that had originally driven the boom. Annual exports of corn increased from 1.1 to 2.4 billion bushels between 1974 and 1980 before falling to 1.2 billion bushels in 1985. With declining commodity prices and farm income as well as higher interest rates induced by increased federal borrowing and the Federal Reserve's efforts after October 1979 to reduce inflation, land values declined substantially, thereby diminishing the assets upon which much of the farmers' debt had been secured. In Iowa, farmland values peaked in 1981 and dropped by 67 percent (in nominal dollars) by 1986 before beginning to climb thereafter.

At the same time, U.S. farmers faced higher costs for their production inputs — including seed, equipment, feed, chemicals, fuel, interest, taxes, and wages — which had grown by 61 percent from 1977 to 1983, while commodity prices had grown by only 35 percent. With declining assets, lower commodity prices, higher input costs and interest rates, and droughts in 1980 and 1983, many Iowa farmers whose fortunes had risen now faced default and foreclosure. While the Midwest accounted for 62 percent of financially distressed farms in the country in 1984, Iowa had the largest number of distressed farms — between 1984 and 1986, one out of five of the state's larger farms faced financial distress.

For many farmers, neither farm income nor land values were sufficient to cover their debt and other expenses. In a sample of 298 Iowa farm bankruptcies between 1984 and 1986, the average debt-to-asset ratio was 182 percent. In an analysis of 135 Iowa farmers, Mark Friedberger found the key predictors of financial trouble were, in order of importance, expansion, lack of inheritance, a switch in lenders, and long-term debt. Other factors included weather, losses in livestock operations (hog producers lost money throughout the first half of the 1980s), and a rise in the failure of agricultural banks in the 1980s.

Lenders as well as farmers were clearly complicit in the run-up in farm indebtedness. They made the loans and in many cases they encouraged farmers to borrow, comforted in the belief that high land values protected their loans. And when the lenders got squeezed by good loan portfolios that turned bad, they squeezed the farmers, pressuring them to sell their assets and in some cases initiating foreclosures. Farmers like Bob and Theresa Sullivan were struck by the suddenness with which their partnership with their lenders turned adversarial. Worried about their loans to the Sullivans, the banks forced the liquidation of 65 percent of the farm's equity. According to Bob Sullivan, "We're doing the same good job farming that we did when you loaned us the money. . . . you've changed, we didn't. . . . We thought we were doing well and everybody worked as a team and all of a sudden we didn't have anything. Economic rather than social criteria came to dominate the relationship between farmer and lender.

The Farm Crisis sharply reduced the demand for new farm equipment, and consequently farm machinery manufacturers laid off thousands of employees. Deere, which suffered less from the farm recession than its competitors, had laid off 14 percent of its workforce by May 1982, with the promise of more layoffs to come. By 1986, employment at Deere's Waterloo Tractor Works had dropped from over 16,000 in 1980 to 6,600. Deere's employment in Dubuque dropped from over 8,000 in 1980 to 4,200 in 1989 with no gains in wages for production workers throughout the 1980s. Overall, Deere's employment declined from 68,000 workers in 1980 to 38,000 in 1988. Beyond the loss of factory employment, Iowa's many farm implement dealers went out of business—an estimated 265 between 1980 and 1986—which had a huge effect on small towns throughout the state.

Deere's major competitor, International Harvester, struggled as well. In late 1984, Harvester announced that it was selling its money-losing farm equipment division in East Moline to Tenneco. Rival J. I. Case would take over Harvester's factories and its network of dealers. In return, Harvester's Farmall tractor plant in Rock Island closed, eliminating jobs for 1,200 to 1,600 workers. Together, Deere and Harvester eliminated 11,000 jobs between 1979 and 1984 in the Quad Cities area. In the 1980s, J. I. Case closed its Rock Island and Bettendorf plants, eliminating 2,150 jobs, and John Deere closed its Plow Works in Moline. With the Deere, Harvester, and Case closings, the Mississippi riverfront in Moline and Rock Island, once the nation's center of farm machinery manufacturing, had by 1990 been reduced to an industrial wasteland awaiting transformation into a postindustrial cityscape emphasizing tourism, consumption, and service employment. The Oliver Farm Equipment Company, which had employed nearly 3,000 workers in the early 1970s, closed its Charles City plant in 1993, costing the remaining 420 workers their jobs.

The effect of the farm machinery recession on local and state employment was sharp and severe. From the employment highs of the 1970s, employment in farm machinery, as well as construction machinery, declined substantially in the 1980s. By 1985, Iowa farm machinery manufacturing employment had plummeted to 14,296, a decline of 50 percent from 1980 levels. Five years later, in 1990, employment fell further, to 12,555, for a 57 percent decrease over 1980. Farm and construction equipment manufacturing in the Quad Cities declined by 57 percent from 1970 to 1990. Black Hawk County, home of Deere's Waterloo Tractor Works, was hit hardest with a 50 percent decrease in manufacturing employment— from 22,101 to 11,923—between 1975 and 1985. Overall, the Deere counties in Iowa experienced a 25 percent decline in manufacturing employment between 1975 and 1985.

Although Iowa's economy was able to recover from the worst effects of the Farm Crisis, the farm machinery industry and manufacturing in general were never able to return to their previous employment highs. Each of the five Deere counties had lower levels of manufacturing employment in 2015 than they did in 1970. Overall, manufacturing employment in the five counties declined by nearly one-third from 1970 to 2015. Statewide, employment in farm machinery manufacturing declined from 21,173 in 1970 (albeit 31,668 in 1975) to 13,678 in 2015. The same is true for employment in construction machinery, which Deere specialized in at its plants in Dubuque and Davenport and which declined from 12,751 in 1970 (albeit 25,515 in 1980) to 10,100 in 2015. Between 1979 and 1983, Iowa lost nearly 60,000 manufacturing jobs. By 2015, 45,115 fewer people were employed in manufacturing in Iowa than in 1970; 10,146 or 22 percent of these lost jobs were in the manufacture of farm or construction machinery. Because manufacturing remains one of the highest-paying industries in Iowa, paying

$11,000 higher than the average statewide wage, this means that the decline in the number of manufacturing jobs has eliminated some of the state's better-paying jobs.

Although manufacturing employment has shrunk significantly, manufacturing's share of gross domestic product in Iowa has declined much less. Manufacturing employment has shrunk from 17.1 percent of the state's employment in 1970 to 10.6 percent in 2016, a 38 percent decrease, while manufacturing's share of Iowa's gross domestic product decreased only a little less than 17 percent, from 22.1 to 18.4 percent. Consequently, manufacturing continues to hold its own as approximately one-fifth of the Iowa economy, more than forty-three other states, including highly industrialized Ohio and Illinois. This raises the question, How has Iowa manufacturing employment been able to continue with many fewer employees?

The answer is increased productivity, often because of automation. Nationally, nearly 90 percent of job losses in recent years can be attributed to a growth in productivity. In the farm machinery industry at least, John Deere was able to become the world's dominant manufacturer by employing automation and various other advanced manufacturing techniques. While this has been good for the company, it has meant fewer employment opportunities as Deere has sought to reduce labor costs. In the 1970s, for example, Deere invested in an entirely new 2-million-square-foot tractor works in Waterloo. In the 1980s, as American industry looked increasingly at Japanese models of factory production, Deere's Waterloo plant became a recognized national leader in the movement toward flexible manufacturing. Around the turn of the twenty-first century, Deere implemented machine cells as part of a $100 million modernization to its Waterloo plant that reduced the need for floor space as well as employees. In 2012, the company announced a $70 million investment in its Waterloo plant that would expand production by 10 percent but would not add any jobs. At the time, Deere employed 6,000 workers in Waterloo, down from around 16,000 in 1980. Deere's Dubuque Works has also become increasingly automated as the plant has adopted robotic welders. Employment there has dropped from 8,000 workers in 1980 to 2,600 in 2017.

As with other economic fallouts, the Farm Crisis represented catastrophe for some and opportunity for others. While some farmers banded together to protest foreclosures, many kept their thoughts to themselves, with some finding opportunities to expand their acreage significantly or purchase foreclosed farm equipment at very low prices, an impact felt by other farmers who suddenly found the value of their assets diminished. One farmer's loss could be another farmer's gain, particularly commercial growers farming on a scale large enough to adopt more efficient technologies.

In 1982, at the height of the Farm Crisis, Iowa had 3,105 farms of a thousand acres or larger, comprising 2.7 percent of all the state's farms. By 2017, there were 8,417 farms of this size, comprising 9.8 percent of all farms. The effect of this growth on farm acreage was even greater: in 2017, these large farms comprised at least 33.7 percent of all farm acreage in Iowa. Measured in gross cash income, Iowa's commercial farms, which earn $350,000 or more annually, comprise only 24.3 percent of Iowa farms but they utilize two-thirds of the state's acreage and generate 79.9 percent of agricultural sales in the state. Whether measured in acreage or revenue, size contributes to relatively few farms accounting for much of the state's agricultural activity.

In 1984, in the midst of the Farm Crisis, Earl Butz was asked what hard-pressed farmers could do. His response: "Get bigger — or increase production on the same amount of land. Or get a job in town." Although the Farm Crisis is part of a longer-term trend toward fewer and larger farms, it certainly seems to have contributed to the realization of Butz's dream. The growth in farm size also reflects the economies of scale that exist for larger farm operations, especially those in Iowa where farmers can take advantage of a higher density of cropland, which enables greater use of laborsaving machinery. The relatively flat and treeless former tallgrass prairie is clearly conducive to cropland density. But the greater efficiencies of large farms come at a price. Big equipment such as 500-horsepower tractors costs a lot of money. When, in 2013, land prices were near their highest in the Corn Belt, U.S. Department of Agriculture researchers estimated that a farmer would need $8 million to purchase the equipment and the 1,100 acres needed to be at the average midpoint of Corn Belt farms.

While the ideal of the family farm continues to predominate in Iowa and the nation, the growing scale of operations required to be competitive has become more prohibitive to both entry into and survival in farming. This is a partly ironic outcome of the Farm Crisis. Although farmers got into financial trouble when they expanded, the farmers who survived and thrived were the ones who were able to successfully take advantage of other farmers' failures. But the years of the Farm Crisis may foreshadow the present and the future. By 2014 and 2015, farm values and revenues had once again declined. By then, the farms that were most at risk were the moderate-sized farms, typically 850 acres, which were being hurt by lower commodity prices and increased debt. More recently, in 2018 and 2019, Iowa farmers have been hurt by the Trump administration's ongoing trade war with China, which has had an impact on the market for soybeans. They may also be experiencing the effects of climate change (see chapter 3); the heavy rains in spring and early summer 2019, for example, resulted in the fifth-latest planting in Iowa since 1960 and the latest in Illinois. Whether these events as well as lower commodity prices will result in a further winnowing out of smaller farms in Iowa remains to be seen.

### Declining Income, Declining Population

Viewing Iowa's agro-industrial economy as a whole, it is clear that the farming and manufacturing sectors continue to be highly productive, but their increased efficiencies have led to fewer opportunities for Iowa farmers and workers to participate in the state's primary economic engines. In the case of farming and agricultural manufacturing, at least, the economic disruption of the Farm Crisis enabled, if not accelerated, a move to greater efficiencies obtained via scale and technology, efficiencies that diminished the need for labor. The upshot of these changes can be seen in the state's incomes as well as its population, both as a whole and in its communities.

In the 1980s, Iowa men experienced declines in real wages at all wage levels. While the wages of men nationwide also underwent declines at most levels (all but the 90th percentile and above), the declines were not as steep. For men nationwide, the median wage worker experienced an 8.5 percent fall in real wages over the decade, compared to a decline of 11.4 percent for Iowa men. Iowa women also experienced sharper wage declines in the 1980s than women nationwide, who actually experienced an increase: –2.1 percent versus +8.2 percent.

By the late 1980s, however, Iowa and the other states in the tallgrass prairie region had recovered from the Farm Crisis and returned to economic parity with the rest of the nation. Corn prices had ended their precipitous decline and began a solid increase in 2006 that lasted until 2012 before beginning to drop. Soybeans followed a similar pattern. The agro-industrial economy of Iowa therefore returned to a more stable and economically comfortable base. Iowa per capita income, which had grown from less than two-thirds of national per capita income in the midst of the Depression to 100 percent of national per capita income in 1978, had declined to 88 percent by 1988. By 2008, the ratio was up to 94 percent and peaked at 97 percent in 2013 before dropping to 91 percent in 2017 on a schedule similar to the decline in commodity prices.

However, with the loss of well-paying and often unionized agro-industrial employment, it is not surprising that income inequality in Iowa has grown since the 1970s, just as it has in the rest of the nation. Income inequality, as measured by the fraction of income accruing to the top 10 percent of earners in the state, increased from 1917 through the 1930s only to decline to a low of 26.7 percent in 1952, when good jobs in manufacturing were relatively plentiful. Since the 1970s, when those jobs began to dry up, the top 10 percent income share in Iowa has increased to 37.7, albeit at a slower pace and to a lower level than in the country as a whole. In 2015, Iowa's income inequality was the fourth lowest of any state in the nation. But the state's middle- and lower-income groups are faring much less well than its higher-income households. Workers in Iowa at the highest income levels (the 90th percentile and above) enjoyed a 28 percent increase in real wages between 1979 and 2017, while workers below the lower 80th percentile obtained only about a 5 percent increase over the same period.

Moreover, in comparison to other states, Iowa's middle class is doing less well in recent years. In the first years of the twenty-first century, from 2000 to 2013, which include the Great Recession of 2007 to 2009, Iowa's middle class declined by 4.3 percent, the seventeenth-largest drop in the nation. In the economic recovery period from 2013 to 2016, Iowa's middle class grew by 0.1 percent, which while positive still ranked the state as fifteenth worst in the nation. Compared to two-thirds of the states, therefore, Iowa's middle class is failing to keep pace.

A number of factors explain this increase in income inequality. Causes that increase incomes at the top include higher pay for chief executives, declining top marginal tax rates, and higher shares of national income for the financial sector. Causes that reduce incomes at the lower end include increased global economic competition that places downward pressure on wages, technological improvements that displace work through automation, and declines in the real minimum wage and in labor union membership. While many of these factors are national or global in origin, Iowa's sharp decline in union membership appears to be a contributing cause of the state's growing inequality: Iowa's nonfarm job force declined from nearly 25 percent union membership in 1977 to 10.9 percent in 2016. Nationally, variation in union membership is a significant cause of income inequality — lower rates of union membership lead to higher levels of income inequality.

In addition, the prospects for union-backed benefits and pay increases for public employees are diminishing. In its 2017 session, Iowa legislators voted to restrict public employee collective bargaining to only one issue — base wages — and placed a cap on the amount that wages can rise. The legislation also requires unions to undertake a recertification vote with each new contract, with recertification contingent on support from a majority of all employees in the bargaining unit, not just a majority of those voting. The legislation also requires that union dues no longer be deducted from a worker's paycheck; they must be paid directly by the worker to the union. The Republican-led legislature's rationale for the revision was that public employees have more say in their wages and benefits than private employees.

This rationale assumes, of course, that private employees are not unionized. The rapid decline in union representation in Iowa and beyond has resulted in private employees being unable to bargain effectively with their employers. The Iowa legislature's solution — intended to even the playing field — ensures that public employees lack this ability as well. The effect on income inequality and Iowa's middle class will be clear. Particularly in rural Iowa, where schoolteachers are among the few workers in the professional class, reducing their bargaining power will only further the hollowing out of the middle class in the state's smaller communities. In addition, the 2017 Iowa legislature also preempted cities and counties from adopting minimum wage laws that exceeded the state's minimum wage of $7.25 per hour, thereby negating the minimum wage increases that four Iowa counties had enacted.

As for population loss, the communities with the highest dependence on meatpacking are the communities with the highest loss of population. Between 1980 and 1990, Iowa suffered a net loss of nearly 137,000 people, or 4.7 percent of its 1980 population. It was one of only four states to decline in population during the 1980s. Community after community in Iowa lost population as residents left for opportunities elsewhere. Of Iowa's ninety-nine counties, only seven grew in population during the decade. Over the 1980s, Waterloo lost 12.5 percent of its residents, while Ottumwa lost 10.6 percent and Dubuque lost nearly 8 percent. Small-town populations also declined and their downtowns continued to shrivel up as businesses, including banks that had accumulated too much farm debt, closed. Mechanicsville's downtown, in eastern Iowa, had once been home to thirty businesses, including two clothing stores and two hotels. By the late 1980s, nearly all were gone. In neighboring Tipton, a downtown department store that had served the community for close to sixty years succumbed in the late 1980s to the stress of the Farm Crisis as well as the arrival of Walmart.

Just as stronger farms swallowed up weaker farms before, during, and after the Farm Crisis, the arrival of Walmart as well as other large discount merchandisers had an effect on small towns that is easily visible in places like Tipton, Anamosa, and Washington, where downtowns no longer offer significant shopping opportunities. Although the presence of a Walmart helped solidify a host town's retail sales, research on Iowa Walmart sales indicates that sales came at the expense of existing merchants both in the host towns and in smaller, nearby communities. Scale economies, which favor larger, better-capitalized firms and farms, altered rural life in Iowa by reducing the number of farms as well as the number of profitable locally owned businesses. Some local businesses, such as Osterhaus Pharmacy in Maquoketa, successfully scaled up, but others were not able to compete against Walmart and other larger retailers.

In addition, as rural populations declined, small towns that could no longer efficiently provide education to their students gave in to consolidated school systems. Schools in towns like Nichols (population 374) and Atalissa (population 311) gave way to the West Liberty (population 3,736) Community School District as the larger town swallowed up the smaller districts in 1961. Statewide, this transformation was huge: the number of school districts in Iowa declined from 4,652 in 1950 to 336 in 2015. To survive, some smaller school districts adopted strategies to attract children from other school districts. Many others, however, succumbed to consolidation.

In spite of the stabilization of Iowa's economy after the Farm Crisis and despite a return from statewide population loss to slow population gain, 67 of Iowa's 99 counties lost population between 2000 and 2017. Among the state's 944 cities and towns, 652, or over two-thirds, lost population between 2010 and 2016. Population gains were typically made in the state's population centers — chiefly the Des Moines, Ames, Cedar Rapids–Iowa City, Davenport, Dubuque, Sioux City, Council Bluffs, and Waterloo–Cedar Falls metropolitan areas. With the steady decline in the number of farms in the state, it is not surprising that the many small towns that traditionally served these farms are losing population.

Outside of the metropolitan areas with cities of 50,000 or more, the micropolitan cities, those with populations of 10,000 to 50,000, are struggling. Of the sixteen nonmetropolitan cities in Iowa in this range, ten lost population between 2010 and 2015. Most of these ten population losers are industrial cities that once had major manufacturing employers: Mason City, Ft. Dodge, Ottumwa, Burlington, Newton, Ft. Madison, and Clinton. The declining industrial employment in these communities affected not only their residents but also the farm families who increasingly sought off-farm employment to offset the volatility of farm prices. Ottumwa and Mason City, which were majority or near majority meatpacking towns, have fallen the furthest, with Ottumwa in particular experiencing a stunning loss of population since 1960: 26.2 percent and 8.4 percent, respectively.

Examining five of these cities more closely, we learn that Ft. Madison, which lost nearly 22 percent of its population between 1980 and 2016, had been the home of the Sheaffer Pen and Art Supply Company, founded in 1913, which at one time employed 1,500 workers. Like their fellow workers in farm machinery manufacturing, Sheaffer employees were represented by the United Auto Workers. After being sold by the Sheaffer family in 1967, the plant closed in 2008.

As an early railroad crossing across the Mississippi River, Burlington had a long history as a center of the Chicago, Burlington and Quincy operations. As the CB and Q consolidated its operations, its repair shop in West Burlington finally gave way. The shop, which had operated from the latter part of the nineteenth century until being shuttered in 2004, was at one time the city's largest employer—with 1,500 workers soon after World War I, it could build or repair fifty locomotives per month. Between 1980 and 2016, Burlington lost 14 percent of its population.

Another Mississippi River city, Clinton was also once home to a major railroad shop—the Chicago and North Western. As in Burlington, many people from Clinton worked in the C and NW yards, which employed as many as 1,500 Clinton residents. As in Burlington as well, as railroads consolidated operations, the C and NW yards closed in 1995. Other major industrial employers that have left the city include Central Steel Tube and DuPont, which manufactured cellophane in Clinton before selling its plant in 2002. At one time, DuPont employed nearly 1,400 people. Between 1980 and 2016, as these businesses left, Clinton lost close to 22 percent of its population.

During that time, Clinton not only lost population, but its workers also lost a major source of leverage for maintaining good jobs at good wages. In 1979 and 1980, Clinton underwent a major strike in which 750 members of Local 6 of the American Federation of

Grain Millers struck Clinton Corn Processing (now Archer Daniels Midland). Local 6 was a strong union that over the years had gained good pay and good benefits for its members. Local contracts were imitated by Clinton's DuPont plant as well. In the late 1960s and early 1970s, the union had used three strikes to obtain five favorable contracts. But by the mid-1970s, high-fructose corn syrup prices had dropped significantly. At the same time, new corporate management looked to reduce costs and squeeze profits from low-profit subsidiaries and therefore brought a new approach to the table that presaged the national decline in labor unions in the 1980s. Clinton Corn began to propagandize against the union, which was followed by a management-union skirmish and a wildcat strike over the discharge of a worker who had a company light bulb in his lunch box. In 1979, Clinton Corn hired strikebreakers and eventually broke the union when a decertification vote succeeded in 1980. In addition to ending union representation in one of Clinton's leading industries, the eight-month strike divided the community, which further eroded the union's position.

Newton is the newest micropolitan city in Iowa to succumb to the loss of a major employer. Newton was the home of the Maytag washing machine company; for nearly one hundred years, the firm employed thousands of white- and blue-collar workers to guide the company and manufacture its products. After it was purchased by Whirlpool in 2006, its new owner found the United Auto Workers organized operation redundant with existing nonunion plants in Ohio and Mexico. Instead of earning $20.00 per hour with good benefits, laid-off production workers faced the prospect of jobs in central Iowa paying little more than half that amount. Maytag's name recognition led to national coverage, including an August 2007 *New York Times* article under the apt title "Is There (Middle Class) Life after Maytag?"

The answer to this question came in the years following. From 2001 through 2005, prior to Maytag's closure in 2007, manufacturing workers in Newton's Jasper County earned a total compensation of about one-third more annually than manufacturing workers across the state. From 2010 through 2016, Jasper County manufacturing workers earned only 73 to 83 percent of what manufacturing workers statewide earned. Over this period, manufacturing jobs in the county dropped from 4,556 in 2001 to 1,483 in 2008 before climbing back to 2,399 in 2016, for an overall decline in manufacturing jobs of nearly 50 percent. Newton has lost 1.7 percent of its population since 1980, most of that since 2010.

Events in Mason City provide a perfect example of the challenges facing Iowa's micropolitan towns. Mason City has been steadily losing population since 1970, and Cerro Gordo County lost 35 percent of its manufacturing jobs between 2000 and 2015. In 2016, given the option of adding 2,000 non-union jobs through a proposed Prestage Foods pork-processing plant with the assistance of $15 million in state incentives matched with over $11 million in local incentives, citizens faced a difficult dilemma. Some could reflect on the 1975 closing of the 1,300-employee J. E. Decker plant that had once anchored the city's industrial base. However, they could also see that the new plant would not offer the same income that Decker had offered four decades earlier: Prestage's $13.00 per hour was below the local average, and many immigrants from other countries were expected to fill the new positions.

Citizens also expressed concerns about the effect of the hog plant's job growth on the community, especially its schools. The introduction of many non-English-speaking children would certainly challenge local schools. Some suggested that opposition to the plant stemmed from resistance to the likely addition of a number of Hispanic Americans or other ethnic groups into this predominantly white community.

Residents were also concerned about the possible effect of the new plant on the environment. They questioned whether such a large plant would entice more concentrated animal feeding operations to locate in or near Mason City to take advantage of what would be the area's proximity to a major consumer of hogs.

Residents and businesses in nearby Clear Lake worried about the impact that these confinement operations would have on the attractiveness of Clear Lake's namesake amenity, which attracts tourists and affluent people with expensive homes near the lake.

Overhanging the debate was the question, whether fully articulated or not: If not this, then what? Although Mason City continues to play a role as a medical and retail center for north central Iowa, work opportunities in these areas have not been enough to compensate for the loss of industrial employment. Mason City is not like Des Moines, where insurance and financial services help drive the economy and population, or for that matter even like Cedar Rapids, where traditional agro-industrial employers such as Quaker Oats have been complemented by major aerospace employer Collins Aerospace.

After much debate and an unlikely partnership between liberal and conservative groups, in early May 2016 the Mason City city council voted (in a tie) not to provide financial incentives to the project, and Prestage found a more receptive community in Eagle Grove, about seventy miles southwest of Mason City. Going forward, Mason City is confronted with major questions about what kind of community it wants to be. Historically, it has been a manufacturing community, but these jobs are drying up and the types of blue-collar employment that many Iowa communities can attract often include meatpacking. Like much of Iowa, Mason City remains tied to the agro-industrial economy. As those jobs shrink in number and lose their union benefits and as family farms become fewer and bigger, the question looms large: What will become of Iowa's economy and its middle class? And without well-paying jobs in manufacturing as well as opportunities on the farm, how will Iowa mitigate the growing income inequality that characterizes the state?

## TWO

## CORN, HOGS, AND WATER

**W**HEN WHITE SETTLERS came to Iowa Territory in the 1830s, they found a land far different from the one they had known in the eastern United States or in Europe. In contrast to the wooded lands of the eastern seaboard, where white oak predominated, forests were relatively uncommon in Iowa and other parts of the tallgrass prairie region. The French explorers who had come before had named this land "prairie," from the French word for "meadow." About 80 percent of Iowa's nearly 56,000 square miles of land was covered with tallgrass prairie, with the remainder of the state covered primarily by woodlands.

Big and little bluestem, Canada rye, prairie cordgrass, Indiangrass, and many other grasses stood tall on the Iowa prairie, with the most common grass, big bluestem, growing to a height of nine feet. Above the ground the prairie was tall, vast, and kinetic. British immigrant John Newhall wrote of the Iowa prairies in 1846: "Sometimes they are spread out in boundless plains; at other times they are gently rolling, like the swell of the sea after a subsiding storm." Visitors also saw the prairie's beauty when colorful flowers bloomed in the warmer months. Biologist Bohumil Shimek said that "the real rich beauty of the prairie was developed only after mid-summer when myriads of flowers of most varied hues were everywhere massed into one great painting." New England transcendentalist Margaret Fuller, traveling in 1843 to Chicago, remarked on the prairie that was still nearby: "In Chicago I first saw the beautiful prairie flowers. They were in their glory the first ten days we were there—The golden and the flame-like flowers."

Despite Fuller's appreciation of the prairie's beauty, her assessment of the prairie's farmers notes that "their mode of cultivation will, in the course of twenty, perhaps ten, years, obliterate the natural expression of the country." Indeed, tallgrass prairie farmers quickly learned that the fertile soils of the prairie offered enormous opportunity for productive cultivation. The region encompassing the Upper Mississippi River Basin, including Iowa, Illinois, Ohio, Indiana, and Minnesota, now has the highest proportion of land in agriculture — primarily corn and soybeans — of any region in the nation.

The stunning landscapes observed by Fuller and others hid the benefits they were providing to the soils underneath. Prairie grasses and prairie flowers have large and complex root systems that actually dwarf, by a ratio as high as 2 to 1, the aboveground plants as well as the root systems of nonnative grasses like those that cover the lawns of modern housing developments. The prairie root systems served many ecological functions. They provided deep access to moisture, even during drought. They enabled prairie grasses and flowers to maintain their ground against invasive vegetation and to recover from the frequent fires that burned on the prairie. In fact, while prairie fires destroy woody material at the surface, through microbial action they stimulate an abundance of soil nutrients. Prairie root systems also provided rich habitat for insects and microorganisms. They effectively incorporated nutrients from the soils while holding the soils in place. And when a plant died, its vast root system provided a rich source of organic matter to the soils that surrounded it. Most prairie plants are perennials, thereby providing a permanent plant infrastructure for enriching the soils. Prairie root systems also influenced soil structure so that prairie soils became rich with relatively large particles that housed a variety of tiny organisms while serving as a sponge that held water in the face of drought or erosion. Prairie soils, therefore, were not only fertile but also retained moisture, which buffered the effects of drought and helped prevent erosion.

Erosion resilience sustained clear water conditions in the many rivers and streams that bisect Iowa and that ultimately drain to the Mississippi and Missouri Rivers, the nation's longest. With both of these great rivers ultimately flowing south to New Orleans and the Gulf of Mexico, the prairie's impact on the environment reached well beyond Iowa.

The tallgrass prairie also depended upon frequent fires ignited by both lightning and Native Americans, who used fire for managing land and hunting buffalo. Fire stimulated the growth of the prairie plants while arresting the growth of trees and other woody plants that might otherwise dominate the grasslands. After a fire, the prairie plants returned earlier the next spring, grew faster, and displayed more flowers. Grazing by buffalo, elk, and deer created distinct microenvironments and therefore fostered biodiversity. In contrast to rainier eastern Iowa, Illinois, and Indiana, the droughts that frequented drier areas like western Iowa, along with ensuing fires, also limited the growth of trees.

What Cornelia Mutel describes as "a sustainable, stable, and self-sufficient system, one where the rivers ran clean, the prairie soils grew thicker and richer, and thousands of plants and animals continued their reproduction and massive annual migrations," was going to be transformed.

### The First Great Plowdown

As Margaret Fuller predicted, much of the tallgrass prairie's complex and delicately balanced ecosystem came to an end as easterners moved west and became prairie farmers. Within the context of a growing nation comprised of predominantly white Europeans seeking economic opportunity, the soils that the prairie had produced seemed simply too fertile and too plentiful to be bypassed or left to Native Americans. Beginning with the defeat of Sauk leader Black Hawk in 1832 and continuing through 1851, the U.S. government forcibly removed Native Americans from Iowa, and the larger herbivores that had also contributed to the preservation and diversity of the prairie were killed by the pioneering farmers and had mainly disappeared by the 1860s. Initially, settlers built their farms in or near the relatively few wooded areas of Iowa, but by the 1840s and 1850s they had begun to farm the prairie. This was no easy task—the dense root systems that gave the prairie its organic wealth made plowing with the tools of 1840s agriculture very difficult.

Breaking the tallgrass prairie came at just the right time, when the Industrial Revolution was developing new tools for agriculture that would make the taming of the prairie more manageable. First in importance was John Deere's 1837 invention of the self-scouring plow, which was able to cut through the prairie sod while shedding the moist dirt that had clung to earlier plows. William Haddock, who came to Iowa as a young man in 1856, described the old plows from back east: "These would be of no use on the prairie. They would not scour. The Iowa plows are light and artistic with bright, shining, tempered steel mold-boards." And with the patenting of barbed wire in the 1860s and 1870s, midwestern farmers were finally able to address the fencing problem caused by the absence of wood on the prairie.

While tallgrass prairie farmers initially planted wheat as much as or more than they planted corn, by the 1870s the prairie had increasingly become known as the Corn Belt. In a sample of Cedar County farmers for 1850, the typical farmer produced 180 bushels of wheat and 400 bushels of corn. By 1880, the typical farmer in the same Iowa county produced 30 bushels of wheat and 2,800 bushels of corn. The tallgrass prairie's rich soils and warm, moist weather were ideal for growing corn, and the small farmers of Illinois and Iowa learned that with relatively little capital expense they could invest in hogs and corn. According to Allan Bogue's account of agriculture in nineteenth-century Illinois and Iowa: "Given the matchless capacity of the prairie triangle to produce bumper corn crops, and given the ability of the hog to convert this cereal into succulent meat, it is little wonder that the corn plant and the hog have come to symbolize the agriculture of the region." In Cedar County, the typical farm household increased its number of hogs from sixteen to seventy-two between 1850 and 1880.

In nineteenth-century Iowa, while corn and other crops had displaced the tallgrass prairie, beef cattle and dairy cows grew rapidly in number by 1900. Initially, when a county was settled, cattle grazed on the open prairie that had not yet been plowed for cultivation. But within about thirty years of initial settlement, farmers were building enclosed pastures for their livestock. Moreover, farmers began to depend on white and red clover and introduced grasses, believing them to stand up better to grazing than the native prairie grasses. Over the nineteenth century, therefore, farmers gradually planted grasses, typically timothy and bluegrass, clover, and eventually alfalfa on the enclosed prairie, thereby reducing the prairie even further. Finally, farmers and other rural residents worked hard to tame the fires that had previously given the tallgrass prairie its hold on the landscape.

The impact of farming on Iowa's prairie was quick and massive. In 1860, total land in farms was 2.7 million acres, 7.5 percent of the state's land area. By 1900, 34.6 million acres were in farms, nearly 96 percent of the state's land total. By 1900, the prairie in Iowa was nearly gone, along with its many native grasses and wildflowers. Taking their place were many invasive plants and animals such as Queen Anne's lace and daylilies as well as house mice. Also gone were many of the animals that had thrived on the prairie, either extinguished or greatly diminished with the loss of their native habitat: buffalo, passenger pigeon, waterfowl, wild turkey, cougar, gray wolf, whooping crane, peregrine falcon, sandhill crane, elk, black bear, and prairie-chicken. In the words of William Haddock, after he had lived forty-five years in Iowa, "as the prairies were settled up they became scarcer and scarcer till now there is neither prairie nor chicken to be seen in the land."

Although by 1900 the prairie had basically disappeared in the

Iowa City area where Haddock lived, the saturated soils of north central Iowa were still not fully plowed under. These wetter lands with their prairie potholes, depressions formed by large chunks of ice left by retreating glaciers, have been succinctly defined by Katherine Andersen as "being less wet than a swamp, but too wet to cultivate." Much of nineteenth-century Iowa, with the exception of the far northeast, southern, and western counties, featured soils at least 10 percent of which were poorly drained. North central Iowa was much wetter, and half or more of the soils in eleven counties are estimated to have been poorly drained in the nineteenth century. One farmer reminisced: "In the year 1865, on arriving at Nevada [in Story County, north of Des Moines] . . . we started across the country northeast. . . . Everything looked like a great lake." Clearly, these wetlands were a major impediment to the complete transformation of the prairie into agriculture.

Drainage was the answer to the problem of saturated lands too wet for farming, and by the end of the nineteenth century north central Iowa was one of the most extensively drained areas in the country, with a reduction in wetlands of 89 percent or more. Starting with an estimated 4 million acres of wetlands in the eighteenth century, by the 1980s Iowa had only 422,000 acres of wetlands remaining. Inspired by the underground drains made of wood and stone in England, Iowa farmers began to employ underground drain tiles in the 1870s. Given the challenges posed by wet prairies, farming was not established in north central Iowa until the 1870s and 1880s, and drainage districts were not fully in operation there until the turn of the century. Drainage tiling was supplemented by an earlier technology: drainage ditches.

Overall, in the Mississippi and Missouri River Basins, drain tiles are employed most intensively in the Illinois-Iowa part of the Corn Belt—the east central Illinois prairie and north central Iowa. Drains originally consisted of clay pipe, but since the 1950s plastic piping has been used. Typically, drain tiles are perforated pipes buried four to six feet belowground. They channel moisture into drainage ditches, streams, and rivers, thereby lowering the water table so that corn and soybeans sink their roots into soil instead of water.

To be effective, drainage required the establishment of drainage districts—farmers, acting alone, could not adequately drain their acres. There were several reasons for this. First, the construction of drainage was not cheap—it was a major capital expense that required farmers to join together. Second, effective drainage required large areas of land—larger than most individual farms. Third, drainage districts required state law to enable them to acquire land for drainage with just compensation through eminent domain.

Many states, including Iowa in 1873, began to pass legislation in the late nineteenth and early twentieth centuries that authorized the creation of drainage districts. By 1930, Iowa farmers had drained 7.3 million acres of wet prairie, 6.1 million acres of which were in drainage districts. About half of this acreage was drained between 1910 and 1920, in part because in 1908 Iowa voters approved an amendment to the state constitution that allowed property owners to establish drainage districts and exercise special assessments to build and maintain drains on property owned by others. Although Iowa law permits two or more private property owners to petition for the creation of a drainage district, members of the county board of supervisors, the legislative body for Iowa counties, serve as trustees for the districts.

As of 1959, Iowa had 6.2 million acres in drainage districts, representing more than 3,000 districts and 18 percent of total farmland in Iowa. While agricultural lands have been drained throughout the United States, Iowa, Illinois, Indiana, and Ohio stand out as the states in the entire Mississippi River Basin with the highest extent of tile drainage. To meet the demand for drain tiles in north central Iowa and beyond, Mason City, the largest city in north central Iowa, began to manufacture clay tiles in the 1880s and was later recognized as the brick and tile capital of the world. In the

1930s, Iowa was said to use more drain tiles than any comparable area in the world. Like the self-scouring plow, the development of the clay tile industry contributed greatly to the conversion of the tallgrass prairie to agriculture.

The creation of drainage districts altered the landscape and ecosystem of north central Iowa in just a few decades. As late as 1903, one could still see considerable standing water. By the mid-twentieth century, 125 drainage districts had been organized in Story County, whereas there were only 2 in 1904. And by 1952, very few prairie potholes contained water throughout the year. The effect on farming and land cover was significant. In 1884, at a time when Story County was fully farmed and well populated and before drainage districting had begun, native hay or prairie accounted for 13 percent of land in the county; by 1947, it accounted for less than 1 percent. During the same period, row crops, corn and soybeans, had grown from 24 percent of the county's land area to 48 percent. With no distinction between wet areas and dry areas, the land became uniform in use and value—nearly all of it was cultivated, and property values varied much less than before.

Loss of wetlands also meant the loss of wetland wildlife. Overall, the prairie pothole region in both the United States and Canada supports between one-half and two-thirds of all game birds in North America. The towns of Plover, Mallard, and Curlew, all located in the prairie pothole region of Iowa, were named by a railroad executive who enjoyed the hunting opportunities presented by the Iowa wetlands. But the loss of wetlands meant a significant loss of waterfowl in Iowa's share of the region. Although both sport and market hunting contributed to the loss of waterfowl, draining in this part of the state eliminated much of the habitat these birds needed.

Other changes better enabled farmers to respond to the growing market for food, driven by the rapid urbanization that began in the second half of the nineteenth century. To help meet this increased demand, Chicago developed into the tallgrass prairie's market town, the place where the crops and livestock of the prairie were graded, processed, stored, marketed, shipped, and traded. Improvements in agricultural technology made it possible for farmers to become more productive. The harvesting of corn would not be as rapidly mechanized as the mechanical reaper had made the harvesting of wheat and other small grains in the first half of the nineteenth century. But Corn Belt farmers were able to save time and energy by employing other inventions of the era: the horse-drawn two-row planter, the straddle-row cultivator, the power corn sheller, and reaper-like mowing machines.

These inventions allowed farmers to make better use of limited time, especially in the spring, to plant and cultivate, and enabled them to use horses to power the new implements. As a result, the horse came to replace the ox, which couldn't move quickly enough to power mechanical implements and lacked the horse's agility to turn around in fields. Whereas sheep outnumbered horses in Iowa in 1850, by 1900 horses outnumbered sheep. This, in turn, affected what farmers grew—grasses and clover for grazing and oats for feed—an estimated three to five acres were needed to produce feed for an adult working horse. Nationally, in 1915 about 25 percent of all farm acreage was used for growing feed for horses.

Major changes took place in farming between 1900 and 1940: the invention of the gasoline-powered tractor, the development of hybrid seed corn, and the invention of the mechanical corn picker, all of which, except the corn picker, were quickly adopted by Iowa farmers between 1920 and 1940. Other key inventions of the period that were adopted included planters, hay balers, silo unloaders, mechanical harvesters, milking machines, and mechanical cultivators. Implements such as cultivators could be driven by a power takeoff, developed in 1918, generated by the tractor's engine. Additionally, the advent of rural electrification, particularly in the 1930s New Deal period, enabled the adoption of electricity-driven mechanization such as milking machines and the lights that made farmwork more manageable after sunset.

Gasoline-powered tractors wasted little time replacing the horse on American farms. The number of horses on farms nationally peaked at 21 million in 1915 and dropped steadily to less than 5 million by the early 1950s. Correspondingly, the number of tractors manufactured increased swiftly, especially from 1915 to 1920 when annual production increased from 20,000 to 200,000, including those produced by John Deere in Waterloo and Hart-Parr in Charles City. At mid-century tractors, many of which were produced in Iowa and across the river in Illinois, were found on nearly nine out of ten farms in the country.

The decline of the horse in farming was also assisted by the adoption of the automobile and the pickup truck for transporting goods and people. No longer was it necessary to use horses and buggies to get to town. By mid-century, horse-drawn buggies were seen only in Amish and Mennonite neighborhoods, where mechanization was shunned. In 1920, horses were kept on 95 percent of Iowa farms. By 1978, only 13 percent of Iowa farms supported or used horses. Correspondingly, the decline in horses freed farmers to replace pasture grasses and oats with row crops such as corn and soybeans. Tallgrass prairie farmers not only gained a huge boost in productivity, but they freed up substantial land for the cash crops that would come to dominate the agricultural landscape.

## Chemical Fertilizers and Hog Farms

Many farming strategies in 1940 did not differ significantly from those in 1900. Tallgrass prairie farmers used a crop rotation system that mixed corn and animal forage crops such as alfalfa, oats, and red clover. Forage crops added nutrients to the soils, reduced stormwater runoff and leaching, and controlled weeds, providing important services to the environment while increasing productivity. In 1945, forage crops comprised about one-third of Iowa's total land area planted in crops. After World War II, however,

farming and the environment were transformed by the adoption
of chemical or synthetic fertilizers, pesticides, and herbicides as
well as modern combines for reaping, threshing, and winnowing.

With the growth of agricultural research at land grant universities as well as the nation's investment in the capture of nitrogen for the manufacture of explosives during World War II, the
era of chemical fertilizers dawned at mid-century. Holly Miller,
who founded Miller Seed and Supply in eastern Nebraska, recalls
that his store first carried nitrogen fertilizer in 1949: "The nitrate,
of course in those days, was taking the place of the legumes . . .
that's what the farmers had been using as rotating their crops. So,
that's what they used the nitrates for." An early adopter of chemical fertilizers in Poweshiek County reported in 1944, after seven
years of using them, that "it gives the land a kick."

Early tests of chemical fertilizers in the 1950s showed gains of
ten or more bushels per fertilized acre over nonfertilized acres.
As productivity gains outweighed increased costs, tallgrass prairie farmers quickly learned to like synthetic fertilizers. In Iowa,
fertilizer use grew from 182,651 tons in 1946 to 2,648,196 tons in
1970, and by 1971 chemical fertilizers were used on 95 percent of
Iowa corn acreage. Iowa farmers also doubled their rate of application from 45 pounds per acre in 1964 to 104.3 pounds per acre
in 1969. Significant increases in application rates took place in
Minnesota and Illinois as well, and fertilizer application became
associated with the corn-growing states of Iowa, Illinois, Indiana,
Minnesota, and the eastern parts of South Dakota and Nebraska.

The application of DDT, the first of many chlorinated hydrocar-
bon pesticides, to farming after the war came none too soon, because the European corn borer had crossed the Mississippi River
from Illinois into Iowa in 1943 and was causing serious crop loss
in central Iowa. In 1945, Iowa State University researchers introduced DDT to Iowa farmers. Previously, farmers had relied on cultural control methods for attacking insect infestations, such as
chopping cornstalks after the fall harvest. Iowa farmers increased

their use of DDT to combat the corn borer before giving way in
the early 1950s to the use of the new hybrid seed corn that was
resistant to the borer.

At nearly the same time, many Iowa farmers saw how DDT
could be used to prevent the fly attacks that reduced milk productivity and weight gain in cattle. More so than corn farmers, farmers raising beef cattle and dairy cows embraced DDT to the point
that by the 1960s they were ignoring extension service guidelines
for safely applying DDT or other chemicals to their animals. In
the early 1950s, corn farmers began to use other chlorinated hy-
drocarbon pesticides, such as chlordane, to eradicate corn root-
worms in tallgrass soils. Combining soil pesticides with fertilizers
and herbicides, Iowa farmers began to revise their crop rotations
from their traditional corn-oats-hay sequence to increased planting of corn on the same soils in consecutive years or, at least, a
corn-soybean rotation.

In addition to fertilizers and pesticides, herbicides also emerged
after World War II. During the war, labor was less available on tallgrass prairie farms to control weeds, and after the war Iowa passed
legislation requiring farmers to take better care against weeds.
With weeds out of control, postwar farmers, reported *Wallaces'
Farmer*, found that the new chemical 2, 4-D was effective in eradi-
cating such noxious weeds as Canada thistle and other broadleaf
plants from their fields. As other growth regulator chemicals were
developed, Iowa farmers found themselves relying increasingly on
chemicals to control weeds.

The transformation of hog farming in Iowa also had a big impact both on agriculture and on the potential for damage to the
environment. Prior to the 1970s, hog farming in Iowa and elsewhere was not a specialization but a practice of the many farmers who raised corn and soybeans. Like cattle, hogs were raised
in pastures. But in the 1960s, Iowa State University animal scientists began to encourage farmers to think about the productivity advantages of confining hogs. At the 1962 Farm Progress

Show in Blairsburg, Iowa, an annual event for farmers in Iowa, Illinois, and Indiana, Iowa State's exhibit—named Pigneyland—demonstrated how hogs could be raised in a building with pens and slotted floors for keeping the pens clean.

At that time Iowa farmers, especially the older ones, hesitated to invest in the buildings and equipment—the concentrated animal feeding operations or CAFOs—required for hog confinement. A few, however, saw CAFOs as an opportunity to fatten hogs year-round. Carl Frederick in Johnson County, who raised 1,600 hogs annually in the mid-1960s, said, "I feel that hogs will be in controlled buildings—they'll never leave buildings from birth to market." Controlled feeding and protection against the weather enabled a Henry Ford–style approach that converted animal husbandry to an industry-based and industry-scaled form of agriculture.

By the 1970s, CAFOs began to transform hog farming in Iowa and the rest of the country. With confinements replacing pasture-raised hogs, hog farms grew more specialized—shrinking in number but increasing in size. In 1959, in Iowa, 134,503 farms were raising hogs, with each raising, on average, only 110 hogs. In 2017, in Iowa, there were 5,660 hog farms, with each raising an average of 4,016 hogs—well over three times the national average. Between 1959 and 2017, the hog population in Iowa grew from 14.8 million to 22.7 million while the number of hog farms dropped by 96 percent. In 2018, Iowa accounted for nearly one-third of the U.S. hog population, more than twice as many as the next-highest state, North Carolina. In Iowa, there were 7 hogs for every person.

Clearly, Iowa had moved into large-scale hog farming. Moreover, as hog farms became fewer in number and larger in size, they became more spatially concentrated. In the past, hog operations were spread throughout the state. Since the late 1980s, however, they have been concentrated primarily in north central and northwest Iowa. As the leading hog-producing state in the nation, Iowa also leads the nation in the production of hog manure—nearly 32 million tons in 2007.

With relatively few hog farms, each with a large number of hogs and concentrated in smaller geographic areas, the environmental and spatial implications of hog farms are evident. Quite simply, hogs produce a lot of manure in relatively small areas. Flies are attracted and the smell is bad, making life unpleasant for a hog farm's neighbors. As with chicken and cattle manure, hog manure has both benefits and costs. In Iowa, at least, manure can be used as fertilizer for row crops. But manure must be stored until it is ready to use. Farmers in Iowa are required to construct storage facilities that meet minimum specifications. But storage facilities, which include both lagoons and tanks built with concrete or steel walls, can leak or overflow, often resulting in significant releases of manure into rivers and streams. In other cases, manure is spilled while being transported. In 2013, 76 manure spills took place in Iowa; in the ten years prior, the number of spills ranged from 41 to 60. The Iowa Department of Natural Resources reports that as of August 2019 there have been 137 manure spills since September 2013.

Even when not spilled, manure that is applied, untreated, to farm fields as fertilizer potentially enters waterways through storm runoff. More generally, flooding increases the likelihood of manure discharges, regardless of whether they are caused by an actual spill. This happened after extraordinarily heavy spring rains and flooding in March 2019 when eight CAFO operators in western Iowa reported flood-related manure discharges. And the flooding associated with climate change in Iowa is increasing the risk of manure discharges from CAFOs.

Manure flowing into water bodies causes significant health and environmental problems. As a natural fertilizer, manure is a source of nutrients, including nitrate, which are both a health and an environmental hazard. Although nitrate pollution is commonly associated with the application of chemical fertilizers, recent research in Iowa comparing nine watersheds shows that nitrate pollution is further compounded by higher concentrations of farm animals and their associated manure. Manure also includes pathogens—the bacteria *E. coli*, for example—veterinary pharmaceuticals, heavy metals, hormones, and the antibiotics used to both treat disease and promote growth in hogs. Recent Trump administration efforts to weaken enforcement of the Clean Water Act serve to reduce the ability to control the impact of CAFOs on water quality.

Various studies have identified the consequences of nitrate, hormones, and pathogens for human and environmental health. Research continues to take place on the role antibiotics play in disrupting the human body's glandular system; in addition, researchers are concerned that the proliferation of antibiotics in the environment will enable the rise of antibiotic-resistant germs. Researchers in Denmark have detected the dissemination of antibiotic-resistant strains of MRSA found in livestock and livestock farmers into the general population. Thus far, researchers have not been able to establish similar links in the United States, but given that the U.S. is second in the world in antibiotic use in farm animals, the threat of antibiotic resistance is real, and therefore policies to limit and regulate antibiotic use and monitor antibiotic resistance are imperative.

Manure from confinement facilities also causes problems with air quality for people working or living on hog farms as well as for their neighbors. Research in Iowa, North Carolina, Germany, and Norway demonstrates the effects of hog CAFOs on the incidence of asthma, acute respiratory symptoms, and airway obstruction. This is true for both adults and children; researchers recorded effects on children as far as three miles away from a CAFO. Researchers in Iowa and North Carolina have also shown that proximity to hogs generates higher rates of influenza among the farmers, meatpackers, and veterinarians who are exposed to them. There is no doubt that CAFOs produce foul odors that exceed those that previously emanated from smaller hog facilities. Researchers have identified these odors as more than an inconvenience—they also produce a variety of physiological and psychological effects, including burning eyes, runny nose, tension, and depression.

Not surprisingly, researchers have found that proximity to CAFOs reduces property values in the United States in a range of 3 to 26 percent and by as much as 88 percent if the property abuts the facility. The impact on property values implies that CAFOs overall have a negative effect on a community's quality of life. In a 2007 study, researchers found that while a larger number of CAFOs led to a small increase in employment, there was no corresponding increase in the other quality-of-life measures related to sustainable development that many Iowa communities seek: population retention, in-migration, and an increase in school enrollment. Moreover, whether due to odors or manure spills that compromise water quality, the environmental amenities that people seek in a place to live or to visit are less likely to be found in CAFO-heavy areas. In other words, there appears to be a zero-sum game between an Iowa whose future is defined by a vision of pleasant small towns and rural areas and an Iowa whose future is tied directly to the growth of CAFOs.

All this raises the question, Why would anyone want to live near a CAFO? One would expect that not-in-my-backyard syndrome would trigger significant opposition when local governments approve the creation of large hog or other animal confinements. In fact, this was the case when several rural counties in Iowa attempted to regulate the proliferation of CAFOs in the state. Legally, however, the counties were up against the fact that since 1947 Iowa law prohibits the application of zoning laws to properties used for agricultural purposes.

In the 1990s, three counties—Hancock, Cass, and Humboldt, each in north central or western Iowa—attempted to regulate CAFOs through what they viewed to be exceptions to prevailing Iowa law. The Hancock County Board of Supervisors argued that a CAFO was not a form of agriculture but a feedlot that, under Iowa law, the county could regulate. In 1995, the Iowa Supreme Court

ruled against the county, stating that CAFOs were a form of agriculture. Cass County attempted to apply its zoning ordinance to
a proposed CAFO, but in 1996 the Iowa Supreme Court employed
its broad definition of agriculture to reject this argument. Afterward, Iowa counties realized that they could not use their zoning powers to regulate CAFOs. Instead, in Humboldt County, the
board of supervisors attempted to use the county's home rule
powers, which give counties and cities the right to regulate the
welfare of their communities, in other words, to regulate CAFOs.
In response, in 1998 the Iowa Supreme Court ruled that a 1995 law
creating statewide minimum requirements for CAFOs implicitly
preempted the adoption of more stringent regulations by local
governments.

When running for governor in 2010, Terry Branstad, who as
Iowa's governor in the 1990s is credited with passage of the 1995
law, responded to a question about local regulation of CAFOs by
stating that "local control is something that won't ever happen in
Iowa." To drive home this point, in 1998 Iowa adopted legislation
explicitly stating that state law precluded local governments from
regulating CAFOs. In 2001 Worth County, in north central Iowa,
attempted to use its home rule powers to regulate the health
and safety of its residents by, among other steps, setting limits
on toxic air originating in CAFOs in the county. After the county
was sued by the "Friends of Agriculture," the Worth County Farm
Bureau, and several interested residents, the Iowa Supreme Court
found in 2004 that its home rule powers were limited by the ability of the state to take away these powers when it so decided.

Since 2003, Iowa has used the Master Matrix process for review-
ing and approving CAFO applications. The Master Matrix process
gives counties a modicum of participation in CAFO site selections,
which are ultimately decided by the Iowa Department of Natural
Resources and, on appeal, by the state's Environmental Protection
Commission, a citizen board appointed by the governor. Counties
can choose to participate in the Master Matrix process; otherwise
they have no say in the permitting of CAFOs. The matrix itself is a

set of forty-four criteria, each of which can be scored for effects on air, water, and community, as well as an overall score. Each of the criteria represents ways by which a CAFO can exceed minimum state standards. For example, the first criterion gives points for "additional separation distance" between a confinement structure and a residence, hospital, nursing home, or childcare facility ranging from an additional 250 to 1,251 feet or more.

Although state law permits Iowa counties to register their recommendations with the state and to file appeals with the state's Environmental Protection Commission, they still have no power to make additional requirements of CAFOs—this has been preempted by the state. Even though the Master Matrix features many desirable standards, such as minimum separations from other land uses, the matrix does not treat them as standards, only as aspirations. One wonders why, if they are desirable, they are not mandatory. Moreover, under the Master Matrix, there is no penalty for locating a CAFO near an impaired waterway. As of 2018, under the federal Clean Water Act's requirement for the listing of impaired waterways, the state of Iowa had inventoried a draft list of 622 impaired water bodies for a total of 831 impairments.

In 2017, two environmental advocacy groups, Iowa Citizens for Community Improvement and Food and Water Watch, presented a detailed petition to the Environmental Protection Commission asking that Master Matrix standards be made more protective of communities and the environment while requiring that the minimum score be increased from 50 to 86 percent. The petition included statements from thirteen Iowa counties requesting stronger local control of CAFOs. In September the commission, following the Iowa DNR's recommendation, rejected the proposal on the basis that it would be too stringent, even though 97 percent of applicants pass the current Master Matrix. It offered no opportunity to negotiate a compromise but said it would review the matrix with "stakeholders."

Clearly, local jurisdictions in Iowa are powerless to regulate CAFOs in the same way they regulate other land uses. Individual property owners are permitted to sue CAFOs under the state's nuisance law, although in 2017 the Iowa legislature adopted a bill that limits damages and requires the plaintiff to provide "objective and documented medical evidence" that the CAFO "was the proximate cause of the person's adverse health condition." In other words, citing the existing research demonstrating the links between CAFOs and illness is not sufficient; instead, the plaintiff must provide evidence of the specific cause and effect.

Rural areas in Iowa face dilemmas when considering the pros and cons of hog farms. On the one hand, residents complain that CAFOs diminish the value of rural living. As a result, said Luke Haffner, he and his wife may leave rural western Iowa: "Rural Iowa is losing people, losing talent and it doesn't care." At the same time, Trent Thiele, who operates a 3,400-hog farm in northeast Iowa, believes that but for his hog farm operation he, his wife, and their five children would need to move to an urban area to earn a living.

Both views are valid, but under Iowa law the power is on the side of the hog farmers, not their neighbors. And if a farm has fewer than 2,500 hogs, it faces even less scrutiny. It no longer has to obtain a state construction permit, and if it has fewer than 1,250 hogs, the farm does not even need to maintain a minimum distance of 1,250 feet from its neighbors. Consequently, after Gary Netser retired to his family's 145-year-old farm near North English, two new confinements totaling 2,400 hogs were built across the road, each with fewer than 1,250 hogs and located more than 1,250 feet from each other. Under state law, nothing could be done about it. While Netser thought the smell and the flies were bad, he found the nonstop squealing to be worse: "It's horrible. It sounds like they're in my front yard."

### Erosion, Ethanol, and Pollution

The growth in the use of synthetic fertilizers and the increase in row crops and concentrated animal feeding operations have had huge effects on the waters of the tallgrass prairie region. By 2000, the Environmental Protection Agency had identified nutrients, including chemical fertilizers, in agricultural runoff as an important source of pollution in the nation's waterways. In addition to CAFOs, runoff was exacerbated by overgrazing livestock, irrigation, and heavy applications of chemical fertilizers to fields.

The EPA also identified sedimentation as a source of water pollution in agricultural areas. In Iowa, sedimentation has accelerated severalfold over its pre-1950 rates. In 2013, researchers found that before settlement, 631 days were required to produce one millimeter of sediment in Iowa's glacial lakes. By 2013, only 59 days were required to accumulate the same amount of sediment. Moreover, most of the sediment found in these lakes was deposited in the prior fifty years, indicating the acceleration of sedimentation in the period of intensive agriculture after 1950.

Storm Lake in northwest Iowa reflects the challenge that accelerated sedimentation poses for tallgrass prairie water bodies. From 2002 until 2017, state and local governments dredged this lake, which encompasses nearly five square miles, while employing watershed conservation initiatives by constructing rain gardens, riparian buffer strips, and detention ponds. As of 2013, 6.2 million cubic yards of sediment had been removed from the lake, necessitating the use of three spoil sites. The 2013 analysis of glacial lakes found that in the period after 1950, annual sedimentation in Storm Lake was four times greater than it was prior to Euro-American settlement. While significant improvements have been made in water clarity, the fact that fifteen years of dredging were required confirms the huge environmental challenge posed by modern agriculture.

More broadly, soil erosion remains a significant problem for the tallgrass prairie states. According to a 2010 U.S. Department of Agriculture Natural Resources Conservation Service inventory of soil erosion on cropland, 54 percent of all water-based erosion takes place in two of the nation's ten agricultural regions—the

Corn Belt and the Northern Plains states of the Dakotas, Nebraska, and Kansas — with the greatest amount, 36 percent, taking place in the Corn Belt at a pace of 3.9 tons per acre per year in 2007. In Iowa, erosion in 2007 outpaced the Corn Belt average at 5.2 tons per acre per year. Working with data collected by Iowa State University, the nonprofit Environmental Working Group found that the NRCS data failed to account for the erosion that takes place after individual storms. Such erosion has significant effects on soils, especially soils on which row crops are grown that are bare of vegetation for more than six months every year. About 30 percent of topsoil is lost through ephemeral gullies, which form under the force of heavy rains, especially in the spring and fall. When data are collected at the township level instead of averaged statewide, Iowa State researchers found that 17 percent of Iowa land was eroding at rates at least twice as fast as the rate estimated by the NRCS, with some townships eroding at rates more than ten times the state average.

Given these soil erosion rates, can Iowa maintain its agricultural fertility? In the past, tolerable soil loss rates of as much as 5 tons per acre per year were considered adequate to maintain fertility. With an average soil loss of 5.2 tons per acre, therefore, Iowa would seem to be managing to retain its soil fertility. More recent research shows that tolerable soil loss rates are much closer to 0.5 ton per acre per year. With soil erosion rates so high in Iowa, the losses to farmers, not to mention society and the environment, are huge. According to Iowa State agronomist Richard Cruse, annual losses in crop yield to Iowa farmers from soil erosion easily exceed $1 billion.

The transition to nearly exclusive row cropping after World War II — seen by some as the second great plowdown — was a dramatic change in Iowa agriculture, as significant in many ways as the original great plowdown that began in the mid-nineteenth century. While corn continued to be a significant crop in Iowa, farmers increasingly planted soybeans. In 1936, only 8 percent of

Iowa farms grew soybeans. By 1964, the percentage had grown to 57 percent. Soybean acreage increased from an average of 1.5 million acres in the 1940s to 11 million acres in 2001. Forage land cover decreased from one-third of crop acreage in 1945 to around only 13 percent in 1997. Instead of roughly half the land being planted in perennials (like hay) or closely spaced annuals (like oats), which hold soils and slow the flow of water, the soils underlying corn and soybeans are now bare about seven months of the year and thus more vulnerable to erosion.

In recent years, row crop conversion has been solidified by the advent of corn ethanol. Beginning in 2005 with the federally mandated Renewable Fuel Standard program and in 2007 with the Energy Independence and Security Act, suppliers of fuel for motor vehicles were required to include a blend of biofuels in gasoline. Congress adopted these laws to promote energy independence and to reduce the amount of carbon dioxide greenhouse gases emitted by burning gasoline. With the mandate, the consumption of corn ethanol increased greatly during the first part of the twenty-first century, growing from fewer than 2 billion gallons in 2000 to nearly 14.4 billion gallons in 2018.

For the Midwest and for Iowa, this meant that corn's traditional and primary role as animal feed was augmented and more recently supplanted by its new role as an energy source. In 1980, nationally, animal feed comprised 86 percent of all domestic corn use. By 2018, the manufacture of corn ethanol accounted for 5.6 billion bushels of all domestic corn use in the United States, slightly more than the 5.5 billion bushels used for animal feed. According to the Iowa Corn Growers Association, corn ethanol accounts for 39 percent of the corn grown in Iowa. Not surprisingly, as the country's leading producer of corn, in 2017 Iowa led the nation in ethanol production, accounting for 26 percent of national output.

The increased demand for corn generated by ethanol appears to have contributed to a significant increase in corn acreage.

Nationally, corn acreage increased from about 80 million acres at the turn of the twenty-first century to 97 million acres in 2012. In Iowa, between 2001 and 2007, acreage in corn increased by nearly 2.5 million acres, a 21 percent increase, corresponding to price increases over that period. This was accomplished in some counties by shifting from a corn-soybean rotation to a corn-corn rotation but in other counties, particularly in the southern part of the state, by converting land that had not been recently cultivated. This included the conversion back to cropping of Conservation Reserve Program land, which had previously received federal subsidies to conserve it from soil and water runoff. Overall, Iowa's CRP acreage decreased by nearly 25 percent, from 1,970,486 acres in 2007 to 1,484,593 in 2015. Since 2015, however, with declining commodity prices, Iowa CRP acreage increased to 1,800,061 acres in 2018, resulting in a 9 percent decrease since 2007.

As a biofuels hotspot, Iowa has become central not only to the production of biofuels but also to their effect on land use, with cropland more intensively farmed for the production of corn as well as the conversion of uncultivated land back to row crop cultivation. Between 2006 and 2011, Iowa experienced a net loss of grasslands to corn or soybean conversion of 376,000 acres, mostly in southern and northeast Iowa. Elsewhere in the tallgrass prairie region, conversion of grasslands to corn production has been even more severe and long lasting than in Iowa. Overall, in the tallgrass prairie states of North and South Dakota, Nebraska, Minnesota, and Iowa, CRP land declined from 10.1 million acres in 2007 to 6.3 million acres in 2018, for a 38 percent loss in land that had provided a diverse ecosystem supporting a variety of plant, animal, and insect life. In the eyes of some, the rise of corn-based ethanol led to the third great plowdown, as grasslands were converted to corn and soybean production.

The conversion to row crops in Iowa and elsewhere in the tallgrass prairie region has been accompanied by an increase in nitrate as well as phosphorus in Iowa's waterways, both of which have been linked to water-quality problems in Iowa and beyond. In the case of nitrogen fertilizer, applications in Iowa rose from an average of 45 pounds per acre of corn in 1964 to 130 pounds per acre in 1978. From there, however, nitrogen fertilizer applications gained only slightly, so that after 1978 applications bounced above and below 130 pounds per acre of corn. In 2010, they were 142 pounds per acre and in 2016 150 pounds per acre, while the national averages for those years were 140 and 145. Similarly, phosphate fertilizer applications, the source of phosphorus in waterways, increased after 1964 from 39 pounds per acre of corn to a range of 55 to 69 pounds per acre between 2000 and 2010, with 75 pounds applied per acre of corn in 2016.

In contrast to a leveling off of nitrogen applications, nitrate-nitrogen concentrations in the Raccoon River, a primary source of water to the Des Moines metropolitan area, increased sharply between the 1930s, prior to the widespread use of chemical fertilizers, and 2004, with the most rapid increase occurring between 1970 and 2004. Nitrate is created by the third step in the nitrogen cycle whereby nitrogen, N, is first converted by bacteria from organic nitrogen into ammonium and then through nitrification into nitrite, $NO_2-$, and then nitrate, $NO_3-$. Nitrate's negative ion means that it does not attach to soils and can be easily leached into groundwater and surface water. Nitrate concentrations are commonly measured as milligrams per liter of nitrate-nitrogen: the amount of nitrogen that is in the form of nitrate.

The Environmental Protection Agency has established the maximum contaminant level of nitrate in drinking water as 10 milligrams per liter of nitrate-nitrogen. Ingesting nitrate can cause methemoglobinemia—the so-called blue baby condition—in infants, which can lead to insufficient oxygen in the blood and has been linked to thyroid cancer in adults. Recent research suggests an association between nitrate in drinking water and cancer (chiefly colorectal cancer) as well as low birth weight, premature births, and neural tube defects. Between 1 and 8 percent of all colorectal cancer cases in the U.S. annually are attributed to nitrate in drinking water. Moreover, recent research estimates that there is a one in a million chance of contracting cancer with a concentration in drinking water as low as .14 mg/l of nitrate-nitrogen, a level one-seventieth the size of the current maximum contaminant level. This suggests that the EPA standard of 10 mg/l may be too high.

Consequently, concentrations of nitrate-nitrogen have caused major concerns for the safety of drinking water, whether it comes from surface water or groundwater. The Iowa Department of Natural Resources reports that 80 percent of the state's residents receive their drinking water from groundwater. According to a *Des Moines Register* examination of Iowa DNR data, more than sixty Iowa water utilities measured concentrations of nitrate-nitrogen exceeding 5 mg/l from 2009 to 2014, including four major cities that draw their drinking water from groundwater: Cedar Rapids (110 times), Iowa City (9 times), Cedar Falls (81 times), and Waterloo (176 times). While 5 mg/l is not regarded as unsafe, the EPA considers it to be a useful indicator for the purpose of identifying states with higher concentrations of nitrate.

Increased concentrations of nitrate have also been found in other watersheds besides the Raccoon. In a 2001 study, the Iowa DNR examined historical records for nitrate-nitrogen concentrations in the Iowa, Cedar, and Des Moines Rivers. Together the three rivers, along with the Raccoon, and their watersheds dominate the central two-thirds of Iowa's land area. In the Cedar River, nitrate-nitrogen concentrations between 1945 and 1951 never exceeded 5 mg/l, while between 1978 and 1998 concentrations frequently exceeded this amount and at times approached 10 mg/l.

When the Iowa DNR compared the 1945 to 1951 data with the 1978 to 1998 data, the nitrate-nitrogen concentrations were three to four times higher for the same discharge rate in the latter period than in the earlier period. The report shows similar increases in nitrate-nitrogen concentrations relative to discharges for the Iowa and

Des Moines Rivers as well. Finally, the correlation of higher nitrate-nitrogen concentrations with discharges implies that nonpoint sources of pollution, rather than point sources such as wastewater facilities, are the more likely source of the higher concentrations. Point sources supply a fairly steady load of nitrate-nitrogen to the environment regardless of rainfall. Nonpoint sources originate primarily from agriculture; they are called nonpoint because they come from multiple sources, like farms, rather than municipal or industrial facilities.

The conversion of agriculture from a mix of corn and forage crops to predominantly row crops of corn and soybeans is strongly correlated with increased concentrations of nitrate-nitrogen. The key to understanding why this is the case is to examine changes over time in base flow, which is exactly what the term implies: the flow of water in a stream or river that is due to runoff not from rain or snowmelt but from moisture that seeps into the ground and then into the waterway. When we recall that the nitrate molecule's negative ion enables it to move through soils easily and to dissolve in water, then it makes sense that the flow of groundwater — or base flow — determines how much nitrate-nitrogen reaches rivers and streams. Also determining base flow is evapotranspiration — the combination of evaporation of water from land surfaces and the evaporation of water from plant surfaces. Assuming a constant rate of precipitation, what moisture is not absorbed in the atmosphere through evapotranspiration ends up in base flow and therefore in rivers and streams.

Perennials, which are in the ground throughout the year, employ evapotranspiration throughout the spring, summer, and fall to absorb moisture from the ground into the air. In contrast row crops, which are planted in the spring and harvested in the fall, are able to employ evapotranspiration only during the summer. Fall and spring, therefore, are the times when the greatest amount of nitrate-nitrogen is likely to leach into the base flow and ultimately into rivers and streams. The rates of evapotranspiration, measured as crop coefficients, have been calculated for different crops for the initial, middle, and end of their growing periods. Higher coefficients mean higher evapotranspiration. For corn and soybeans, the beginning and end of the growing period coefficients are generally lower than they are for forage crops, like alfalfa, while in the middle of the growing season they are comparable. Other studies have shown that perennial crops have significantly higher water demands and hence, evapotranspiration, than do annual crops like corn and soybeans. With their lower rates of evapotranspiration, row crops increase base flow and consequently the concentration of nitrate that leaches into groundwater and then into the rivers and streams of Iowa and other states in the Upper Mississippi River Basin.

In Iowa, therefore, the tallgrass prairie gave way not only to agriculture but to a form of agriculture that made extensive use of chemical fertilizers and concentrated animal feeding operations. Through the intensity of row cropping, the application of nitrogen and phosphorus fertilizers, and the extensiveness of drain tiles, farming had major consequences for water quality, both in the state and in the broader ecosystem that culminates in the Gulf of Mexico. Concentrated animal feeding operations, unwanted and uncontrolled by many local governments, also added to the excess nutrient load created by chemical fertilizers. A small farm state, Iowa would come to have a huge impact on the environment.

## ~ THREE ~

## CHALLENGING IOWA AGRICULTURE

D RINKING WATER for Iowa's capital city is fed by two rivers that join in that city: the Raccoon and the Des Moines. The Raccoon River is partly located in the artificially drained region of northern Iowa—on average, 64 percent of the row crop acreage in the 2.3-million-acre Raccoon River watershed is artificially drained. The river's significance for the quality of Des Moines's drinking water is not to be understated. From 1980 to 1996, among forty-two water basins feeding the Gulf of Mexico, the Raccoon River Basin had the highest level of nitrate-nitrogen concentrations. The Des Moines River was also among the highest sources of nitrate-nitrogen, ranking fifth out of the forty-two water basins. Together, the two rivers confronted the Des Moines Water Works with one of the nation's highest, if not the highest, concentrations of nitrate-nitrogen pollution.

Faced with the impact of row cropping and artificial drainage on its primary sources of drinking water, the Des Moines Water Works, serving 500,000 people, began to look at options for ensuring the safety of its drinking water. In 1991, in response to repeated violations of the Environmental Protection Agency's drinking water standards, the water works purchased what was reported to be the world's largest ion exchange nitrate-removal facility at a cost of $4.1 million. Des Moines was not alone in facing the health threats posed by nitrate pollution in its drinking water sources. According to a 2014 estimate by staff at the Iowa Department of Natural Resources, 30 percent of Iowa's 880 water supplies are highly susceptible to contamination from nitrate. Nationally, the U.S. Department of Agriculture Economic Research

Service estimates that water utilities spend $1.7 billion per year to reduce nitrate pollution caused by agriculture. Clearly, the water pollution induced by intensive agriculture has caused significant problems for many communities, including many that lack the resources of a relatively large city like Des Moines.

By May 2013, nitrate levels in the Des Moines and Raccoon Rivers had reached nearly 18 mg/l and 24 mg/l, respectively, much higher than the EPA's maximum contaminant level for drinking water of 10 milligrams per liter of nitrate-nitrogen. Bill Stowe, director of the Des Moines Water Works, commented: "The optimal solution to prevent nitrate concentrations from entering our source water is through watershed protection programs and good land management practices." In the winter of 2014–15, the water works ran its two-decade-old nitrate-removal equipment for 97 consecutive days at a cost of $540,000. By July 2015, it had spent $1.5 million since December 2014 on nitrate removal, and throughout 2015 it needed to run its equipment for 177 days, more than in any other year. These dollar figures reflected unprecedented high levels of nitrate in the water sources, resulting in the water works' assertion that it would need to replace its aging equipment at a cost between $76 and $183.5 million by 2020.

### Board of Water Works Trustees of the City of Des Moines v. Sac County Board of Supervisors et al.

In March 2015, at a loss to meet the growing costs associated with removing nitrate from its sources of drinking water, the Des Moines Water Works filed a lawsuit that took aim at the drainage districts supervised by county boards of supervisors in three counties northwest of Des Moines — Sac, Buena Vista, and Calhoun — through which the North Raccoon River flows. The lawsuit carried huge implications for the shared responsibility of providing clean water to Iowans. Filed in federal district court, it claimed that row crop agriculture in the three counties had resulted in nutrient pollution in the Raccoon River, with its consequences being felt not only by the Des Moines Water Works but as far south as the Gulf of Mexico. Moreover, because nutrients are piped into the Raccoon River from the counties' vast systems of drainage ditches and drain tiles, the lawsuit claimed that the pollution was attributable to a point source and was therefore regulated under the point source provisions of the federal Clean Water Act. This was an important argument: it gets to whether agriculture is generally exempt from the regulatory provisions of the Clean Water Act.

The Clean Water Act's regulatory provisions, including its requirements for the National Pollutant Discharge Elimination System, which provides permits for the discharge of pollutants, exempts nonpoint sources of pollution from the need to obtain such permits. Given the act's definition of point source pollution, this means that agriculture has generally been exempted from its regulatory requirements. The Des Moines Water Works suit hit at the heart of this exemption by identifying the major source of the Raccoon River's nitrate pollution as the ten drainage districts that occupy the three counties named in the suit: "the artificial subsurface drainage system infrastructure, such as those created, managed, owned and operated by the Drainage Districts, consisting of pipes, ditches, and other conduits that are point sources which transport high concentrations of nitrate contained in groundwater."

The lawsuit employed the same language found in the Clean Water Act's definition of point source pollution and thereby made it clear that the Raccoon River Basin drainage tiles and ditches constituted point sources. Overall, the suit built on evidence of high nitrate levels collected at various ditches and drains that flow into the Raccoon River, the correlation of high nitrate levels in these ditches with high nitrate levels at the water works' intakes on the Raccoon River, the short-circuiting by drains of "natural conditions that otherwise keep nitrate from entering streams and rivers" during the bulk of the year when there is no vegetation to absorb it, the water works' history of nitrate removal going back to the early 1990s, the state and national challenges of nitrate pollution, and the broad systems of drainage tiles and ditches in the Raccoon River watershed associated with nitrate pollution. It charged that the drainage districts in this area had failed to obtain the permits required under the Clean Water Act and Iowa state law for point source pollution, maintained that reliance on voluntary conservation efforts under the state's nutrient reduction strategy was inadequate, and alleged that the nitrate pollution in the Raccoon River constituted a nuisance and a taking of property imposed upon the Des Moines Water Works.

The immediate results of the lawsuit were clear: water quality became the hot topic in Iowa and elsewhere in the Midwest, and Iowa's agricultural establishment lined up against the lawsuit while the public supported it. The state's leading newspaper, the *Des Moines Register*, ran frequent articles on Iowa's water-quality issues in 2015 and 2016. The University of Iowa's Public Policy Center ran two well-attended conferences on the issues in 2015 and 2016. The general public in Iowa supported the lawsuit, with 60 percent in favor, but split over how to pay for it. The lawsuit also caught the attention of farmers and drainage districts in Illinois. One observer commented that "the State of Illinois, with an estimated 22 million acres of corn and soybean production— nearly 10 million of it drained by subsurface tiles—watches closely the developments to its west."

The Iowa Farm Bureau, one of the most powerful and effective lobbies in Iowa, was a leading opponent of the lawsuit. The Iowa Partnership for Clean Water, which launched a half-million-dollar public relations effort to discredit the water works and its director Bill Stowe, was backed by the Iowa Farm Bureau. The Farm Bureau has long opposed Iowa's leading potential source of funding for environmental protection and remediation. In 2010, it unsuccessfully opposed a referendum in which 63 percent of the public approved the creation of the Natural Resources and

Outdoor Recreation Trust. Since then, it has successfully and repeatedly lobbied the state legislature in opposition to funding the trust, which would, in part, fund conservation efforts to prevent nitrate pollution.

The Iowa Farm Bureau and the Iowa Corn Growers Association joined other private donors in contributing $934,000 to combat the lawsuit. The Agribusiness Association of Iowa, which represents major state, national, and international agricultural, seed, and fertilizer interests, also assisted with paying for the three counties' legal defense, creating an agricultural legal defense fund to which "hundreds of individuals and organizations throughout the state" contributed. Despite prodding by the *Storm Lake Times*, which earned itself a Pulitzer Prize for editorial writing on efforts to fight the lawsuit, and eventually by the boards of supervisors for the three counties, the Agribusiness Association declined to identify the donors to the legal defense fund. Joining the agricultural establishment was Republican Governor Terry Branstad, who commented that the Des Moines Water Works "had declared war on rural Iowa."

Although the lawsuit challenged the near exemption that agriculture has enjoyed under the Clean Water Act, it was not aimed directly at agriculture or even at row crop agriculture; it was aimed instead at the extensive drainage systems for agriculture. Nevertheless, if farming in these three counties came under the point source provisions of the Clean Water Act, this would have an enormous effect on agriculture in a region known nationally and internationally for its productivity.

In the end, despite the attention that it created, the lawsuit was unsuccessful. Rather than being fully argued in federal court, it was stopped by a state court decision. The federal district court ruled that the issue of whether drainage districts could be sued was a matter of state law and that this issue had to be resolved by the Iowa Supreme Court before any further review by the federal court. On January 27, 2017, the Iowa Supreme Court ruled that

drainage districts, even though they were managed by county supervisors, could not be sued because they did not control the use
of nitrogen fertilizer by farmers and, thus, they had no liability.
On March 17, 2017, the U.S. district court dismissed the case. Soon
thereafter, the water works board of directors voted to end the suit.

Sadly, Bill Stowe, who spoke eloquently and acted forcefully
regarding the impact of Iowa agriculture on water quality, succumbed to pancreatic cancer in 2019. Shortly before his death,
the environmental advocacy groups Iowa Citizens for Community
Improvement and Food and Water Watch filed suit in Iowa district court against the Iowa Department of Natural Resources for
failure to adequately ensure clean water in the Raccoon River. The
suit calls for the Iowa DNR to develop a remediation plan for the
river's watershed with "mandatory agricultural water pollution
controls" and with a prohibition on new or larger concentrated
animal feeding operations in the watershed.

## The Dead Zone and Iowa Agriculture

Most of the fertilizers that contaminate the Gulf of Mexico come
from the production of corn and soybeans concentrated in the
tallgrass prairie region of the Midwest — 52 percent of the nitrogen and 25 percent of the phosphorus. Although Iowa occupies
only 5 percent of the Mississippi River Basin, a 2000 study found
that 25 percent of the nitrate flowing into the Gulf of Mexico from
the Mississippi originates in Iowa. The Mississippi watershed is
the third-largest in the world, representing 41 percent of the conti-
nental United States. The watershed is heavily agricultural; farms
account for approximately 70 percent of its 1.2 million square
miles. Globally, therefore, the Mississippi watershed is very important, and Iowa plays an outsize role in shaping a critical environmental issue for the Gulf of Mexico.

Most fundamentally, in addition to its impact on the safety
of drinking water, the heavy use of synthetic fertilizers contributes to eutrophication: the excessive growth of aquatic plants

commonly induced by the nutrients from synthetic fertilizers. The resulting blue-green algae blooms cut off sunlight, resulting in fish kills. They also produce microcystins that irritate skin, eyes, and throats in humans and can be toxic to the liver: high doses can cause liver failure.

Through the flow of water into and down the Mississippi River, fertilizer-induced eutrophication, along with stratification by temperature and salinity, has produced the oxygen-starved Gulf of Mexico Dead Zone. As blue-green algae blooms die, decomposition reduces oxygen in the water, creating dead zones of hypoxia where little or no oxygen remains dissolved in the water. The Dead Zone has stretched each summer, since at least the 1980s, up to eighty miles offshore from the Mississippi River delta westward to the Texas coastal waters. Within this zone fish, shrimp, and crabs leave to find more oxygen while less mobile fauna undergo stress or die. The consequences for the fishing industry can be substantial.

With the rapid growth of the Dead Zone in the 1990s, Congress enacted the Harmful Algal Bloom and Hypoxia Research and Control Act of 1998, which called for, in part, the completion of a report on hypoxia in the northern Gulf of Mexico. The 2001 report of the Environmental Protection Agency's Mississippi River/Gulf of Mexico Watershed Nutrient Task Force—the Hypoxia Task Force—identified agricultural nutrients as a source of Gulf hypoxia and called for measures that would reduce the size of the Dead Zone to no more than 1,930 square miles by 2015. Nonpoint agricultural sources in Iowa, Indiana, Illinois, southern Minnesota, and Ohio were prominently identified in the report as sources of harmful nutrients. States whose waters entered the Mississippi were expected to develop nutrient reduction targets, strategies, and assistance programs by 2003 that would result in voluntary efforts by farmers to increase wetlands and vegetative buffer strips and adopt best management practices to reduce nutrient runoff on their properties.

In a follow-up report, released in 2007, the EPA's Science Advisory Board reaffirmed the 2015 goal, although it questioned the likelihood that the goal would be met. Importantly, it added that to reduce the size of the hypoxic zone and improve water quality, there needed to be a 45 percent reduction in both nitrogen and phosphorus entering the Gulf from the Mississippi/Atchafalaya River Basin. The 2001 report had identified only nitrogen as a source of Gulf hypoxia, but the 2007 report noted the role of phosphorus in the onset, extent, and duration of the zone. The board assigned substantial responsibility for Gulf hypoxia to Iowa and the remainder of the intensively tile-drained Corn Belt, finding that 29 percent of the yearly nitrate-nitrogen flow came from the Mississippi River sub-basin between Clinton, Iowa, and Grafton, Illinois. In the spring, the board reported, the Upper Mississippi River Basin and the Ohio-Tennessee River Basin accounted for nearly all the nitrate-nitrogen flow to the Gulf.

By August 2015, the Gulf Dead Zone had grown in one year from about 5,050 square miles, slightly smaller than the state of Connecticut, to 6,474 square miles. By summer 2017, it had grown to 8,776 square miles, about the size of New Jersey, a nearly 36 percent increase over 2015 and the largest zone since measurements began in 1985. In 2018, it shrank to 2,720 square miles, slightly less than one-third of the previous summer's high. Scientists making the measurements speculated that local weather conditions, including a storm at the beginning of their survey, may have increased the amount of oxygen in the water. In 2019, scientists measured the Dead Zone at 6,952 square miles, the eighth largest in thirty-three years of measurements. As of 2018, the three-decade average size of the zone, 5,375 square miles, still made it the second largest in the world.

As early as 2009, the EPA's independent Office of Inspector General had questioned the agency's approach to achieving any significant reduction in nutrient pollution in waters flowing into the Gulf of Mexico, criticizing the EPA's lack of accomplishment since Congress had created the Hypoxia Task Force in 1998. Its report noted, first, that the EPA's reliance on states to implement nutrient reduction strategies had failed largely because the states saw implementing such strategies via subsidies or regulations as both expensive and politically unpopular. Second, states in the Upper Mississippi River Basin had failed to consider the impact of nutrients on downstream states or the Gulf of Mexico. Third, the report concluded, the EPA had failed to monitor state adoption of nutrient standards: in the eleven-year period, no state had yet developed a full set of numeric nutrient standards.

In its September 2014 report, the Office of Inspector General stressed the seriousness of agricultural nutrient pollution and criticized the EPA for permitting states to focus on water-quality problems only within their borders and not beyond. The report noted that a majority of the twelve task force member states had not yet completed their nutrient reduction strategies by the 2013 deadline, and of these only Iowa and Minnesota had committed to specific nitrogen and phosphorus reduction goals, and only Minnesota had committed to a specific timetable — 2025 — for meeting its goals. The report recommended that to be effective, the EPA and the states should develop specific measures for assessing the impact of nutrient reduction strategies on both state and regional bodies of water and the Gulf of Mexico.

The task force's 2015 report pushed the 1,930-square-mile goal for shrinking the Dead Zone from 2015 to 2035. Clearly, this was an admission that previous efforts to reduce the size of the Dead Zone were not successful. The state of Iowa had a hand in the decision to extend the reduction target date: Bill Northey, secretary of the Iowa Department of Agriculture and Land Stewardship, served as the task force's state cochair (along with a federal cochair). The 2015 report did contain summaries of each member state's nutrient reduction strategies, but it was not able to cite any common metrics that all states could use to track the effectiveness of their conservation and management practices. With the EPA unwilling or unable to play a strong leadership role in curbing Gulf hypoxia and the courts unwilling to tell the EPA otherwise—despite petitions and lawsuits intended to force the agency to establish federal limits on nitrogen and phosphorus in the Gulf of Mexico—states like Iowa were left to themselves to develop criteria for regulating the introduction of nutrients into their waterways.

## The Iowa Nutrient Reduction Strategy

In May 2013, just as the Des Moines Water Works was using its nitrate reduction equipment for the first time since 2007, director Bill Stowe said of the state's approach to improving water quality: "The recently published Nutrient Reduction Strategy is inadequate in that it lacks vision, goals, measurable outcomes, or timelines for agricultural (non-point) discharges. Without significant action, Des Moines Water Works will be forced to continue treating degraded source waters, and our customers will continue to pay for that extensive treatment in their rates." Stowe was referring to the Iowa Nutrient Reduction Strategy, which was unveiled in the same month in response to growing national concern over the impact of chemical fertilizers—including both nitrate and phosphate—on water quality throughout the Midwest and the Gulf of Mexico.

In compliance with the 2008 Hypoxia Task Force's recommendations, Iowa prepared its nutrient reduction strategy in 2013 with revisions following annually through 2017. Although a lengthy report, the strategy made two points very quickly and clearly. First, to meet the task force's goals for reducing the Gulf Dead Zone, Iowa needed to reduce nitrogen and phosphorus entering its waters from nonpoint sources by 41 and 29 percent, respectively. Second, the strategy placed great emphasis on scientific evaluations of various conservation practices for reducing nutrient flows into Iowa waters. Prepared primarily by scientists at Iowa State University as well as the Iowa Department of Agriculture and Land Stewardship, the Iowa Department of Natural Resources, and the

U.S. Department of Agriculture, the strategy eschewed any policy recommendations. In fact, it clearly stated that conservation practices such as using cover crops, combining cover crops with wetland restoration, and employing woodchip bioreactors to absorb nutrients were only examples, not specific recommendations.

The strategy focuses on three scenarios, each of which would meet the task force's goals of reducing nitrogen but would require dramatic and significant changes in agricultural land use in Iowa. Estimated start-up investment costs for the three scenarios range from $1.2 billion to $4 billion. Alternatively, initial investment and operating costs for the three scenarios range between $77 million and $1.2 billion per year.

Scenario 1 (NCS1 in the report) calls for 60 percent of corn and soybean farmland to be planted with cover crops to hold the soil and trap nitrate during fall, winter, and spring when the ground is bare. This scenario also calls for 27 percent of agricultural land to be treated with a wetland, which means that wetlands would be re-created to help filter nutrients. Finally, 60 percent of tile-drained land would remain drained, but water flowing through the drains would be cleansed of nitrate by the use of woodchip bioreactors.

The other two scenarios would also make major changes to Iowa's agricultural landscape. Under Scenario 2 (NCS3), 95 percent of corn-soybean and continuous corn acres would have cover crops grown on them in the off-season; the remaining 5 percent would be converted from corn and soybeans to grassland, pastureland, or the federal government's Conservation Reserve Program; and 34 percent of agricultural land in many of Iowa's northern counties would be treated with re-created wetlands. Under Scenario 3 (NCS8), 31.5 percent of all agricultural land would be served by wetlands, 70 percent of tile-drained land would employ woodchip bioreactors, 70 percent of all agricultural streams would be bordered by agricultural buffer strips to reduce nutrient flow, and 70 percent of all applicable lands would have controlled drainage—fields would be drained just prior to planting and harvesting rather than year-round. In addition, various strategies for reducing phosphorus would be employed, a nitrification inhibitor would be used with fall-applied nitrogen, and spring-applied nitrogen would be side-dressed—applied after corn plants are established.

With no specific funding programs to reach the lofty goals set by these three scenarios, the Iowa Nutrient Reduction Strategy is basically a well-researched goal with no accompanying plan of action. The strategy is not a strategy at all. It is not a plan of action. Instead, it consists only of examples accompanied by broad policies, such as combining "in-field and off-field practices," coordinating conservation programs, piloting small watershed projects, exploring opportunities for nutrient trading and other "innovative approaches," encouraging the development of new technologies, and strengthening "outreach, education, and collaboration" as well as "public awareness and recognition." It recommends no changes in policies and no specific funding programs, instead stating that "initially, Iowa will rely on existing funding sources." Instead, it emphasizes that adoption of any of the scenarios is voluntary. Ironically, it makes clear the fact that adoption will not be easy but will instead be costly.

Without market or other incentives for transforming Iowa's agricultural landscape, it seems far-fetched to expect farmers to voluntarily adopt the strategy's nutrient reduction scenarios. Instead, the strategy offers itself as "a dynamic document" that "will evolve over time as new information, data and science [are] discovered and adopted." In other words, the strategy's authors appear to expect that science will provide the solutions to nutrient overload and that the scenarios in the report may be supplanted by new ideas that are cheaper and more effective. This may explain why the strategy has no deadlines for achieving its nutrient reduction goals: we are apparently waiting for new science to emerge.

Given the Des Moines Water Works' challenges with nitrate in its drinking water and the lack of a serious state strategy for promoting clean water, Bill Stowe remarked in August 2015 at a meeting of state and local officials: "We hear a great deal about the few practices that are being exercised. We hear a lot about cover crops, even though maybe 2 percent of our acreage is affected by cover crops. We hear about bioreactors when maybe there are 10 bioreactors in the state. The agronomy folks at Iowa State have been very clear that 60 percent of the land in this state would have to be impacted by conservation practices to get us even close to the under-resourced, untimed goals of the Nutrient Reduction Strategy. Nothing like that is happening in the real world, and you know it."

Collaboration and voluntary efforts seem unlikely to produce the dramatic changes in agriculture identified in the Iowa Nutrient Reduction Strategy. As Stowe commented, 60 percent of corn and soybean farms, 14 million acres, would need to be cover-cropped — and such a dramatic change is not likely to happen if it relies on voluntary actions. According to a 2017 Environmental Working Group analysis of aerial and state cover crop data, only 2.6 percent of Iowa soybean and corn acreage was cover-cropped in the fall, winter, and spring of 2015–16. A 2019 follow-up study found that by 2017, 3.9 percent of Iowa row crop acres were cover-cropped, an increase of 315,000 acres — a step in the right direction, but just a step.

Correspondingly, the state has not appropriated resources that will have any serious effect on nutrient reduction. Since 2010, when Iowa voters authorized the creation of the Natural Resources and Outdoor Recreation Trust, to be financed with an increase in the state sales tax and used for a variety of purposes, including improving water quality, no sales tax increase has been approved by the Iowa legislature. In May 2014, one year after the unveiling of the nutrient reduction strategy, Republican governor Terry Branstad vetoed $11.2 million in FY 2015 funds for water-quality and conservation programs administered by the Iowa Department of Agriculture and Land Stewardship.

By 2016, Branstad was willing to propose significant new funding for water quality to help implement the nutrient reduction strategy. There would be a catch, however: no new tax revenue would be legislated. Instead, Branstad proposed a change in the state's one cent sales tax for education. In exchange for extending the penny sales tax an additional twenty years, a portion of the sales tax, approximately $4.1 billion over thirty-two years, would be diverted to water-quality improvement measures. The proposal was quickly criticized for pitting education against water quality, and while there were competing proposals to fund water-quality measures, they all failed in the 2016 legislature. One of the failed proposals, adopting a three-eighths of one cent increase in the state sales tax to fund the Natural Resources and Outdoor Recreation Trust, was supported by a broad coalition of environmental groups as well as the Iowa Soybean Association and contingently by the Iowa Corn Growers Association. It was opposed by the Iowa Farm Bureau.

In 2018, after Republicans had gained control over the Iowa legislature, it united behind water legislation, which acting governor Kim Reynolds hailed as the first piece of legislation she would sign after taking over for former governor Branstad, who had been appointed ambassador to China. But because of the defeat of the Des Moines Water Works lawsuit, the impetus to pass strong legislation, especially in the face of opposition by the powerful Iowa Farm Bureau, resulted in a much weaker piece of legislation, which failed to establish adequate financial support or accountability mechanisms that would realistically result in any significant reduction in nutrient flow from Iowa waters to the Gulf of Mexico.

The adopted legislation (SF512), backed by the Iowa Farm Bureau and the state's agriculture secretary, uses existing water and gambling taxes to provide $282 million over twelve years. The legislation, while providing ongoing support for cover crops and other water-quality improvement practices, falls far short of the Iowa Nutrient Reduction Strategy's multi-billion-dollar estimate for funding to meet Iowa's goals for reducing nitrogen and phosphorus. The bill does not require water-quality program recipients to quantify the expected decline in nutrients, nor does it describe any means for verifying that such reductions actually took place. It does not give preference to projects that have the greatest chance of meeting the nutrient reduction strategy's goals or that have their plans evaluated by the state's Nutrient Research Center. In other words, farmers will receive grants for measures that should lead to improved water quality, but there will be no way of knowing how successful they will be in significantly reducing Gulf hypoxia.

Judging by this bill, it appears that neither the Iowa Farm Bureau nor the dominant wing of the controlling Republican Party favors water-quality legislation that requires any degree of accountability or performance on the part of farmers. In a prescient article published in 2016 by the *Storm Lake Times*, editorial writer Art Cullen observed, "That's the problem with all the legislative talk. They want to throw money at the problem and wash their hands rather than arrive at a real solution."

### Climate Change

Despite the outcome of the Des Moines Water Works lawsuit, it clearly framed and stimulated the debate over water quality and agriculture in Iowa. By focusing primarily on the effect of nitrate on rivers and streams, however, it may have diverted attention from other environmental issues exacerbated by Iowa's reliance on row crop agriculture. Among these is climate change, including the impacts that Iowa agriculture has on climate change as well as the impacts that climate change is expected to have on agriculture and the state's environment.

In Iowa and elsewhere in the tallgrass prairie states, agriculture plays an outsize role in contributing the greenhouse gases that are causing climate change. Per capita emissions of greenhouse gases in Iowa are much higher than the national average. According to a 2018 Iowa Department of Natural Resources inventory, in 2016 the state's greenhouse gas emissions accounted for slightly less than 2 percent of national greenhouse gas emissions. At the same time, Iowa's 2016 population was close to 1 percent of the U.S. population that year. Consequently, per capita greenhouse gas emissions in Iowa are twice as high as the national average. Iowa's reliance on agriculture, along with its low population density, likely contributes to the state's high per capita production of greenhouse gases. As of 2016, agriculture accounted for 30 percent of Iowa's greenhouse gas emissions compared to only 9 percent for the United States.

To appreciate agriculture's effects on climate change, it is important to remember that greenhouse gases are given their name because they act like a greenhouse — they trap heat, specifically infrared radiation, in the atmosphere. It is not merely the fact of greenhouse gases that concerns climate scientists but their growing abundance, in which agriculture plays a major role. Although the increase in greenhouse gases is associated with industrialization and the burning of fossil fuels — coal, natural gas, and oil — agriculture also matters. Whereas carbon dioxide is the chief greenhouse gas associated with the burning of fossil fuels, accounting for 82 percent of greenhouse gas emissions, two other gases associated with agriculture — nitrous oxide and methane — are also greenhouse gases.

Nitrous oxide, which accounts for 6 percent of U.S. greenhouse gas emissions that originate in human activities, primarily stems from the management of agricultural soils, most importantly through the application of chemical fertilizers. Not surprisingly, nitrous oxide emissions from row crops concentrate in the tallgrass prairie states, with Iowa being at the geographic center. Methane, which is a distant second to carbon dioxide at 10 percent of total greenhouse gas emissions, is also connected to agriculture— slightly over one-third of it is produced in the United States by digestion in domestic ruminants as well as by the manure that farm animals produce. As a top cattle producer as well as a leading poultry and hog state, Iowa is a significant source of methane.

In 2017, manure management accounted for 29 percent of Iowa agriculture's share of greenhouse gas emissions. Because manure also accounts for 5 percent of U.S. nitrous oxide emissions, in a state like Iowa the fertilizers used to grow the corn produced to feed livestock have a nearly double effect: producing nitrous oxide both directly and through the production of manure. At the same time, grain grown in Iowa is shipped to other places where livestock is raised, contributing to transportation's production of the greenhouse gas carbon dioxide. Finally, agriculture-related manufacturing also contributes to greenhouse gas emissions. In 2016 and 2017, two major fertilizer production plants were constructed in Iowa—a $2 billion facility in western Iowa and a $3 billion plant in eastern Iowa. These plants consume significant amounts of natural gas, thereby contributing to carbon dioxide emissions. The Iowa Department of Natural Resources estimates that the two plants contributed to a 181 percent increase in greenhouse gas emissions from ammonia and urea production between 2016 and 2017.

Given Iowa's importance as a producer of greenhouse gases, it is imperative that the state develop plans for reducing greenhouse gas emissions. This is exactly what was done by its 2008 Iowa Climate Change Advisory Council, whose report made a number of recommendations for reducing greenhouse gases. While some of these point to practices that would reduce emissions of nitrous oxide and methane, others speak to agriculture's potential to be a significant resource for reducing carbon emissions. Although the Iowa Nutrient Reduction Strategy makes no mention of climate change mitigation (the word "climate" is not found in the document) as a by-product of nutrient reduction, among the 2008 advisory council's recommendations are three practices very similar to those found in the strategy: more efficient management of nutrients leading to less nitrogen runoff and leaching, redesign of drainage ditches and construction of wetlands so that fewer nutrients enter the waters, and employment of conservation tillage, specifically no-till farming. The first two practices decrease nitrous oxide emissions by reducing nitrate pollution in Iowa water bodies. Conservation tillage, in addition to reducing the phosphorus entering Iowa waterways, helps lock carbon in Iowa's soils that would otherwise be emitted into the atmosphere.

Taken together, the Iowa Climate Change Advisory Council estimated that these three practices could account for about one-third of the reduction in greenhouse gases that can be achieved by the agricultural sector, with land management accounting for the bulk of the reduction. Another 9 percent would come from improved manure management, primarily from capturing methane for energy production in lieu of burning fossil fuels. Collectively, land management techniques like no-till farming and cover crops not only reduce carbon emissions into the atmosphere but serve as carbon sequestration sinks, playing a role more commonly associated with forests.

In recent years, carbon sequestration in soils has been popularized by the "4 per 1000" initiative, announced at the December 2015 United Nations Climate Conference as a program for increasing the stock of soil carbon by 0.4 percent annually. Recent research in this area suggests that there is uncertainty regarding how much we can count on soil sequestration to mitigate climate change, in part because global temperature increases will increase the amount of microbial activity that releases soil carbon. Nevertheless, the mechanisms for carbon sequestration—including cover-cropping and conservation tillage—remain critical to adapting to climate change–induced events, such as flooding, if not significantly reducing the rise in global temperatures.

The preservation of grasslands against their significant loss to row crops is also an important way to protect against carbon loss.

Using agricultural and forest biomass for energy production could account for much of the remaining reduction in Iowa greenhouse gas emissions associated with agriculture. Overall, the Iowa Climate Change Advisory Council found that using biomass as energy feedstock could account for 47 percent of Iowa's projected reduction in agriculture-related greenhouse gases by replacing fossil fuels as energy sources to produce electricity, heat, and steam. This includes burning animal manure, residue from crops such as dried corn stalks, and excess biomass such as dead and dying trees converted to woodchips. In addition, the council identified biofuels produced from cellulose as a source of energy with lower greenhouse gas emissions than corn-based ethanol. Despite their promise, however, the production of cellulosic biofuels has not yet been able to overcome significant technological and financial barriers as well as the fact that they can sometimes require land that would otherwise be used to grow food.

Although not directly related to agriculture, Iowa's climate, particularly the strong winds in the northern and central part of the state, has produced a rapid increase in wind-generated energy production. As recently as 2000, Iowa produced very little wind energy, but within thirteen years it emerged as a leading producer of electricity from wind, employing nearly 4,700 wind turbines to generate 34 percent of the state's electricity in 2018, second highest in the nation. Over roughly the same period, Iowa's dependence on coal dropped from 76 percent of net electricity consumption in 2008 to 45 percent in 2018. Moreover, Iowa ranks sixteenth among states in its potential for rural utilities to take advantage of solar-powered photovoltaics.

Nevertheless, climate change is a global phenomenon, and unless there are global solutions to greenhouse gas emissions, the impact on climate in Iowa and elsewhere will be significant. Climate change is resulting in higher temperatures throughout the world as well as increased precipitation in much of the United States and Europe. For the United States, the ratio between daily record high and low temperatures has moved from 1.12 to 1 in the 1950s to slightly over 2.18 to 1 in the second decade of the twenty-first century. Globally, July 2019 was the hottest month on record. Climate change is also causing an increased number of heavy precipitation events. At the same time, there is evidence of increased drought as measured by both intensity and duration. Unless we accomplish major reductions in greenhouse gas emissions by the middle of the twenty-first century, global temperatures will very likely continue to rise.

According to the 2018 *Fourth National Climate Assessment*, the Midwest has become wetter from April to June over the past thirty years as well as more humid, thereby creating a more welcoming environment for mold, pests, fungus, toxins, and pathogens. Increased rainfall also means a higher likelihood of flooding. While daily maximum temperatures have not yet risen in the Midwest, daily minimum temperatures have, resulting in warmer winters and earlier springs and a climate more favorable to pests and pathogens. Going forward, temperatures in the Midwest are projected to increase faster than in any other region in the country. By the middle of the twenty-first century, with increased temperatures, rainfall, floods, and droughts, commodity productivity in the Midwest is expected to decline to the level of the 1980s. Corn productivity is expected to decline by 5 to more than 25 percent, with soybean productivity declining by over 25 percent in the Lower Midwest with a possible increase in the Upper Midwest.

Trends and expectations for Iowa are similar to the rest of the Midwest. The average temperature in Iowa has increased by one degree since 1900. Precipitation has been increasing since the 1870s, while there has also been an increase in intense rain events over a similar period. The increase in humidity is associated with a higher incidence of summer thunderstorms, and the frequency of two-inch or more rain events in Iowa since 1900 has increased to its highest levels in the years since 2000. As a whole, the Midwest experienced a 37 percent increase in very heavy precipitation between 1958 and 2012. A study of 774 stream gauges over fifty years in the Midwest, including the Corn Belt states of Iowa and Illinois, found an increase over time in the incidence of floods.

At the same time, winter temperatures are increasing six times faster than summer temperatures and nighttime temperatures have increased more than daytime temperatures. Ironically, maximum summer temperatures have decreased. This is attributed to wetter weather and increased evapotranspiration from crops, both of which generate more water vapor, effectively suppressing summer daytime temperatures. This is expected to change as the twenty-first century progresses—by the middle of the century, the high temperature in the hottest five-day period of the year is expected to rise from 92 degrees to 98 degrees, and once every ten years the peak will grow to 105 degrees.

Iowa's weather between 2008 and 2014 reflected the paradoxical mix of excessive precipitation, flooding, and drought predicted by climate scientists. In 2008, heavy snow and rainfall in the spring and early summer led to the worst floods ever experienced by eastern Iowa cities like Cedar Rapids and Iowa City. The University of Iowa, whose campus is bisected by the Iowa River, suffered the flooding of twenty-two buildings and nearly $750 million in recovery expenses. Cedar Rapids, through which the Cedar River travels, was inundated with river waters 19 feet above flood stage, covering 9.2 square miles of land, including most of downtown. The floods of 2008 were followed by a drought that began in summer 2011 and lasted through 2012. That was followed by flood years in 2013 and 2014 during which the University of Iowa, for example, spent approximately $9 million to install barriers to help protect the campus from flooding.

In general, Iowa climate scientists predict that the increase in intense rain events in the summer will result in increased summertime flooding. This weather pattern certainly seems to have been the case with the flooding of the Cedar River in September 2016—at that time, the second-highest flood in Cedar Rapids's recorded history. And Iowa set a record for rain and snow in the twelve months from June 2018 to May 2019, when a broken flood wall caused water to pour into downtown Davenport. For residents of western Iowa, along the Missouri River, 2019 included three major storms and flood events in March, May, and September that resulted in hundreds of people being forced indefinitely from their heavily flooded homes.

Both drought and excessive precipitation pose serious risks to Iowa agriculture. The negative result of drought on crop yields as well as farm animals is clear. In 2012, corn yield was reduced by about 20 percent over the previous four-year average; soybeans experienced a 10 percent decline. Livestock producers had to contend with less efficient weight gain and higher feed costs. Excessive precipitation can also hurt agriculture. Heavy spring rains can delay planting or require replanting, in either case shortening the growing season. Heavy rains also quicken soil erosion while moist soils, along with higher temperatures and humidity, can stimulate plant diseases and the growth of weeds. Very significantly, given Iowa's water-quality problems, heavier precipitation speeds up the flow of nutrients into waterways, especially when more rain leads farmers to install more drain tiles. Farther downstream, the heavier precipitation will increase the flow of nutrients into the Gulf of Mexico, thereby directly linking climate change in the Midwest with increased hypoxia in the Gulf of Mexico.

The year 2019 was the second-wettest year in U.S. history, and the flooding that took place in Iowa and the Midwest that spring was an important part of this story. Excessive spring rainfall significantly delayed planting in Iowa and Illinois. Nationally, farmers were unable to plant on 19 million acres, of which 70 percent were in the Midwest. The town of Hamburg in southwest Iowa was two-thirds submerged by floodwaters in March, and in the first half of the year eighty of Iowa's ninety-nine counties were designated for federal assistance by the Federal Emergency

Management Agency. According to central Iowa farmer Aaron Heley Lehman, president of the Iowa Farmers Union, "This has definitely been a bad year for almost all farmers in Iowa, even if you weren't on river bottom ground and having your grain bins explode and your land underwater for weeks and weeks at a time," he said. "It was still a very rough year."

Additionally, rising water temperatures will combine with nutrients to increase the incidence of blue-green algae blooms, thereby exacerbating health problems and limiting public recreation—in the summer of 2016, algae blooms led the Iowa Department of Natural Resources to issue a record number of advisories—thirty-seven—for swimming in state-owned lakes; these declined in 2017 and 2018 to the single digits before increasing to twenty-four in 2019.

Flooding and excessive temperatures also impose dangers for Iowa's residents. Flooded industrial facilities, such as those in the 2008 flood in Cedar Rapids, can release carcinogenic substances into the water supply. Residents of flooded areas are also confronted with extensive mold in their homes associated with respiratory diseases. Even without flooding, higher levels of precipitation raise humidity levels, thereby increasing the incidence of mold. And higher temperatures, particularly in drought periods, can have very significant health effects: the elderly, who constitute a proportion of Iowa's population higher than the national average, are especially susceptible to heat-related deaths.

Climate change is also expected to have dramatic, if not yet fully understood, effects on wildlife and vegetation in Iowa. With warmer winter temperatures and shorter winters, wildflowers are blooming earlier and migratory birds are returning earlier in the spring. Some species will find the warmer temperatures inhospitable—trout, for example, thrive in cold-water streams with little sediment. Warmer temperatures and increased flooding will upset their environment, and some species may decline.

Iowa has now reached a time when the environmental consequences of ecosystem loss are multiplied by climate forces. This presents obvious challenges, but perhaps opportunities also exist. The challenges, of course, come from adapting to the change in climate—higher temperatures, more intensive rain events, and droughts—caused by the increase in greenhouse gases stemming from the agro-industrial era. Iowa's climate challenges also stem from the recognition that the state's production of greenhouse gases is double the per capita rate of the nation's average—Iowa bears a disproportionate responsibility for generating greenhouse gases. By recognizing the role that agriculture can play in reducing the emission of greenhouse gases and in sequestering atmospheric carbon in the state's soils, Iowa could catalyze the adoption of conservation practices that would improve its degraded water resources. Increasing conservation tillage, harvesting crop residue for energy feedstock, and burning cellulosic biofuels could give Iowa a comparative advantage in reducing greenhouse gases. Of the estimated reduction of 564 million metric tons of carbon dioxide equivalent identified by the 2008 Iowa Climate Change Advisory Council as necessary to mitigate the effects of climate change, 233 are expected to come from agriculture, forestry, and waste management. The state has already led the way in great part because of its success in harvesting one of its chief natural assets: abundant wind energy.

Beyond wind energy, Iowa has been less successful in taking a leadership approach to climate change. Despite thorough research prepared by two expert panels—one on the impacts of Iowa on climate change and the other on the impacts of climate change on Iowa—the state barely acknowledges the existence of climate change. After its reports were issued in 2008 and 2011, the Climate Change Advisory Council was dissolved in 2011, and there remains no ongoing panel charged with advising the state on climate change or monitoring the state's progress toward meeting goals for greenhouse gas reduction. In public discussions with state representatives and other stakeholders, references to climate change are minimized and even discouraged. In October 2019, the University of Iowa Public Policy Center sponsored a statewide event with a focus on heat and flooding, but reference in the event's title and description was to extreme weather, not climate change.

Not only is Iowa at a crossroads, it is at a nationally important crossroads that will have significant consequences for water quality and climate change. While Iowa's leadership in wind energy is the clearest sign that it has the potential to take a different path, one that embraces the environment and mitigates climate change, there are signs of other progressive changes. The Farmers Electric Cooperative in tiny Frytown, for example, provides 20 percent of its customers' electrical needs through solar energy facilities, including a massive solar farm constructed in 2013 and expanded in 2016.

The University of Iowa has set a goal of employing 40 percent renewables by 2020 and to use zero coal by 2025. A significant part of this goal is to be met by working with farmers to grow *Miscanthus* on 2,500 acres of marginal farmland in southeast Iowa without displacing row crop production. The native Asian plant, which requires little water or fertilizer, is rich in carbohydrates and biomass per planted acre and can be burned as a cellulosic biofuel in the university's power plant. This is an extension of work that the university began in 2003 when it began to burn oat hulls from the Quaker Oats plant in nearby Cedar Rapids. In addition to reducing the amount of coal that the university must burn, *Miscanthus* farming will provide perennial cover crops that better absorb nutrient runoff than row crops and will also sequester carbon by decreasing tillage. Moreover, the university's investment in this renewable resource helps rural Iowa economies, while purchasing coal sends money out of state.

Farther west, Charles City has employed permeable pavers on many streets in its Green Streets Project to reduce sediment flow into the Cedar River. The Whiterock Conservancy, near Coon

Rapids in western Iowa, holds 5,500 acres in the Middle Raccoon River valley. The land is used for recreation and conservation but also for production agriculture, employing major water conservation practices such as cover crops and buffer strips. The University of Iowa's Iowa Flood Center has taken the lead by obtaining a $97 million grant from the U.S. Department of Housing and Urban Development that funds efforts in nine Iowa watersheds throughout the state to employ strategies such as vegetative buffer strips, cover crops, bioreactors, and wetland construction that will limit flood damage while absorbing nutrients. While some Iowa farmers and town leaders may discount the environmental threats of climate change or the Dead Zone, they do understand what happens when flooding takes place, and by developing watershed-based strategies that both increase flood resilience and improve water quality, the Flood Center is counting on a win-win approach to building support to enhance the environment, both in Iowa watersheds and beyond.

Against the backdrop of Gulf hypoxia and climate change, the question facing all Iowans is, How can the state's citizens build on these and other initiatives to develop a sustained and comprehensive approach that significantly improves water quality while addressing weather forces? Iowa is a small state, but its national and international profile in agriculture gives it an important role to play — either to the detriment of the environment or to its benefit.

## ~ FOUR ~

## WHY IS IOWA SO WHITE?

I N THE SPRING OF 2011, I traveled with a group of University of Iowa faculty and staff to the central and northern parts of the state as members of the Faculty Engagement Corps. The corps' purpose was to introduce faculty and staff to parts of the state they might not otherwise visit. We stopped in medium-sized towns like Webster City and Marshalltown, small towns like Goodell, and the state's largest city, its capital of Des Moines. In Marshalltown, we met with school officials to discuss the challenges posed by the city's growing number of Hispanic American children, many of whose parents had immigrated to the area to work in the Swift pork-processing plant. Everyone we met with on the three-day tour was white, and even when driving through Des Moines, where we visited the art museum and talked with state natural resources and education officials as well as business lobbyists, we saw no people of color.

It is quite possible that the faculty and staff on our tour would not even have noticed that we met with no people of color, except that one of our colleagues, who is African American, commented on this after the trip was over. In response, planners for the next year's trip scheduled a visit to Waterloo, home to one of the state's largest African American populations.

Such is diversity in Iowa. You can drive through the state or walk through the University of Iowa campus as I have and not see a single African American or Latin American person and, unless you are a member of those groups, you may not think anything of it. In 2017, Iowa was the nation's sixth-whitest state, trailing Maine, Montana, New Hampshire, Vermont, and West Virginia, with 85.9 percent of its residents white—white being defined as not African American, Native American, Hispanic American, or Asian American.

If we define Iowa's history as beginning with statehood in 1846, then Iowa's history seems to be the story of white people. In 1850, whites comprised 99.8 percent of the new state's population. The state's white share of the population would not dip below 99 percent until 1970. From that year forward, the number and percentage of nonwhites in Iowa would begin to grow, but not so fast as to challenge Iowa's position as one of the whitest states in the nation. Between 1980 and 2015, the number of African Americans grew more than 2.5 times, from 41,700 to 110,050. Over the same period, Asian Americans increased sixfold, from 11,577 to 73,564. The state's small population of Native Americans nearly tripled, from 5,455 to 15,924. Most dramatically, from 1980 through 2015, the number of Hispanic Americans grew from 25,536 to 182,606, a seven-fold increase, and Hispanics became the largest minority population in the state. By 2018, the state's Hispanic American population had grown to 194,432. In 2017, the African American, Asian American, and Native American populations in Iowa were 120,218, 82,346, and 16,222.

Despite rapid growth from small numbers, much of Iowa continues to look white. This is because Iowa's African American, Native American, Asian American, and Hispanic American populations are concentrated in relatively few places. In 2016, 60 percent of the state's African American population lived in only four counties: Black Hawk, Linn, Polk, and Scott. Reflecting the rapid growth of Iowa's Hispanic American population, twenty-three of Iowa's ninety-nine counties are 5 percent or more Hispanic— of these, eleven are more than 10 percent Hispanic, with Crawford (27.3 percent), Buena Vista (24.8), Marshall (19.9), Muscatine (17.2), and Louisa (16.2) leading the state. Each of these counties has at least one major meatpacking plant. Nearly 46 percent of the state's Hispanic population lives in Polk, Woodbury, Scott,

Marshall, and Johnson Counties. But three-quarters of the state's counties have Hispanic populations of less than 5 percent of the total county population. In 2016, 38 percent of the state's Native American population lived in just three counties: Woodbury, Polk, and Tama. Finally, in 2015, 63 percent of Asian Americans lived in five counties: Polk, Johnson, Story, Linn, and Scott.

Iowa's whiteness, however, belies its history, both before and after statehood. As with its environmental and economic issues, Iowa is at a crossroads regarding diversity. State forecasts project that the percentage of the population that is white will decline from 91 percent in 2010 to 76 percent in 2050, with at least a doubling in the number of African Americans, Asian Americans, and Hispanic Americans. How did Iowa become predominantly white? How was it able to remain white for so long? Going forward, how well is it handling the process of moving from a predominantly white to a more diverse population? And how can the state positively address its growing heterogeneity and become more sustainable, not only in an environmental and economic sense but also with regard to social justice?

## Native Americans in Iowa

How did Iowa become so white? The quick answer, of course, is that Euro-American settlers—eager for new land in a nation that added population at an astounding rate of roughly 33 percent every decade between 1790 and 1860—took it from Native Americans. Native Americans had lived in what is now Iowa for millennia; at least fourteen Indian nations are identified as having lived in the state: Ioway, Otoe and Missouria, Omaha and Ponca, Pawnee and Arikara, Santee and Yankton Sioux, Sauk, Meskwaki, Potawatomi, Winnebago, Illinois, Huron, Mascouten, Ojibwa, and Miami.

Prior to Euro-American settlement, Iowa's Native American population engaged in partnerships with French, British, and Spanish traders. This economic system was based on the exchange of pelts from beaver and other fur-bearing animals, trapped by the Ioway and other tribes, and traded for European manufactured goods such as weapons, tools, woven cloth, blankets, and metal pots. By about 1720, two tribes dominated the state: the Otoe and the Ioway. After 1730, the Sauk and the Meskwaki (or Fox, as the French called them), allied nations that fled Wisconsin after war with the French and the Chippewa, moved into Iowa, settling there and in Illinois in the 1780s. By the early nineteenth century, as the position of independence that the Ioway enjoyed under Spanish rule weakened, the Sauk and the Meskwaki became dominant in eastern Iowa and northwest Illinois.

The Sauk and the Meskwaki lived in proximity to each other, but in separate villages. The Sauk were concentrated in three villages, one on the west side of the Mississippi and two on the east, the chief of which was Saukenuk, near where the Rock River flows into the Mississippi. On the eve of Illinois statehood in 1818, Saukenuk was the largest community in Illinois and the center of activity and leadership for the Sauk nation. The most important Meskwaki village was also on the east side of the Mississippi near the Rock River, but four other Meskwaki villages were located on the west side of the Mississippi in what is now Iowa.

While the Ioway depended upon fur trapping for trade goods, the Meskwaki exploited another natural resource: deposits of lead in and around modern-day Dubuque. The Dubuque area, along with northwest Illinois and southwest Wisconsin, has significant lead deposits that had been mined by Indians for at least four thousand years. With the arrival of European traders, the Sauk, Meskwaki, and Winnebago tribes that inhabited this region were able to expand their trade connections and support their local economies by trading lead as well as furs, food, and crafts. Native American women, along with children and older men, performed the actual mining as well as the farming and craft making in their communities. Through intermarriage with both French and British traders, partnerships were established in which Native

Americans mined and Europeans traded, all within a blended Creole culture.

Given the colocation of Sauk and Meskwaki in both Illinois and Iowa, the fate of Indians in Iowa is intertwined with their removal from Illinois and what ultimately became known as the Black Hawk War. Bookending the 1832 war was a series of treaties that nearly extinguished the Indian population of the state and, for the most part, transformed the Midwest from Native American to white. In the first of these, in 1804, Indiana territorial governor William Henry Harrison induced a group of five Sauk and Meskwaki men to sign a treaty that vacated the tribes' rights to lands east of the Mississippi River between the Illinois River to the south and the Wisconsin River as far east as the Fox River—land that comprised much of northwest Illinois. The treaty affected the Meskwaki because it reflected an agreement between the U.S. government and the "united Sac and Fox tribe," a legal conflation of the two tribes that would persist as the government negotiated subsequent treaties.

As long as white Europeans remained east of the Appalachians, Sauk and Meskwaki access to land in Illinois was not threatened. But by the 1820s, circumstances had changed dramatically. Prior to 1822, the fur trade and the federally regulated factory system of trading posts sought to provide fair prices to Indians while helping them avoid debt and alcohol. The factory system succumbed to pressure from John Jacob Astor's American Fur Company to open up the frontier to free market capitalism, which employed debt and alcohol to gain the upper hand over Indians. Indebtedness created pressure on Indians to catch more fur-bearing animals, thereby putting more pressure on the ecosystem on which they depended, an ecosystem that was being further strained as white settlers moved into the Midwest.

In the wake of these changes to the fur trade economy came white Europeans hungry for land. Ohio's population was only 42,159 in 1800—by 1830, it had grown to nearly 938,000. Indiana's population grew from less than 3,000 in 1800 to 343,000 in 1830. For the most part, immigration into states like Indiana and Ohio was white — in 1830, the population of both states was at or near 99 percent white. A tsunami of white Europeans, therefore, headed to Illinois and beyond to Iowa, threatening Indian primacy in the Midwest.

As white settlers moved westward in Illinois in the 1820s, the federal government and the traders on the frontier put increasing pressure on the Sauk to vacate Saukenuk and relocate west of the Mississippi River. Many Sauk removed themselves, following the advice of their leader Keokuk. Other Sauk, as well as some Meskwaki, were influenced by Black Hawk, who denied the Treaty of 1804 and the follow-up Treaty of 1816, in which Sauk and Meskwaki leaders had appeared to agree to give up lands east of the Mississippi. By 1829, Black Hawk and his followers claimed that, the treaties notwithstanding, the Sauk still possessed Saukenuk. After Black Hawk and other Sauk returned to Saukenuk in 1831, as they had every spring in the past, the U.S. Army and the Illinois militia forced them to sign articles of agreement and capitulation, in which the Sauk agreed to leave Illinois and never cross the Mississippi River again. The following April, Black Hawk led a group of as many as two thousand back across the river to return to Saukenuk. They continued up the Rock River, however, and eventually into the Wisconsin portion of what was then Michigan Territory. White settlers reacted, and the Illinois governor called out the militia, joined by the U.S. Army. In August, Black Hawk and his people were trapped on the eastern banks of the Mississippi River and massacred by government forces at the Battle of Bad Axe, although Black Hawk managed to escape.

The massacre that ended the Black Hawk War was not enough, however. No longer was it enough for the Sauk and the Meskwaki to remain on the west side of the Mississippi River — now they would be forced to vacate their villages in eastern Iowa, and the Meskwaki, who had not led the return to Illinois but were considered part of the "united Sac and Fox tribe," would be punished just the same as the Sauk. In exchange for their alleged misdeeds, in 1832 the U.S. government required "a cession of a tract of Sac and Fox country" along a line drawn fifty miles westward from the Mississippi into what would become Iowa. This entailed the eventual opening of nearly 6 million acres or roughly one-sixth of the current state of Iowa to white Europeans of land once reserved for Native Americans. The ceded land included the Dubuque lead mines that the Meskwaki had controlled for decades.

The consequences for the Meskwaki and the Sauk were devastating. The 1832 treaty handed the coveted lead mines over to the United States, and soon thereafter white settlers began to move in. Within twelve years of the Black Hawk War, the Meskwaki and Sauk villages had been transformed from thriving communities with a population of nearly 6,000 in 1833 to less than 2,500 in 1845. Declining game populations as well as liquor and disease contributed by whites influenced this downward spiral. By that time, the Sauk and the Meskwaki had sold much of their land in the eastern half of Iowa. Under the Treaty of 1842, all Sauk and Meskwaki were to leave Iowa by 1845, to be removed to Osage County, Kansas. Iowa would be transformed from a place lightly populated by Native Americans into an overwhelmingly white state of farmers who would convert the tallgrass prairie into some of the most productive farmland in the world.

## The Meskwaki in Iowa

There was one important exception, however, to the complete elimination of American Indians from Iowa. The Meskwaki were not as prepared as the Sauk chiefs to leave Iowa. Rather than leave, many of them chose to stay or to return from Kansas. They did this not with a grand display of defiance, as Black Hawk had attempted, but simply by being persistent and elusive. The Meskwaki took advantage of the fact that in the 1840s and 1850s,

Iowa was still somewhat sparsely settled. Soldiers could catch some but not all Meskwaki, and many would continue to return to Iowa. Moving back to Iowa enabled them to return to the rivers they had formed their culture around while asserting their independent identity.

Whites in Iowa objected to the lingering Meskwaki and sought to have the U.S. Army eject them. But unlike Illinois's response to Black Hawk's return, white opposition did not materialize into a call by Iowa's governor for mobilization of the state's militia. Moreover, the Meskwaki had supporters among two citizen groups that petitioned the state to permit them to purchase land for their permanent occupancy. Two of the tribe's supporters for a return to Iowa were Iowa's governor, James Grimes, elected as a Whig in 1854, a contributor to the founding of the Iowa Republican Party and an opponent of slavery, as well as Josiah Bushnell Grinnell, also an opponent of slavery. As a consequence, in 1856 the Iowa General Assembly adopted legislation permitting the Meskwaki to remain in Tama County along the same Iowa River where they had lived before their expulsion to Kansas. The Meskwaki had made special efforts to develop positive relations with their prospective neighbors, and this effort seems to have paid off with the state legislature.

The Meskwaki paid $1,000 for eighty acres of land in Tama County. Funds were raised from their annuities — periodic payments for the land they had been persuaded to sell to the U.S. — as well as the sale of craft goods to whites. Because they were not citizens, the Meskwaki could not make a direct purchase, but Governor Grimes agreed to accept the tribe's money and buy the land on their behalf, holding it in trust for them. This arrangement was maintained by subsequent Iowa governors until 1896, when it was converted to a federal trust, similar to the arrangement by which the federal government retains title to various Indian reservations.

Since the 1850s, the Meskwaki community has grown from 80

to 8,000 acres. Viewed against the millions of acres of prime Iowa farmland that the Sauk and the Meskwaki sold in the 1830s and 1840s, this is very limited compensation. But compared to what happened to other tribes forced out of Iowa, the Meskwaki were able to obtain a degree of sovereignty. This included the ability to resist the impact of the 1887 Dawes Act, which attempted to instill the idea of individual ownership of land, which for the Meskwaki of Kansas as well as other tribes resulted in serious loss of land. Meskwaki ownership of land in Iowa helped prevent this from taking place, and instead tribal holdings grew in the nineteenth and twentieth centuries.

While the state of Iowa permitted the Meskwaki to return, this did not reduce the tensions between the tribe and the surrounding white community. Issues of crime enforcement jurisdiction and fishing and hunting regulations have confronted the Meskwaki and their neighbors for decades. Interracial conflict has occurred over the years, with bad feelings expressed by both sides. Ironically, now that the Meskwaki run a very successful casino, the largest employer in Tama County, antagonisms have evolved from white criticism of Meskwaki poverty to white envy of Meskwaki prosperity. What the casino has afforded the Meskwaki and white communities, however, is the opportunity to work together. That the casino places the Meskwaki in the economic driver's seat for the county certainly upends the low status to which whites in the Midwest had relegated Native Americans for more than 175 years.

### African Americans and Civil Rights
### in the Nineteenth Century

Iowa's slave state neighbor, Missouri, had a rapidly growing African American population, increasing from 25,660 in 1830 to 118,503 on the eve of the Civil War in 1860. But Iowa had a small black population of its own: in 1840, the U.S. Census Bureau counted 172 free blacks and 16 who were enslaved. John Chambers, Iowa's second territorial governor, who had negotiated the 1842 cession with the Sauk and the Meskwaki, brought enslaved people with him to the territorial capital in Burlington. U.S. Army officer Dr. John Emerson brought his slave Sam to live in what is now Iowa in the 1830s. After Emerson's death Sam, under his new name of Dred Scott, sought his freedom on the basis that Wisconsin Territory, which included present-day Iowa, forbade slavery. Similarly, when General Joseph M. Street, who had fought in the Black Hawk War, was named as agent to the Sauk and Meskwaki tribes in 1836, his household in Wapello County included nine enslaved or indentured servants. By bringing slaves into the new territory taken from the Indians they had vanquished, both men reflect a multi-dimensional white supremacy that aimed to keep both Native and African Americans subservient to white dominance.

Consistent with this view of white supremacy, early Iowa legislators shuddered at the prospect of a large number of nearby slaves leaving the South—after all, Iowa was "upon the borders of a slave state, and if we had not something to keep them out, we should have all the broken-down negroes of Missouri overrunning us." The speaker of these words was Ed Langworthy, whose family had moved into Dubuque after the Black Hawk cession to profitably mine lead. He had made money by keeping Indians out of Dubuque, and he felt the same way about African Americans.

Langworthy did not succeed in convincing the 1844 Iowa constitutional convention to establish a law barring African Americans from living in Iowa—that would come in 1851, after statehood in 1846. Before statehood, delegates feared that such a law would cause Iowa to lose the opportunity to become a state, because an exclusionary law restricting the free movement of citizens could be deemed unconstitutional. But the Iowa territorial legislature, dominated by Democrats, with Whigs as the minority party, had already approved laws in 1839 restricting the civil liberties and civil rights of black residents in the territory. In that year the Iowa legislature, with no apparent controversy between Democrats and

Whigs, adopted a set of "black codes" that restricted "blacks and mulattoes" from voting, serving on juries, testifying in court, serving in the state militia, or attending public schools. One year later, the legislature added the prohibition of interracial marriage to the list. Free blacks were permitted to live in the state only if they could provide adequate documentation from a court within the United States that they were free. In addition, each free black was required to post a bond of $500 against being a charge on the county—being convicted of a crime—as well as for good behavior. When Iowa's constitutional convention did meet in 1844, it continued the authority of the 1839 and 1840 black codes while adding that only white males could serve in the legislature, a law that would not be overturned until 1880.

With regard to white supremacy in Iowa, Iowa's territorial legislators were, like army officers Emerson and Street, doubly advantaged. Their rise to positions of status as elected officials as well as in their various professions was due in part to the opportunity to settle a new and fertile land that had been opened up by punitive treaties. And as soon as they had the opportunity, in the first session of the Iowa territorial legislature in 1838–39, these officials worked hard to make certain that the other group of nonwhites in America, African Americans, would be no more than second-class citizens. Iowa's emergence by 1850 as a nearly all-white state was no accident. Like much in politics, it was done on purpose.

Iowa exclusionists did themselves one better in 1851, when they persuaded the legislature to adopt a law forbidding black and mulatto settlement into Iowa, although current black and mulatto residents were permitted to stay and own property. Since Iowa had become a state in 1846, the argument that an exclusionist law could prevent statehood had ceased to have value. Consequently, Iowa became the first state in the nineteenth century to adopt a racial exclusion law. Strangely, the final legislation required that the bill would become law only if its text was printed in a Mt. Pleasant newspaper published by an abolitionist, which it never was.

Thereupon, the 1851 law was not published in the 1851 Iowa Code and consequently took on a ghostly appearance that stimulated exclusionists to continue to petition the legislature to fully adopt laws excluding blacks and mulattoes from residency in Iowa.

Iowa's white supremacists were not met with silence, however, either by white progressives or by the state's small black community. Although a minority in the headlong movement of white Americans westward into Iowa, small communities of religion-based abolitionists cropped up in Iowa. Consistent with their opposition to slavery, these groups also opposed the black codes erected by the Iowa territorial legislature — for them, second-class citizenship would not be the end goal of abolition. Chief among these groups were Congregationalists, Quakers, Seceders (whose belief system is described as Associate Reformed Presbyterianism), and Presbyterians. Each group was concentrated in small villages in southeast Iowa, giving them good proximity to each other and to the then state capital in Iowa City. In addition, their location within sixty to eighty miles or so of the Missouri line and not far from Illinois meant that they were in a good position to receive runaway slaves from Missouri and deliver them to safety in Illinois and eventually to Canada. They would be joined by other communities, farther west in Iowa, that became links on the Underground Railroad.

Beginning with the 1840–41 legislative session, leaders in these groups began to challenge Iowa's black codes. This began a process of several decades whereby Iowa moved from being a state in which white supremacy was legal to a state that was among the nation's leaders in legislating equality in civil rights and liberties for whites and blacks. Iowa's small black community entered the fray in 1855 when a group of "Colored citizens of Muscatine County" petitioned the legislature for repeal of the 1851 black exclusion law. Best known among the petitioners were Alexander Clark, whose parents had been emancipated, and Thomas Motts, who, like Clark, was a barber. Sixty percent of Iowa legislators voted to table the petition, similar in proportion to the 57 percent of legislators voting in favor of the 1851 exclusion bill.

The politics of race was beginning to change, however, particularly with regard to the extension of slavery. The 1854 Kansas-Nebraska Act, which negated the Missouri Compromise, the 1820 act that had made Iowa a free state and Missouri a slave state, opened up the possibility that Nebraska could also become a slave state. Reflecting Iowa's dismal record on race under the dominance of its Democratic legislators, it is not ironic that its U.S. senators supported the act and supported Illinois senator Stephen Douglas's proposal to allow residents of the two territories to determine whether they would be slave or free. What is ironic is that the outrage in Iowa to having slavery on two borders helped end their political careers and move the state into a stronger antislavery stance. James Grimes, the Whig who had endorsed the return of the Meskwaki to Iowa, also opposed the extension of slavery, and with an Iowa population increasingly concerned about the extension of slavery to neighboring Nebraska, he was elected as governor in 1854.

In 1856, Iowa supported the Republican presidential candidate John Frémont, who also opposed the extension of slavery. Despite Iowa's stance against the extension of slavery, however, an 1857 public referendum that would grant black men the right to vote, following on another petition by Muscatine's African Americans, was resoundingly defeated. While the ascendance of the Republican Party meant that Iowa was speaking decisively against the power of the slave states to extend slavery, its white citizens still did not welcome African Americans to enjoy the same privileges that they possessed. Opposition to slavery did not necessarily translate into tolerance for African Americans but was compatible in Iowa and other northern states with white supremacy.

The Civil War altered the situation radically. Republicans in Iowa's legislature, prompted by attempts to enforce the 1851 exclusion law, finally voted in 1864 to formally permit blacks to live in

the state. During the Civil War, Iowa whites had become increasingly concerned about the prospect of southern blacks liberated
by the Union Army moving into the state. One of these former
slaves was Archie Webb, who had lived on an Arkansas planta-
tion. With the Union advance, Webb ran away to the Union camp
and from there accompanied an Iowa soldier to Iowa. Living in
Des Moines in 1863, Webb and other former slaves were seen as
a threat by local whites, who engaged the sheriff to enforce the
black exclusion law. In response to a writ of habeas corpus filed
on Webb's behalf, an Iowa judge ruled that the 1851 law violated
the privileges and immunities clause of the U.S. Constitution and
that Webb could remain in Iowa.

With the end of slavery, the issue of black suffrage became par-
amount. President Lincoln spoke favorably of black suffrage in
his final speech before he was assassinated by a white suprema-
cist. At its 1865 convention, Iowa's Republican Party approved a
resolution supporting the right of African American men to vote.
Although some Republicans feared a bold stance on black suffrage would doom them in the gubernatorial race that year, their
candidate, Governor William Stone, spoke eloquently and forcefully about the importance of fully implementing the belief that
all men are created equal. This had the effect of isolating the opposition, the Union Anti–Negro Suffrage Party and its gubernatorial candidate, Thomas Hart Benton, Jr., into an apparent denial
of a basic tenet of the Declaration of Independence. Stone and his
Republican ticket won the 1865 election decisively.

Because both Democrats and Republicans had made black suffrage a key issue in the race, it seemed that Iowa's electorate had
turned around on the question of African American civil rights
and liberties. Following upon their 1865 success, in 1868 Republicans pushed for amendments to the state constitution that would
ensure black civil rights, including suffrage, which at that time
was available to black men in only five other states. With a presidential ticket that year headed by the popular Ulysses S. Grant, the
prospect for approval of the amendments appeared strong, and in-

deed 57 percent of the electorate favored black suffrage compared to 62 percent who voted for Grant. Eleven years after decisively rejecting black equality, the Iowa electorate had now fulfilled Grant's hope that Iowa would be "the bright Radical star" that would demonstrate commitment to equal rights for blacks. Iowa joined Minnesota as the only two states to approve black suffrage by referendum prior to adoption of the 15th Amendment to the Constitution outlawing racial discrimination at the voting box.

By 1880, the Iowa legislature and the Iowa voting public had eliminated the last vestiges of the state's black codes. The 1880 referendum, however, on the question of whether black men could serve in the legislature indicated that while there had been a revolutionary evolution of white attitudes toward blacks, the revolution might still be actively resisted. Sixty-three percent of voters in 1880 favored allowing blacks to serve in the legislature, but many voters elected to either vote only on various officeholders and not on the referendum or not to vote at all: 58 percent of eligible voters abstained from voting on the referendum. Moreover, there was effectively no campaigning by Republicans for the referendum. In 1868, when Grant swept to victory in Iowa and nationally and the Republicans made black suffrage a key issue, only 10 percent of voters abstained. By 1880, with Grant no longer at the head of the ticket, with Iowa Republican interests directed at the upstart Greenback Party, and with the end of Reconstruction and the nation's attention to issues of race, Iowa Democrats and conservative Republicans would be freed from conforming to state and national opinion and could instead express anxieties about African Americans in their midst by sitting out the final referendum on black equality. In 1884, the Republican-dominated Iowa legislature approved a civil rights law that prohibited discrimination in a variety of public accommodations, but its limitations in coverage as well as enforcement became the target of the state's civil rights activists after World War II.

Leadership on civil rights was also exercised by Iowa's courts as well as by African Americans willing and able to employ the courts to obtain their rights. In its first case, Montgomery v. Ralph, 1839, the Iowa Supreme Court decided in favor of a slave named Ralph whose master, Jordan Montgomery, in Missouri, had permitted him to work in the Dubuque lead mines to earn $550 (plus interest) to buy his freedom. After five years, Montgomery hired slave catchers to retrieve Ralph, whom he believed did not intend to repay him. A white man, Alexander Butterworth, who had a mine adjacent to Ralph was able to file a writ of habeas corpus to prevent him from being shipped back to Missouri. The Iowa district court judge, Thomas Wilson, transferred the case to the Iowa Supreme Court in July 1839. The court's two justices (Wilson had recused himself) ruled that Ralph had been rendered free by the fact that he lived in a territory whose freedom was guaranteed by both the Northwest Ordinance and the Missouri Compromise. Moreover, the runaway slave laws of the time did not apply because Ralph had not run away. The court ruled that Ralph "should be discharged from all custody and constraint, and be permitted to go free while he remains under the protection of our laws."

The decision by the Iowa Supreme Court in the case of Ralph began a series of three cases in which Iowans asserted equal rights for African Americans that were well ahead of the rest of the nation. In 1857, in the infamous Dred Scott case, where the slave whom Iowa knew as Sam made a similar argument regarding his stay in free territory, the U.S. Supreme Court moved in the opposite direction of the 1839 Iowa Supreme Court, instead ruling that black people had no rights that white people need recognize.

Two other Iowa Supreme Court cases, decided soon after the Civil War, followed in the footsteps of Ralph's case, and both preceded national vindication of black civil rights by many decades. In the first, the unstoppable Alexander Clark of Muscatine filed suit on behalf of his twelve-year-old daughter, who had been denied enrollment in that city's white school, being told that she needed to attend a school for black children set up by the school district. Muscatine was not alone among Iowa communities in maintaining separate schools for blacks or simply denying them admission to public schools. In 1868, in Clark v. Board of Directors, the court ruled that under the Iowa Constitution and Iowa law, the state had provided for the provision of education "without regard to color or nationality," and therefore the Muscatine school board had no more authority to establish separate white and black schools than it had to establish Irish or German schools. The court concluded that it was the Muscatine school board's duty "to admit the plaintiff to said school, and to equal privileges with the other pupils therein." According to legal scholar Paul Finkelman, this was the first successful school desegregation case in U.S. history. Unfortunately, other school districts continued to maintain segregated schools in the nineteenth century. In Keokuk, which had one of the state's largest black populations, two black mothers sued on behalf of their children to obtain entry to the city's white schools. By 1875, both the lower courts and the Iowa Supreme Court had ruled in their favor, and by the next year the Keokuk schools were integrated.

In 1873, in Emma Coger v. North Western Union Packet Company, the Iowa Supreme Court decided in favor of schoolteacher Emma Coger, daughter of a white father and a black mother, who had been summarily evicted from first-class passage in a section reserved for women on a steamboat departing downriver from Keokuk. The steamboat company considered that only white women should be permitted in the first-class section, but the court ruled that Coger was entitled to the "same rights and privileges while upon defendant's boat, notwithstanding the negro blood . . . which were possessed and exercised by white passengers." By grounding its decision in the state's 1857 constitution, which remains Iowa's constitution, the Iowa Supreme Court affirmed the principle of equality embedded in Iowa law. By the 1880s, therefore, Iowa had obtained a basic core of law that treated blacks and whites as equals. Despite these pioneering decisions, both during and after the Civil War many whites made it very clear that they did not welcome blacks to Iowa.

The increased number of African Americans moving from the

South to Iowa during and after the Civil War years raised the level of white anxiety toward black newcomers that had first appeared in the decades leading up to the war. Through Democratic newspaper editorials, public meetings, and newspaper caricatures, many whites in the Midwest made clear their antagonism toward freed slaves moving north. Racial antagonism began in earnest when Union forces began to ship black families north to relieve the burden they imposed on northern troops. As the Civil War's purpose began to shift from resistance to southern aggression and secession to a war of emancipation, the movement of blacks made freeing slaves less abstract to the daily lives of midwesterners. Although they were still only half of 1 percent of Iowa's growing population, the wartime immigration of escaped slaves helped African Americans increase their numbers from 1,069 in 1860 to 3,608 in 1865 and then 5,762 in 1870.

The rhetoric that followed, chiefly from the Democratic Party, helped lay the foundation for a white racial narrative that continues today in Iowa and the Midwest. Midwestern whites resented the inordinate attention and resources that they felt the federal government was showering on black immigrants at the expense, they thought, of white families and soldiers. In addition, they felt threatened by the competition for jobs that they perceived from former slaves. Leslie Schwalm summarizes the white reaction to black immigration during the Civil War: "For those Midwesterners whose understanding of white supremacy had been premised on their right and ability to exclude first Native Americans and then African Americans from the region, the physical mobility of former slaves suggested an undesirable change in racial boundaries and practices in a post-slavery nation." The Iowa Democratic Party confirmed this perspective when it proclaimed at its 1862 convention: "This is the Government of white men and was established exclusively for the white race; that the negroes are not entitled to, and ought not to be admitted to political or social equality with the white race."

## African Americans in Iowa after
## the Nineteenth Century

Whether purposely or not, African Americans obliged white sentiment by staying away from Iowa as well as nearby Minnesota and Wisconsin. By 1940, Iowa's population was 0.7 percent black while Minnesota's and Wisconsin's were only 0.4 percent. That Iowa bordered the slave state of Missouri may explain the difference among these three states — one-quarter of Iowa's 1870 black population was born in Missouri. Of the four neighboring states that border the Upper Mississippi, only Illinois, at 4.9 percent African American, stood out in 1940. In Iowa, after the quadrupling of the black population during and immediately after the Civil War, the pace of growth slowed to less than 20 percent between 1880 and 1910, and the state's black population even declined in two consecutive decades between 1920 and 1940. Even so, Iowa's 1940 black population (16,694) exceeded both Wisconsin's (12,158) and Minnesota's (9,928). Nevertheless, the fear that emancipation meant an end to Iowa's white numerical dominance did not materialize.

While African Americans were only a small percentage of the state's population, their primary locations shifted dramatically between the end of the Civil War and 1940. In 1870, Iowa's largest concentration of African Americans lived in Lee County, home of Keokuk, in the southeast portion of the state along the Mississippi River, reflecting the employment of black laborers by riverboat commerce as well as proximity to Missouri. By 1940, the black population had shifted toward the state's urban centers, with Polk County (Des Moines) having the largest population followed by Black Hawk County (Waterloo). At the same time, rural counties in southeast Iowa that had attracted comparatively large numbers of blacks during and after the Civil War experienced declining black populations between 1870 and 1940. With fewer blacks living in counties such as these, Iowa's pattern of many

African Americans living in a few areas took hold. In 1870, 44.7 percent of the state's black population lived in the four counties with the largest black populations: Lee, Henry, Polk, and Scott. By 1940, this percentage had grown to 61.5, and it remained at about the same level in 2016, in both instances being concentrated in the state's most urbanized counties.

It is a matter of debate why Iowa blacks began to move to more urbanized areas in the state. Undoubtedly the state's growing industrialized cities offered opportunities that attracted African Americans, particularly poor farmers who struggled against the increased commercialization of agriculture following the Civil War. Another view, however, is that active racism pushed blacks in Iowa and elsewhere in the Midwest from rural to more urbanized areas. In his book *Sundown Towns*, James Loewen contends that many small towns, particularly in the Midwest, used formal and informal restrictions to evict blacks from their midst, figuratively if not literally commanding them to be gone from town by sundown.

Loewen has very limited information on Iowa, identifying only one community, New Market in Taylor County on the Iowa-Missouri border, as a sundown town. Nevertheless, he identifies a general demographic phenomenon in which counties throughout the United States experienced a decline in their black populations between 1890 and 1930. In Iowa, according to Loewen, the number of counties with fewer than ten African Americans increased from twenty-eight to thirty-eight between 1890 and 1930, while the number with no blacks decreased slightly from thirteen to twelve. In 2010, when Iowa's black population had grown by more than five times since 1930, the comparable cutoff for counties would be those with fewer than fifty African Americans. The number of counties with fewer than fifty African Americans was also thirty-eight.

Relative to the size of the total black population in Iowa, therefore, the number of counties with comparatively few African Amer-

icans remained the same between 1930 and 2010. Regardless of
whether one considers that blacks were attracted by greater economic opportunities in larger communities or were pushed out of
rural counties, the effect in Iowa as well as elsewhere in the Midwest was the same. Both historically and currently, Iowa features
plenty of communities—roughly one-third of the state's ninety-
nine counties—in which it is very unlikely that a resident would
even see a black person. This means that the only contact that
many Iowans have with African Americans is through what they
see in the media: entertainers, athletes, criminals, politicians, or
civil rights activists. Without any direct contact with blacks, white
Iowans in many communities experience African Americans as
narrowly defined stereotypes.

Newton and Jasper County provide prime examples of what this
means. In 1870, Jasper County's black population was only 69, but
by 1900, 190 African Americans lived there. In spite of their success in establishing a community in the county's largest city, Jasper County's black population declined from 54 in 1940 to only 40
in 1980. This in spite of the fact that Newton was home to one of
the most successful companies of the twentieth century, Maytag,
whose employment growth contributed to Newton's population
increasing by 4.5 times between 1890 and 1930. Clearly, Newton's
industrial growth suggested a place of opportunity, but apparently not for its African American residents.

While Newton's black population was shrinking, Waterloo's was
soaring. In 1910, only 29 African Americans lived in Black Hawk
County, including its chief city, Waterloo. By 1920, this number
had grown to 856, as blacks moving to Waterloo from the South
joined thousands of other African Americans moving north during the First Great Migration. While Maytag appears to have made
little use of African Americans, Waterloo's Illinois Central Railroad maintenance and repair terminal saw in them an opportunity to employ non-union labor in the midst of a national attempt
by skilled workers to achieve recognition of their unions. When

skilled shopmen in Waterloo convinced unskilled immigrant workers to walk off the job with them, the Illinois Central successfully used its southern network to recruit African Americans from Mississippi and nearby states. Restrictive covenants by property owners resulted in African Americans becoming concentrated in a triangular area immediately northeast of the Illinois Central yards. By 1920, this twenty-block area was 94 percent African American. Not surprisingly, the Illinois Central's employment of blacks as strikebreakers meant that race relations in Waterloo got off to a rocky start. Nevertheless, by 1940, 1,528 blacks lived in Waterloo.

During a coal miners' strike, African Americans were also recruited from Virginia to mine coal in southern Iowa. Buxton in Monroe County and its predecessor mining camp, Muchakinock, were owned by the Consolidation Coal Company, which had been purchased by the Chicago and North Western Railroad in 1881 to supply coal to the railroad. Beginning as a majority-black community in 1900, Buxton gradually became more evenly divided between black and white miners, many of whom were Swedes, Slovaks, and immigrants from the British Isles. In contrast to other Iowa communities, Buxton featured racially integrated schools that provided opportunities for black teachers, who would be shunned by other racially integrated schools in the state up into the 1940s. Under Iowa law, the company was able to set up other integrated facilities such as a YMCA to serve Buxton's 5,000 or so residents.

Buxton did not last. By World War I the camp began to lose population, in part because workers were moving to a new coal camp at nearby Haydock. Gradually, as Iowa coal-mining ceased to operate in the 1920s, black families left Buxton for larger communities in Iowa—typically Cedar Rapids, Des Moines, and Waterloo. In Des Moines and Waterloo, African Americans were segregated into small, constrained communities. In these and other Iowa communities, the former black residents of Buxton encountered discrimination both in and outside the school system. Des Moines schools did not hire their first African American teacher until 1946, and former residents of Buxton noticed the difference when they switched from Buxton's schools to others in the state.

Buxton was an anomaly in the African American experience in Iowa. Policies there regarding race were implemented by a private company practicing welfare capitalism, through which the Consolidation Coal Company attempted to stem unrest by providing workers with good pay and living conditions. Nearly all the employees were miners, a relatively low skilled and dangerous job. Given that Consolidation appears not to have practiced wage discrimination, the social and economic structure of Buxton was very flat. While there were a few managers and store owners, the bulk of the community was of the same class. Moreover, nearly all the residents were immigrants of some form or another — whether from the South or from Europe. Despite outward differences in appearance, Buxton's blacks and whites shared a common economic and immigrant experience — everyone was a newcomer to Iowa. Moreover, while the number of blacks and whites varied, African Americans were never a small minority.

By World War II, African American immigration into the Midwest had accelerated with the Second Great Migration, in which many blacks left the South for northern cities. While Iowa's black population would grow with this immigration, its pace would be significantly slower than in the more urbanized states of the Midwest, including not only Illinois but also Wisconsin and Minnesota. By 1970, Iowa's black population of 32,596 was the smallest of all four states, and by 2010 its black population of 89,148 was tiny in comparison to Minnesota's, with 272,570, the next-lowest black population of the four states.

## Civil Rights in Iowa after World War II

By the end of World War II, it had become clear that the relatively few African Americans who lived in Iowa were not the first-class citizens that Buxton had permitted them to be. Instead white Iowans treated them as second-class citizens, isolating them

from the state's predominantly white residents and denying them
access to the public accommodations and employment opportunities routinely available to whites. In an era in which both blacks
and some whites were beginning to pay attention to civil rights,
community leaders in Davenport, Waterloo, Burlington, and Des
Moines, among other cities, documented the challenges faced by
African Americans.

In Davenport, the League for Social Justice, a small group of
activists associated with St. Ambrose University, concluded in
its 1951 report that the city's African Americans were treated as
second-class citizens. At that time, only about 3.3 percent of Davenport's 75,000 residents were black, and they were concentrated
in two small areas in poor-quality and overcrowded homes. One
of the white students who worked on the study commented that
she had lived in Davenport all her life but had never known a
"single Negro." Regarding employment, the study's authors reported that "we found no Negro schoolteachers in Davenport; no
Negro office workers; no Negro firemen or policemen. And 18 large
concerns—factories, offices, and department stores which employ more than 10,000 workers—have less than 175 workers on
their payrolls." Fourteen of seventy-nine physicians refused to
treat black patients, and many of the remainder preferred to see
African Americans after hours when they weren't serving white
patients. Thirty-six of fifty-four dentists refused to treat black patients. Of five cemeteries, two refused blacks and one practiced
segregation in the placement of graves. No Davenport barbershop
accepted African Americans; they had to cross the river to Illinois
to get a haircut. Although Davenport public schools were not segregated, thanks to the Iowa Supreme Court cases of the 1860s and
1870s, life was highly segregated in these and many other aspects
at mid-century.

A similar survey in Waterloo in the mid-1950s also showed that
African Americans were discriminated against in employment
as well as in restaurants, theaters, bars, and other retail estab-

lishments, and were unable to rent or buy outside their historic neighborhood. Even though Waterloo blacks were graduating from high school at a higher rate than they had in the 1920s or 1930s, their career paths were blocked because employers hired them only for the most menial jobs. And the 1949–51 Burlington Self-Survey concluded that "the position of the Negro group in the city as seen from this view of the Negro family is extremely marginal, restricted and limited in opportunity."

Not only were blacks few in number in Iowa, therefore, by the middle of the twentieth century they had been marginalized into second-class citizenship, concentrated in the few areas in which they were permitted to live, and removed from the public accommodations and places of employment to which most Iowa whites were accustomed. But by mid-century, Iowa blacks began to successfully rebel against their "invisible man" status by contesting the right of restaurants and theaters to impose segregated service or completely deny them service. Although the Iowa legislature had adopted the Civil Rights Act of 1884 to protect against discrimination in public accommodations, efforts by the Iowa Civil Liberties Union and the NAACP to obtain convictions for discrimination under the act were often unsuccessful. Eighty-seven percent of Iowa county attorneys in the middle of the twentieth century believed that discrimination in public places was not a problem. Black attorneys in the state knew better, however—to them the invisible was obvious.

The Griffin–Katz Drug Store battle demonstrated the ability of Iowa's black community to employ not only the law but also aggressive community organizing to make the case for African American access to public accommodations. In 1948, Edna Griffin joined two other African Americans at Katz's lunch counter in downtown Des Moines, where two of them attempted to order ice cream sundaes. Katz's employees told them that the drugstore did not serve African Americans. Griffin and her colleagues filed criminal charges against Maurice Katz for violating Iowa's

Civil Rights Act. She followed this by organizing pickets, sit-ins, and boycotts against Katz Drug Store, pioneering strategies that would be used more than a decade later in attempts to desegregate lunch counters in North Carolina. After a jury convicted Katz of violating the Civil Rights Act, he appealed, ultimately to the Iowa Supreme Court. To keep pressure on him—he had been required to pay only a $50 fine—Griffin filed a $10,000 damage suit against him, for which she received a token dollar. Other suits as well as protests followed, and by December 1949 Katz had agreed to pay Griffin $1,000 and cease discrimination.

At nearly the same time, a partnership between Waterloo's black community and the United Packinghouse Workers of America demonstrated how aggressive labor organizing could be used to achieve more equitable access to employment. Nationally, the UPWA practiced multiracial organizing for a practical reason: to forestall the employment of African Americans as strikebreakers. In Waterloo, the union represented employees at Rath Packing Company. In the mid-1950s, when Waterloo's black population was growing by 87 percent, the number of African American employees at Rath grew to around 1,000 out of about 6,500 employees. Rath tended to put black employees into the dirtiest jobs. Local 46 of the UPWA fought back by successfully pushing management for more opportunities for blacks in traditionally white jobs, such as Rath's sliced bacon department, which the company liked to showcase with a staff of white women wearing white uniforms in a clean environment. Local 46 then pushed to integrate other departments at Rath and also looked at discrimination outside the plant, using legal challenges, sit-ins, and public picketing in the early 1950s to challenge bars and restaurants that would not serve blacks. Unfortunately, as legacy firms like Rath faced more competition, they began to lay off workers, which disproportionately hurt African American employees. By the end of the 1950s, the number of black workers at Rath had dropped from a mid-1950s high of nearly 1,000 to only 299.

As the national civil rights movement turned more militant in the 1960s, so did the movement in Iowa. Moreover, the theme that resounds in Iowa and the nation today—relations between black citizens and the police—emerged as a significant issue in Des Moines. A much older issue—the struggle for territory—also emerged in the form of white appropriation of African American space in the historically black commercial and entertainment area along Center Street. Just as white settlers had coveted land occupied by Native Americans in the nineteenth century, so did white economic and government elites seek land in Des Moines that had been occupied by blacks in the middle of the twentieth century. In both instances, the U.S. government facilitated acquisition of land. In Des Moines in the 1950s and 1960s, this meant the federal government's urban renewal and interstate highway programs, which both acquired and redeveloped land, thereby resulting in the loss of homes for black residents and buildings for black businesses. According to Hobart DePatten, a resident of the Center Street area and the son of a business owner, "Urban renewal was our 9/11."

Other issues continued to mount in the 1960s as Des Moines African Americans expressed stronger dissatisfaction with the state of race relations in Des Moines and Iowa, especially the increasingly complicated relationship with the police and the lack of housing, employment, and education opportunities. In the midst of growing conflict, activists Mary Rhem and Charles Knox organized the Black Panther Party of Des Moines in summer 1968. Like other Black Panther chapters, the Des Moines branch organized breakfast programs for children and other social service programs. They spoke out, as well, against police actions that they felt hurt their community. On April 13, 1969, the police arrested Knox for resisting orders to stop speaking on a public-address system at a rally to promote a free breakfast program. Knox began to gain support on university campuses, and University of Iowa students led demonstrations at the Des Moines courthouse. On

April 26, a bomb of unknown origin leveled the Black Panthers' headquarters, after which another conflict with the police ensued. In the next year, with Knox facing court charges, the Black Panthers of Des Moines ceased to operate.

By the 1960s, it was clear that the achievement of basic civil rights was not sufficient to overcome black marginalization and near invisibility in Iowa. Instead, the black community's relationships with the police and other major institutions, as they pertained to criminal justice as well as education and employment opportunities, became increasingly important. This situation does not appear to have changed dramatically since the 1960s. What does appear to have changed, however, is the flow of African Americans into Iowa. Although black population growth in Iowa continued in the immediate post–World War II era, the numbers never approached those of its more urbanized neighbors like Illinois and Wisconsin. After 1970, when the rate of growth for Illinois's black population began to decline from the 60-plus percent range of the 1940s and 1950s, the rate of growth in Iowa maintained a steady pace in every decade except the 1980s, during the Farm Crisis, when the state lost population overall. Iowa's black population grew at 44 percent (the highest since the 1870s) in the first decade of the twenty-first century, while Illinois's black population declined for the first time in history.

More than half of the 386,000 African Americans who left Chicago and Cook County between 2006 and 2015 stayed in Illinois or moved to Indiana. Another 46,000 moved to Georgia or Texas. But a slightly smaller group stayed in other states in the Midwest— moving to Wisconsin (19,231), to Minnesota (15,989), and to a lesser degree to Iowa (7,204). When I moved to Iowa City from Florida in 2008, I first heard about the alleged "Chicago issue" or "Chicago problem" that Iowa City was facing, and I knew immediately that these words were not directed at me, a white suburban Chicagoan. It quickly became clear to me, instead, that "Chicago" was code for black people. Other cities in Iowa, including Burlington, Cedar

Rapids, Clinton, and Dubuque, that have also undergone black in-migration have subsequently developed racial narratives in which "Chicago" is code for African Americans moving into what had once been a predominantly white community.

By 2008, the narrative had developed into one in which Chicago's African Americans had been evicted from public housing when that city undertook its Plan for Transformation, through which much of its public housing was demolished and replaced with mixed-income housing. Iowa, with its good schools, better employment opportunities, lower crime rates, and lower housing costs, offered an attractive alternative. Some black Chicagoans had indeed been evicted from public housing, but the size of the out-migration from Chicago and Cook County was much greater than the 16,846 households affected by the city's Plan for Transformation — hence the belief that Chicago's public housing program caused the out-migration of blacks to communities throughout the Midwest is a myth. But the perception that Iowa offered a favorable alternative to Chicago for African Americans is not. Nevertheless, Iowa has not yet become the Promised Land that journalist Nicholas Lemann identifies as the objective of African Americans leaving the South in the First Great Migration.

In Iowa City, white residents reacted to the stigma of the "southeast side," a phrase that in 2009 and 2010 appeared commonly in that city's media. A set of three violent incidents on Iowa City's southeast side in 2009 had led the city to impose a controversial youth curfew, and racial tensions rose. A small interracial group, much like the group that had studied racial challenges in Davenport sixty years earlier, met to examine the issues. The group's report, published in 2013, found that African Americans living in Iowa City were significantly poorer than other Iowa Citians, with 40 percent of blacks living in poverty versus 16 percent of whites. Although African Americans were not subject to the overt employment discrimination found in the Davenport, Waterloo, and Burlington studies of sixty years earlier, the Iowa City study found that the black rate of unemployment was several times higher than the white rate and that disproportionately low percentages of city and county employees were persons of color.

The 2013 report also found that black youth in Iowa City's schools were more likely than white youth to be in special education classes and less likely to be in advanced placement classes. Black youth were substantially more likely to be suspended as well as to be referred to the police by Iowa City schools than white youth. In the five school years between 2011 and 2016, African American juveniles accounted for a disproportionately high 54 percent of grade 6 through 12 suspensions. Statewide, black youth were 4.8 times more likely to be suspended than white youth. Iowa City black youth were 9 times more likely to be arrested than white youth in 2009, a ratio that declined to "only" about 5.5 in 2011. More recent juvenile data for Iowa City do not include arrest data but instead focus on county attorney petitions for formal court proceedings in juvenile court. In federal fiscal year 2015–16, black youth in Johnson County were 1.5 times more likely than white youth to have their cases petitioned to court. Across the state, black youth are 4.8 times more likely than white youth to be arrested.

For adults, the 2013 Iowa City report found that African Americans were arrested in Iowa City in 2011 at a rate 6 times their proportion of the population (28 percent vs. 4.8 percent). Iowa City is not unusual in this respect. According to the Sentencing Project's 2018 information, Iowa is third in the nation (behind New Jersey and Wisconsin) in the rate at which African Americans are imprisoned relative to whites—a ratio of 11 to 1. Iowa's top or near top ranking in black-white incarceration disparity goes back to at least 2007, when it led the nation with a black incarceration rate 13 times higher than the rate for whites. Iowa's high incarceration disparity is due in part to its highest-in-the-nation ratio of black to white arrest rates for marijuana possession: 8.3 times higher for blacks than for whites in 2010, even though nationally black and white marijuana use is nearly the same. Iowa's minimum mandatory sentencing rules for robbery convictions, the only such rules in the Midwest, are also seen as contributing to the disproportionate incarceration of African Americans. Overall, Iowa is second only to Montana in its ratio of black to white rates for drug possession arrests, with a black arrest rate more than 6 times higher than that for whites. Finally, as of late 2019, Iowa is the only state in which a felony conviction results in a lifetime loss of voting rights. With a higher incarceration rate for African Americans, therefore, Iowa's disenfranchisement law means that a disproportionate number of blacks permanently lose their right to vote.

Together, the Iowa City and Iowa data on juvenile school suspensions, arrests, juvenile court petitions, and adult incarcerations that fall disproportionately on African Americans suggest a continuum — a school-to-prison pipeline that results in a higher proportion of black youth facing suspension or arrest, eventually leading to incarceration as adults. Statewide, Iowa is not only a leader in incarceration rates for black adults, it also ranks high among all states in the black-white differential in high school suspensions. According to 2011 and 2012 data collected by UCLA's Civil Rights Project, Iowa is effectively tied for fourth place, with Alabama, Indiana, Michigan, and Missouri, among states with a 20 percentage point gap between black and white high school suspension rates. Although the UCLA study does not directly connect high school suspensions with later incarcerations, the fact that Iowa ranks so high nationally for disproportionate suspensions and incarcerations among blacks and whites implies that there is a pattern.

African Americans in Iowa's largest metropolitan area, Des Moines, face problems similar to those faced by blacks in Iowa City. Because Des Moines's Polk County is home to 32,261 African Americans — 28 percent of the state's black population as of 2018 — the challenges encountered by blacks in Des Moines are representative of those encountered by all black Iowans. Des Moines area blacks are generally not well off. In 2016, the annual black median income in Polk County, at $26,725, was 44 percent of the $59,844 earned by all households in the county. Thirty-nine percent of Polk County blacks lived below the federal poverty line compared to 10 percent of whites. Contributing to these economic disparities is the fact that the black unemployment rate in Polk County was 16.7 percent compared to only 3.5 percent for the county as a whole. In fact, in 2015, the state of Iowa had the highest black unemployment rate in the nation at 14.8 percent, even though its overall unemployment rate was 3.6 percent, one of the lowest in the nation. By 2017, Iowa ranked seventh worst among states in the ratio between both white and black unemployment and white and black homeownership.

Despite Iowa's pioneering civil rights cases, African Americans in Polk County remain invisible. In 2016, over the entire Iowa General Assembly and all the city councils and school boards in Polk County as well as the Polk County Board of Supervisors, there were only seven African Americans, five in the General Assembly and two on school boards. In 2014, the Des Moines Police Department was only 3 percent black, while the city's population was 10 percent African American. In 2015, there were no black members of the Iowa State Patrol. Instead, African Americans lead a marginalized existence in Des Moines and more generally in Iowa, with high unemployment, incarceration, and suspension rates, lower educational achievement, and little to no presence in public life. Even at the comparatively progressive University of Iowa, given its low number of black faculty and administrators, black students, staff, and faculty often feel like tokens or involuntary spokespersons for all African Americans. In the words of UI Center for Diversity and Enrichment director Nadine Petty: "The status quo here on this campus is White." Based on the African American presence in leadership positions in the state, it appears that the same statement can be made about Iowa.

### Hispanic Americans in Iowa

Hispanic Americans have a much briefer history in Iowa than Native and African Americans, but their presence runs deeper in history than might be expected. As far back as the late nineteenth and early twentieth centuries, Mexicans were encouraged to work in Iowa, either in agriculture or industry or for the railroads. But regardless of whether we look at this earlier period or at more recent history, the immigration of Hispanic Americans into Iowa as well as elsewhere in the Midwest has been significantly determined by such transnational economic factors as the demand by industry and agriculture for physically challenging, unskilled, and poorly compensated labor, the availability of various ethnic and economic groups to do such work, the politics and economics of various sending nations that affected migration flows, and the immigration policies of the U.S. government. Consequently, at the time of the first significant flow of Mexican-origin individuals into Iowa, between 1910 and 1930, the proximate causes were the decline in immigration from southern and eastern Europe associated with World War I, the tightening of U.S. immigration restrictions in the 1920s, and the Mexican Revolution that began in 1910, as well as the land confiscation that preceded it.

In 1900, only 29 Mexicans were recorded by the U.S. Census Bureau in Iowa; by 1920, the state's Mexican population had grown to 2,560. Initially, labor contractors recruited single men to work for the railroad or in Iowa's sugar beet industry in north central Iowa in and around Mason City. In the early 1920s, as a strategy to promote labor stability and lower wages supplemented by family income, the Great Western Sugar Company and the Atchison, Topeka and Santa Fe Railway began to encourage male workers to bring their families with them to Iowa. The largest number of Mexicans in the 1920s, about 1,000, were located in eastern Iowa, with many living in five barrios — Holy City in Bettendorf, Cook's Point in Davenport, and El Cometo, La Yarda, and La Istafiate in Ft. Madison, where the Santa Fe railroad employed many Mexicans as *traqueros* to lay and maintain track.

Compared to Texas, where many Mexicans had lived before coming to Iowa, Iowa provided a more welcoming environment. However, although Iowa was not the Jim Crow South, this did not mean that most Iowans would see Mexicans as anything but non-whites whose presence in the state was viewed with prejudice and distrust. Mexicans were welcome in Iowa, but only to do physically demanding labor at low wages and to live in boxcars or shacks in flood-prone neighborhoods lacking paved streets, electricity, and running water. In the national immigration debates of the early twentieth century, restrictionists argued against Mexican immigration while antirestrictionists, chiefly representing agricultural and industrial interests, favored it. But both sides employed racism to characterize Mexicans, with the antirestrictionists maintaining that Mexicans were better suited to physically demanding labor than other ethnic groups and therefore vital to the U.S. economy. Although the level of antagonism expressed by whites varied from place to place, the strongest anti-Mexican views found expression in Ft. Madison.

Iowa's small Hispanic American population grew rapidly in the last three decades of the twentieth century at the same time that the state's meatpacking industry underwent the revolution in organization, technology, and staffing described in chapter 1. New firms, using new technologies and operating in smaller communities, attracted Hispanic and other foreign non-union workers—such as Bosnians and Chin Burmese in Waterloo and Columbus Junction and Laotians in Storm Lake—to work at relatively low wages. Just as Iowa railroad companies had once welcomed Mexicans to lay and maintain track, meatpacking companies seeking to squeeze dollars looked to Hispanic workers to perform dangerous work at low wages. From just under 17,500 in 1970, Iowa's Hispanic population grew to just under 82,500 in 2000 and then nearly doubled to 151,544 by 2010. By 2016, the State Data Center of Iowa estimated that 182,606 Hispanic individuals lived in Iowa. One-third of this population was estimated to be foreign born, with about 70 percent originating from Mexico, 5.5 percent from El Salvador, and 10.5 percent from Guatemala.

As in the earlier part of the twentieth century, U.S. immigration laws have had a huge effect on Hispanic immigration into Iowa and the Midwest and their reception by the Anglo-American community. Prior to the 1986 passage of the federal Immigration Reform and Control Act, workers from Latin America frequently crossed and recrossed the U.S.-Mexico border. The act combined legalization of 2.3 million undocumented individuals with a hardening of the border and increased employer sanctions for hiring undocumented workers. The law had the unplanned effect of reducing the back-and-forth flow between the United States and Mexico, thereby encouraging undocumented migrants to stay in the U.S. Moreover, it encouraged family reunification—if workers were no longer able to rejoin their families in Latin America, then their families were encouraged to join them in the U.S., whether legally or illegally. With increased sanctions against employers hiring undocumented workers, businesses compensated for the added risk by paying lower wages to undocumented workers or anyone who looked undocumented. With legalization, many of the formerly undocumented began to move away from the Southwest and California to other areas of the nation, including the Midwest. Anti-immigration sentiment began to grow, first in California with Proposition 187 and then nationwide.

Mexican and other Hispanic Americans moving to Iowa faced a situation made complex by the transformation of the meatpacking industry, including changes that affected the working-class whites formerly employed in the plants, as well as by changes in immigration laws, which rather than solving problems helped make immigration a major political issue in the country by the end of the twentieth century. In Perry, for example, where Latin Americans moved to take employment at the Iowa Beef Packers (now Tyson) plant, they praised the jobs, the affordable housing, and the safe neighborhoods they found there. At the same time, they felt that they lived in someone else's America and that they could best cope with their hypervisibility in a small white town by keeping to themselves—by becoming invisible. Contributing to this feeling was their belief that white Americans saw them as just laborers. Many wished, in the words of one Hispanic American, that Anglo Americans would treat them "not like we're invading the country, not like strangers, but like neighbors, like people who have just arrived but are not foreign to this country or to the community." Contributing to the sense that they were welcome only as laborers are the dominance of the English language in Iowa and the calling out of Hispanics for speaking Spanish.

Hispanic Americans in Iowa face disparities similar to those that separate white and black Americans. Iowa Hispanic Americans are about half as likely as whites to meet American College Testing college readiness standards. Grade 4 reading scores for Hispanic Americans were 18 points lower than they were for white students in 2015. The 2017 Annie E. Casey Foundation scores on education, health, employment, income, and family structure showed that Hispanic American youth in Iowa ranked eighteenth in the nation—behind Illinois, Minnesota, and Missouri—with an index score of 458, well below the white Iowan score of 744. UCLA's Civil Rights Project analysis of 2011 and 2012 data found that Iowa ranked tenth in the nation with a 6 percentage point gap between white and Hispanic secondary school suspensions. At the same time, the rate of Hispanic American incarceration in Iowa is below the national average. Also, the Hispanic unemployment rate in Iowa is among the lowest in the nation. Overall, Hispanic Americans are in a stronger position in Iowa than African Americans, but in educational success they significantly trail white Iowans.

What distinguishes the Latin American experience in Iowa is the prospect of arrests and deportations. According to the Pew Research Center, as of 2014 there were approximately 40,000 unauthorized immigrants living in Iowa, a number that had not changed significantly since 2009. Comparing this number to the 182,606 Hispanic Americans estimated to be living in Iowa in 2016 is tricky, because the high number of undocumented residents

suggests that the official state estimate is an undercount. Nevertheless, it does indicate that the percentage of undocumented
Hispanic Americans in the state is significant. Moreover, given
the concentration of Hispanic Americans in relatively few places
in Iowa, the presence of undocumented people in Iowa communities is felt even more. What this means, of course, is that the
prospect of arrests and deportations is likely to affect residents of
most, if not all, Hispanic American communities in Iowa.

Arrests and deportations of Hispanic Americans in Iowa have
loomed large since they began moving to Iowa in bigger numbers.
Fewer than 300 Hispanic Americans lived in Marshall County in
1990. By 2000, the Hispanic population had grown to 3,523, in large
part because of the Swift pork-processing plant in Marshalltown.
In 1996, federal agents raided the plant, detaining 148 workers for
being undocumented. On December 12, 2006, the Day of the Vir-
gin of Guadalupe, U.S. Immigration and Customs Enforcement
officials conducted a raid at six Swift plants, including the one in
Marshalltown, where 90 workers were deported or transferred to
detention centers in other states. Fear and uncertainty as well as
loss of income struck the Hispanic community in Marshalltown.
Losses were palpable across the community as retail sales declined
in the wake of the raid, the sale of homes to Hispanic Americans
decreased, Latin American businesses suffered losses, and Swift
had a harder time finding dependable employees. Social relations
were affected as well—the raid gave license to some Anglos to say
ugly things about Hispanics, but it also stimulated community
bonding as other whites reached out to assist Hispanics and to
join in moving the community forward. Ironically, in 2000, Governor Tom Vilsack had cited Marshalltown as a model community
in Iowa for its efforts to welcome immigrants and refugees.

Other raids, arrests, and deportations have affected Iowa's
Latin American residents. Of these, the best known is the May 12,
2008, raid at the Agriprocessors kosher meat-processing plant in
Postville; 389 workers, mainly Guatemalans and Mexicans, were

detained, including 305 who were arrested on criminal charges rather than the more typical charges associated with deportations. At the time the largest single-employer raid in U.S. history, the Postville raid effectively put Agriprocessors into bankruptcy and reduced the town's population by more than 20 percent. Like Marshalltown, the consequences for families were traumatic, with individuals displaying symptoms of post-traumatic stress disorder. Like Marshalltown, Postville had received positive attention for its growing diversity, including a population of Hasidic Jews, demonstrating how immigration could help transform a declining small town into a place where people from different cultures could work together to grow the local economy. And like Marshalltown, U.S. immigration policy and a major raid had disrupted a community's efforts to chart a new economic and intercultural future. While both communities demonstrate resilience, both still show the effects of the raids.

The aftershock of the Postville raid pervaded Iowa's Hispanic American communities. Throughout the state there were reports of preparations for further raids and discrimination based on the confusion of immigrant status with race or ethnicity, and people avoided public spaces. Fear also spread among households in which some members were undocumented and others were not. Moreover, an analysis of births among white and Latina mothers throughout Iowa before and after the raid showed an increase in the incidence of low birth weight babies for both U.S.-born and foreign-born Latina mothers but not for white mothers. Because low birth weight is associated with emotional stress, the study concluded that the Postville raid had a stress-inducing impact on Latina mothers throughout the state regardless of whether they were U.S. citizens or not.

With the election of Donald Trump as president in 2016, immigration arrests began to increase after declining significantly after 2009. Arrests in Iowa, Minnesota, Nebraska, and the Dakotas increased by two-thirds in fiscal year 2017. Moreover, unlike

during the Obama administration, the arrests increasingly tar-
geted individuals with no criminal records. Not surprisingly, fear
of further raids and arrests increased in Iowa, fears that were realized with the May 9, 2018, raid on a concrete plant in Mt. Pleasant
that resulted in the arrest and detention of thirty-two men from
Mexico and Central America. At nearly the same time, federal
officials detained twenty-five other individuals from communities across the state, most of whom were from Mexico. Anxiety
has grown in Mt. Pleasant and so have community divisions—
for example, some churches minister to and raise money for
families whose breadwinners were arrested while others with-
hold support, believing that the men were in the U.S. illegally and
therefore deserved to be arrested. With Trump-era raids such as
the one in Mt. Pleasant, anxiety and preparation for further raids
once again spread to other communities in the state.

With the 2016 election, it became very clear that many Iowans
were becoming more united against undocumented immigration.
A state that had voted for Barack Obama for president in 2008 and
2012 voted for Donald Trump in 2016 in part because of Trump's
stance on immigration. In the Iowa caucuses, Trump voters were
nearly twice as likely to rank immigration as their most important
issue as they were to rank any other issue. In a September 2015
poll of likely Republican caucus goers, 47 percent advocated de-
portation of all 11 million undocumented immigrants estimated
to be in the country—among Trump supporters, the proportion
was 73 percent.

In August 2018, news of the death of University of Iowa under-
graduate Mollie Tibbetts both strengthened and challenged Iowans' certitude about immigration. When an undocumented immigrant from Mexico was arrested and charged with her murder,
President Trump and Iowa Governor Kim Reynolds wasted no
time in blaming "the broken immigration system" for her death.
A ratcheting up of anti-immigrant rhetoric soon followed, leading Tibbetts's father to ask white nationalists not to "appropriate

Mollie's soul in advancing views that she believed were profoundly racist." The anti-immigrant rhetoric highlighted Iowa's conflict over the economic benefits of immigration, particularly in an agro-industrial state. Tibbetts's alleged murderer had worked for four years on a large dairy farm in Poweshiek County. Craig Lang, who co-owned the farm, is a former president of the Iowa Farm Bureau, a former member of the Iowa Board of Regents, and an unsuccessful Republican candidate for state secretary of agriculture.

Employers in year-round animal care operations, especially dairy, as well as meatpacking plants hire foreign workers because they will do jobs for relatively low wages in adverse conditions that white Americans will not do. Overall, Iowa employs 84,000 immigrants, many of whom work in dairy, hog, poultry, or cattle operations. Consequently, even though many Iowans support Trump's anti-immigration stance, many others understand that but for immigrants their communities would be a lot worse off. The fact is that the state's agro-industrial economy depends on the availability of foreign labor, much of which comes from Mexico and Guatemala. In the words of northwest Iowa dairy farmer Darin Dykstra, who milks 3,000 cows three times per day: "It's not a glamorous job. We have 36 Mexican or Guatemalan workers and one American guy. Americans just don't want to do the work. So if you take away the work force that we have in the United States now Americans aren't going to appear magically out of nowhere to do the work. . . . If you're going to take the labor supply away in agriculture, dairy particularly, it's going to fall apart. It just will."

### Asian Americans in Iowa

Immigrants from Asia, often refugees, have also contributed to Iowa's increased diversity over the last fifty years. Among these are the Tai Dam, an ethnic minority originally from northwest Vietnam. The Tai Dam opposed Vietnam's communists; after the Viet Cong victory in 1975, they sought refuge at a camp in

Thailand. From there, they sought asylum by writing thirty U.S. governors. Only Iowa governor Robert Ray responded. Using his executive authority, he began a program that eventually relocated more than 1,000 Tai Dam to Iowa, many of whom settled in the Des Moines area. They were joined by other refugees from Southeast Asia, including Laotians and Vietnamese. Governor Ray responded to the Vietnamese "boatpeople" crisis of the late 1970s by sponsoring an additional 1,500 refugees fleeing the communist takeover of that country. As a consequence, Iowa's Asian American population grew from 3,420 in 1970 to 11,577 in 1980, an increase that, along with a growing African American population in that decade, began to chip away at Iowa's white predominance.

More recently, since 2006, Iowa has received approximately 7,000 refugees from Burma and 3,000 from Bhutan. Approximately two-thirds of this population have limited English skills and therefore face challenges not only in language but also in transportation, employment, health (including hepatitis B, internal parasites, and malnutrition), education, participation in civic life, and childcare. In the 2014–15 school year, about 34 percent of Asian American K–12 students were enrolled in English Learner classes in Iowa, a percentage that is very close to the 37 percent of Hispanic children enrolled in these classes. Poverty rates for Asian Americans are higher than the overall state average but lower than those of Hispanic American and African American populations. As of 2017, while Indians and Chinese accounted for the largest shares (totaling one-third) of Iowa's Asian American population, Vietnamese (including the Tai Dam) and Burmese (including Chin Burmese) were third and fourth, accounting for 13.9 and 8.9 percent.

The Burmese, many of whom have spent years in refugee camps, are escaping Myanmar's long-running civil war. According to Iowa state senator Janet Petersen: "These are by far the neediest refugees we have ever had. Many of them don't understand the concept of public schools and public education. They've never

even had running water. Their needs are enormous." In 2015, Burmese students in Des Moines public schools surpassed the number of Mexican students in need of English-language proficiency.
Language issues and the lack of funding for translators make it
difficult for adults to deal effectively with social service agencies
and help their children with homework. Burmese individuals
who are able have found employment in meatpacking at Tyson
facilities in Perry, Waterloo, and Columbus Junction. But because
many of Iowa's Burmese were originally settled in other states
by the U.S. government, they are not eligible for federally funded
services. Given this higher-need population with fewer resources,
including diminished federal funding, the task of resettling the
Burmese successfully has been especially challenging.

As with Iowa's Hispanic American population, federal immigration policy under the Trump administration also threatens
refugees like the Burmese. In September 2019, the administration reduced the 2020 cap on refugee admissions to 18,000, a 40
percent decline from the 2019 cap and a nearly 80 percent decline
from the close to 85,000 refugees admitted during President
Obama's final year in office. At the same time, Trump issued an
executive order granting state and local governments the authority to reject refugee resettlement. As with Hispanics and African
Americans, refugees like the Burmese are an important source of
population growth and employment for Iowa—if their numbers
are limited, who will live and work in the state?

Exacerbating Iowa's immigration tensions is its 4th District
congressman, Steve King, who made his name by campaigning
for the state's 2002 English-only law, a law which makes life that
much harder for refugees like the Burmese. King, who claimed
that Mollie Tibbetts's death was caused by lax enforcement of immigration laws, has a long history of making white nationalist
comments and being reelected by his northwest and north central Iowa constituents, although in 2018 he won by a much smaller
margin. He is known throughout the country for his xenophobic

comments. As such, he is a national face of Iowa, perhaps as well known as veteran Iowa senator Charles Grassley, who plays a much more substantive role in Congress than does King. King's status as a recognized spokesperson for Iowa confirms what its history shows us: Iowa's position as the nation's sixth-whitest state is no accident. Iowa's whiteness is not a natural state of being; it is a constructed reality that the state, aided by the federal government, attempts to maintain.

Yes, Iowa's population is becoming more diverse, but its whiteness was deliberately created, and it is not going away easily. With the assistance of federal treaties, Iowa was transformed from a sparsely settled state of Native Americans into a rapidly growing state of Anglo-Americans. Despite being known for its pioneering court decisions on African American access to public schools and public accommodations, as well as its vote, in 1868, in favor of black suffrage, Iowa was the first state in the nineteenth century to adopt, in 1851, a law prohibiting residency by African Americans. The federal government assisted local government efforts to restrict the residency of African Americans by employing federal highway and urban renewal laws to expel blacks from their historic home in Des Moines's Center Street district. The federal government continues to discourage Hispanic American residency in Iowa through the employment of raids that separate families and create an atmosphere of fear across the state. And the federal government, under Trump, is trying to do the same with refugees like the Burmese.

Local governments, through their police departments and public schools, engage in practices that result in African Americans and, to a lesser degree, Hispanic Americans spending less time in the classroom. Iowa's top or near top incarceration rate for African Americans, relative to white incarcerations, also contributes to the belief that compared to other states, Iowa is less welcoming of African Americans. While the 1851 exclusion law was overturned in 1864, its spirit continues in the state's prisons and even in its classrooms, where Iowa ranks near the top in black youth suspensions.

Iowa continues to maintain the appearance of a white state. As its population becomes more diverse, Iowa will need to think harder about what kind of state it wants to become.

## ← FIVE →

## THE BEST STATE IN AMERICA?

ON TUESDAY, February 27, 2018, Iowans woke up to watch reporter John Dickerson interviewing Iowa governor Kim Reynolds on *CBS This Morning.* Joined by Brian Kelly, chief content officer of *U.S. News and World Report*, they were there to discuss the fact that *U.S. News* had just announced that Iowa was number 1 in the news outlet's 2018 Best States ranking. Governor Reynolds, who as the state's lieutenant governor had succeeded Terry Branstad in 2017, was proud of the state's ranking and made a point of it when her Democratic gubernatorial opponent, Fred Hubbell, answered in the negative when asked if Iowa was the best state in the nation. She said, "Well, Fred, if you don't think Iowa's the best place to live, then you just don't know Iowa." Hubbell could have answered the question differently by simply drilling down into the *U.S. News* database and examining the areas in which Iowa was trailing many other states, including the economy and economic opportunity, the environment, and equity.

*U.S. News* ranked Iowa 9th in the nation in Quality of Life, a category that was added for the first time in 2018. Quality of Life reflects two indexes, each weighted equally: Natural Environment and Social Environment. Iowa ranked 10th on the Social Environment index—composed of Community Engagement, Social Support, and Voter Participation—but only 18th on the Natural Environment index. Furthermore, among the four Natural Environment subindexes, Iowa ranked between 24th and 38th on three of them and 9th on the fourth—Urban Air Quality—rankings that fell well below Iowa's overall ranking of 18th. It should come as no surprise that Iowa fared comparatively well on Urban Air Quality—it doesn't have large cities—but the low ranking for Drinking Water Quality (26th) is consistent with the state's high level of nitrate pollution. Iowa ranked low on the other two Natural Environment subindexes—Industrial Toxins (24th) and Pollution Health Risk (38th). Both these measures reflect the consequences of manufacturing, mining, electric power generation, and hazardous waste treatment—but not agriculture. The health effects, for example, of Iowa's concentrated animal feeding operations or the weed killer glyphosate, whose ties to non-Hodgkin's lymphoma are presently being litigated, are not reflected in the rankings.

Moreover, the *U.S. News* rankings do not examine how Iowa affects the environment of neighboring states, specifically the growing research results and public recognition of the fact that Iowa farmers' use of chemical fertilizers has had a very significant impact on the level of nutrients in the Gulf of Mexico and the growth of the Dead Zone there. An April 2018 report by University of Iowa research scientists confirmed Iowa's role in contributing to the Dead Zone. The scientists reported that from 1999 to 2016, Iowa contributed an average of 29 percent of the long-term nitrate load to the Mississippi/Atchafalaya River Basin, which feeds into the Gulf of Mexico—comparable to what earlier studies had reported. Over the same period, Iowa contributed 45 percent and 55 percent to the long-term nitrate loads in the Upper Mississippi River Basin and the Missouri River Basin.

The Iowa scientists noted that while nitrate loads in the Mississippi/Atchafalaya River Basin have declined slightly in the non-Iowa portion of the basin, overall loads have increased, suggesting that Iowa has played the principal role in raising nitrate loads in the basin and, consequently, the Gulf of Mexico. They concluded that significantly reducing nitrate loads from Iowa would yield a much better chance of meaningfully reducing the Dead Zone: "With the role of $NO_3$-N as a strong driver of Gulf hypoxia, focus on reducing loss of this pollutant from its primary source areas like Iowa is crucial." Subsequent research by two of the Iowa authors showed that between 2003 and 2018 the five-year running annual average for nutrient loads was 73 percent higher at the end of the period than it was at the beginning. Nutrient loads from Iowa to the Missouri River grew by 132 percent during this period, versus 55 percent for Iowa nutrient loads to the Mississippi River. Clearly Iowa, particularly western Iowa, is key to addressing the nutrient flows into the Gulf of Mexico and solving the Dead Zone problem.

By not examining the impact of Iowa's use of agricultural chemicals on the environment, either in Iowa or beyond, the *U.S. News* Best States ranking underestimated its negative effects. And by ignoring the production of greenhouse gases, the ranking failed to consider how Iowa or any other state is faring as it faces climate change. In fact, research reported in the first volume of the *Fourth National Climate Assessment* shows that by the middle of the twenty-first century Iowa and other states in the Midwest will experience the highest increases in average annual temperatures. The increases will be noticeable—between 4.2 and 5.3 degrees—as will be the increase in the hottest-day temperature—6.7 degrees. And the once-in-ten-years highest temperature is expected to increase by 13 degrees by mid-century, again the highest in the nation. Projections for the twenty-first century show that spring precipitation will continue to increase in northern states like Iowa. Intensive precipitation events, which are most likely to produce flash floods, will also increase in Iowa.

Iowa has already experienced significant consequences from increased precipitation and flooding. Between 1988 and 2016, Iowa ranked fourth in the nation in the number of counties receiving a presidential disaster declaration for flooding, trailing Texas, Missouri, and Kentucky. Between 1953 and 1989, a thirty-six-year period, there were fourteen presidential disaster declarations for flooding in Iowa. From 1990 through 2017, there were twenty-seven such declarations for Iowa, one per year on average. From 2010 through 2017, there were twelve in a seven-year period. Many, but not all, of the declared disasters took place in eastern Iowa in the Skunk, Iowa, Cedar, Wapsipinicon, Turkey, and Upper Iowa River Basins. While not reflected in the *U.S. News* Natural Environment indexes, it is clear that even though Iowa is a landlocked state, its abundance of rivers and streams renders it among the states most vulnerable to flooding.

In some respects, Iowa is a leader in mitigating climate change, but in others it trails behind other states. Iowa ranks 2nd in the fraction of its total energy production—34 percent—derived from wind. But Iowa's energy consumption is also high, ranking 5th per capita in 2017. Not surprisingly, therefore, despite its growing reliance on wind, given Iowa's continued dependence on coal—45 percent of net electricity generation in 2017—and its high energy consumption, the state also ranks relatively high in energy-related carbon dioxide emissions per person—13th in 2016. Iowa's high ranking can be attributed to its cold winters and comparatively scattered population.

Since 2010, Iowa has done little to nothing either to address the state's contributions to climate change or to develop strategies for adapting to it. One exception is the Iowa Department of Transportation, which has researched the impact of climate change on the viability of the state's roads and bridges, which are clearly threatened by increased flooding. The state discontinued its Climate Change Advisory Council in 2011. Although it continues to measure its production of greenhouse gases, unlike Minnesota, Michigan, and Illinois, Iowa has set no goals for reducing them. Even when confronted with evidence that climate change is leading to increased flooding, the state has been unwilling to admit that it is a causal factor. When the Iowa Flood Center was preparing a 2015 application to the Obama administration's National Disaster Resilience Competition, which the federal government explicitly established to help communities and states respond to climate change, representatives of the Iowa governor's office informed the Flood Center that it should not directly mention climate change contributing to flooding. It remains to be seen whether continued flooding in Iowa will alter this attitude. For the more recent period, 2013 to 2017, Iowa was one of seven states with the most federally declared flood disasters, and so the challenge of adapting to climate change remains.

According to *U.S. News*, Iowa ranked 4th in its Opportunity category. Again, Iowa's high ranking masks issues identified in earlier chapters. In the Best States ranking, Opportunity consists of the Economic Opportunity, Equality, and Affordability indexes. Because housing prices in Iowa are comparatively low, the state ranked 3rd in housing affordability. For the Economic Opportunity index, Iowa has comparatively low income inequality, but it also has a modest median household income — $56,247 in 2016 — which resulted in a modest ranking of 26th, substantially behind neighbors Illinois (16th) and Minnesota (13th) with their median incomes of $60,960 and $65,599. This puts Iowa at a disadvantage in growing its population among four-year college graduates, who typically identify job opportunities and competitive wages as very important but who are much less likely to identify Iowa as possessing these attributes.

Among the *U.S. News* Opportunity indexes, Iowa fared least well with Equality, ranking 36th. Iowa's low Equality ranking was driven by low rankings in employment gaps by Disability (36th), Gender (22nd), and Race (36th) and income gaps by Gender (40th) and Race (27th). *U.S. News* defines gaps in race by comparing non-Hispanic whites to minorities — African Americans, Hispanic Americans, and Asian Americans. These low rankings for race are consistent with Iowa's historical and contemporary record for the various education and employment gaps between whites and African Americans described in chapter 4. Similarly low rankings for Iowa are found in the *U.S. News* data in the Crime and Corrections category. Iowa ranked 32nd in this category, primarily because of low rankings in the Equality in Jailing (39th) and Least Juvenile Incarceration (41st) indexes. These two indexes reflect the huge disparity between white and black incarceration rates in Iowa as well as the higher arrest and juvenile court petition rates for African American youth in cities like Des Moines and Iowa City. While Hispanic Americans in the state are faring better in overall employment than African Americans, the anxiety and fear associated with being Hispanic in Iowa, especially after major federal raids, result in a lower quality of life not captured by the *U.S. News* rankings.

In 2019, *U.S. News* published its next edition of the Best States analysis. This time, Iowa was no longer the best state — its overall ranking fell to 14th. This drop reflected significant declines in Health Care, Economy, and Infrastructure. But it also reflected a new category: Natural Environment, which had previously been lumped with Social Environment in the Quality of Life category. *U.S. News* ranked Iowa 32nd in its Natural Environment category, including 41st in Air and Water Quality and 25th in Pollution. As in 2018, Iowa continued to rank far from the top in overall Equality (24th) and Equality in Jailing (39th).

Overall, when we dig deep into sustainability issues in Iowa, especially those related to the environment or equity and diversity, we find that Iowa is not doing so well compared to other states. Yes, Iowa has affordable housing, good health care, a respected education system, and a pleasant social environment, but its highly productive agro-industrial system creates serious environmental problems, and its ability to smoothly transition to a more diverse population is held in check both by its history and by contemporary problems associated with assimilating Native Americans, African Americans, Hispanic Americans, and Asian Americans. Iowa's future includes growing diversity and climate change, which the state's agricultural system both contributes to and is affected by but is not proactively preparing for.

We have learned that Iowa is at a crossroads. What kind of state does it want to be? A state in which there is growing income

inequality? A state with a degraded environment that is unpre-
pared for climate change? A state that has an outsize and negative impact on major ecosystems like the Gulf of Mexico? A state
that continues to struggle to support racial and ethnic diversity
and justice? If we view the state through Scott Campbell's three-
dimensional definition of sustainable development, it is clear that
despite its ranking as the 2018 *U.S. News* Best State, Iowa's sustainability performance is not going well.

What is to be done? What follows is not a set of specific policy
prescriptions but a set of twelve general principles derived from
the three points of Campbell's sustainability triangle: economic
development, environmental protection, and social justice issues
of economic opportunity and equality.

## *Iowa Should Support and Grow Its Middle Class*

The loss of well-paying jobs, especially in manufacturing as well
as through the decline in the number of farmers, has contributed
to a decline in Iowa's middle class and to the growth of income
inequality in which more people are either doing well or doing
poorly. Although the decline of the middle class is a national problem, between 2000 and 2016 Iowa fared worse than two-thirds of
the states. What can be done to help the state do better?

1. Iowa should undo its attempts to gut the rights of public employee unions. As of early 2017, labor unions represented more
than 119,000 public employees in Iowa, including 56,000 teachers.
These workers constitute an important part of the state's middle
class. By neutralizing their right to bargain for wages and benefits
in 2017, the state legislature weakened the state's middle class,
especially in smaller communities, where teachers constitute a
significant part of the middle class that has otherwise moved to
bigger cities.

2. Iowa should do a better job of supporting higher education.
Historically, a college education has meant higher income and
therefore a higher probability of becoming middle class. Because

of declining state support for higher education in Iowa, it is becoming more difficult for its citizens to afford a college education. Since 2001, the state portion of university budget expenditures has declined precipitously at the University of Iowa (from 63 to 34 percent in 2016) and Iowa State University (from 68 to 35 percent) and less sharply at the University of Northern Iowa (from 70 to 56 percent). In response, the state's universities have raised tuition, putting a college education out of reach for more middle- and lower-income households. The economic payoff for higher education in Iowa remains, but the cost of obtaining that higher income has gone up, which prevents students from earning their degrees at a four-year public university or burdens them with loans that will reduce their buying power. By failing to keep pace with the costs of higher education, the state of Iowa is weakening the ability of its residents to obtain salaries that will put or keep them in the middle class.

3. Iowa should raise its minimum wage. Iowa's minimum wage of $7.25 an hour is among the lowest in the Midwest—behind Illinois, Ohio, Missouri, Minnesota, Nebraska, Michigan, and South Dakota and tied with North Dakota, Indiana, Kansas, and Wisconsin—and among the lowest in the nation: twenty-nine other states have higher minimum wages. On January 1, 2020, twenty-one states raised their minimum wage—Iowa was not among them. By setting a low floor, the Iowa legislature undercuts income and thereby reduces the size of the middle class. Moreover, in 2017 the legislature prevented local governments from raising the minimum wage. Four counties had already adopted higher minimum wages, and a fifth was in the process of doing so. Three of the counties that had adopted a wage increase—Johnson, Linn, and Polk—comprise more than one-fourth of the state's total employment. The three counties, home to Iowa City, Cedar Rapids, and Des Moines, are among the fastest-growing areas in the state, reflecting a rate of growth that the state's shrinking counties can only wish for. In 2017, the U.S.

Census Bureau named Des Moines the Midwest's fastest-growing city, a status that should be the envy of the rest of the state if not the entire Midwest. Given Des Moines's rapid growth, one would assume that the state would not want to interfere with a local jurisdiction's record of success in economic growth, preferring instead to look for ways to replicate whatever Des Moines is doing so well. Apparently, that is not the case.

4. Iowa should make itself more attractive for recreation, the arts, and entertainment. Iowa can grow its middle-income population by making the state a more appealing place to live. Individuals with more education and higher income potential have greater choices about where they live and consequently value activities outside of work that include recreation, the arts, and entertainment. Des Moines provides an excellent example of doing exactly this. Up until the 1990s, Iowa's capital city was seen as boring. Through the adoption of the same City Beautiful ideas that turned Chicago from a dirty nineteenth-century metropolis into a city of great parks, museums, and public spaces, members of Des Moines's business elite and government embarked on a plan to convert downtown into a vital entertainment, recreation, and cultural center.

Like Chicago, Des Moines has built its transformation around a major water amenity—the Des Moines River—which cuts through the middle of the city. Reflecting this shift, many young Iowans who would have previously fled the state have remained, and the city's population, which shrank from 1960 to 1980, has grown by nearly 14 percent since that time. The city's attractiveness to millennials is seen in its Court Avenue entertainment area and the ascendance of the Des Moines Social Club arts and entertainment venue, as well as the accelerated demand for downtown and near downtown lofts and apartments.

While other communities in Iowa may lack the scale to duplicate Des Moines's success, they can share some of the capital city's key strategies that appeal to middle-income tastes. Charles

City's development of white-water kayaking on the Cedar River attracts visitors and has led to similar projects in Manchester and Elkader. While Des Moines is hub to some 224 miles of off-street bike trails, smaller communities and regions in the state have also succeeded in creating trails that are attractive for day, evening, and weekend bicycling. Among these is the 3.5-mile Jewell to Ellsworth trail in rural Hamilton County, which connects these two small towns along a former Union Pacific right-of-way. Ellsworth schoolkids can bike to the consolidated school in Jewell, and recreational riders can enjoy Sweet Treats ice cream in Jewell. Both larger cities and smaller towns, such as Kalona and Bellevue, can support brewpubs, which attract a steady clientele, seemingly because the love of craft beer crosses urban and rural lifestyle preferences. The same seems to be true for coffee shops, which have enjoyed success in places like Charles City, Webster City, and Oskaloosa. Finally, even small communities can benefit from the arts. Maquoketa has converted part of its downtown into the Maquoketa Art Experience, and tiny St. Ansgar and Osage host the Cedar Summerstock Theater, reported to be the Upper Midwest's only regional college summerstock venue.

Partnerships like the one between St. Ansgar and Osage, as well as the one between Jewell and Ellsworth, reveal the potential for greater collaboration among Iowa's smaller communities in establishing regional recreation, arts, and entertainment networks. These networks can address the lack of scale that can challenge projects in smaller communities. One example of this is the Grant Wood Mississippi River Region organization, which obtained a $1.9 million state Parks to People grant to develop and promote events, places, and "experiences" in Jackson, Jones, and Dubuque Counties in eastern Iowa. Another example that Iowa communities may seek to emulate can be seen in the nine towns in southeast Minnesota, just north of the Iowa state line, that have formed the nonprofit Root River Trail Towns to promote the sixty-mile Root River trail system and the towns that comprise it.

### Iowa Should Restore Its Water Quality and
### Increase Planning for Climate Change

Iowa has the ability to become a better steward of the state, the region, and the globe. Because agriculture plays such an important role in affecting the environment, it also plays a significant role in the production of the greenhouse gases that generate climate change. Iowa farmers could take the lead by adopting practices to reduce the greenhouse gases that currently emerge from agriculture and, through conservation tillage and cover crops, to use the soils to store carbon.

5. Iowa should fund the Leopold Center for Sustainable Agriculture and embrace Aldo Leopold's land ethic. Internationally known conservationist Aldo Leopold was born and raised in Burlington, Iowa. Trained as a forester, he worked nearly twenty years for the U.S. Forest Service before chairing the Department of Wildlife Management at the University of Wisconsin. Leopold's most famous work, *A Sand County Almanac*, published in 1949, ends with an essay titled "The Land Ethic." Leopold argues that there is no ethic that governs the relationship between humans and the land. Instead, the relationship is defined strictly by economics — land is property — and therefore the relationship is defined solely by privileges and not obligations. However, he considers land — "soils, waters, plants, and animals" — to be part of the community to which humans have ethical obligations. He writes, "In short, a land ethic changes the role of *Homo sapiens* from conqueror of the land-community to plain member and citizen of it." And he concludes with a succinct definition of the land ethic: "A thing is right when it tends to preserve the integrity, stability, and beauty of the biotic community. It is wrong when it tends otherwise."

Clearly, plowing under Iowa's prairie followed by despoiling waters in Iowa, the Mississippi River Basin, and the Gulf of Mexico is a violation of the land ethic. But it is also clear that Iowa's economic use of the land will not be returned to the era when Native Americans lived freely in the state and white settlers did not. Founded in 1987 during the Farm Crisis, the Leopold Center for Sustainable Agriculture at Iowa State University was an attempt to begin to rebalance the relationship between the economic and the ecological use of the land. The state legislature employed a tax on fertilizer sales to fund the center to support agricultural innovation that was both economically and environmentally sustainable. Each year the center distributed state funds for projects related to alternative crop and animal operations, such as the production of hops and aronia berries, which would allow small farmers to compete against the big corn, hog, and soybean farmers who dominate the state. The center, which was among the first sustainable agriculture centers at a land grant university, awarded more than five hundred grants to researchers in ecological initiatives, marketing and food systems, and policy initiatives—all related to sustainable agriculture. In 2017, however, the Iowa legislature voted to transfer funding for the Leopold Center to Iowa State's Iowa Nutrient Research Center, which unlike the Leopold Center does not have to share its findings with the public.

Embracing Leopold's land ethic is no doubt a challenge to the way in which agriculture is practiced in Iowa. But if the state is to begin to make headway in meeting its environmental obligations to its waters and soils, a fuller consideration of the ethic is needed. Defunding the Leopold Center was a step in the wrong direction.

6. Iowa should take its critical role in water quality more seriously. When it comes to water quality, Iowa is clearly in the driver's seat. The state's farming operations are among the most intense users of fertilizers in the Mississippi River Basin. This has clear implications for Iowa's waters. Iowa accounts for more than its share of nutrient pollution flowing to the Gulf of Mexico—as noted, the most recent estimate is 29 percent of the nutrients flowing from the twelve states that comprise the Mississippi River/

Gulf of Mexico Watershed Nutrient Task Force, the Hypoxia Task Force. Iowa's elected agriculture secretaries—Bill Northey and, more recently, Mike Naig—have served as state co-chairs (along with a federal cochair) of the Hypoxia Task Force since 2010. Appointed undersecretary of agriculture in 2018, Northey continues to serve on the Hypoxia Task Force as the U.S. Department of Agriculture representative. Iowa has therefore been a major contributor to nutrient pollution in Iowa, Mississippi, and Gulf waters while being in a position to influence state and federal policy regarding nutrient contamination.

Given Iowa's influence, both environmental and political, on water quality in the state, region, and nation, its record has been weak. The Environmental Protection Agency and the Hypoxia Task Force have failed to move decisively against the causes of Gulf hypoxia. Iowa's leadership position on the Hypoxia Task Force has undoubtedly influenced this outcome. Within the state, efforts to reduce nutrients in its waterways have been ineffectual. Since the beginning of the Iowa Nutrient Reduction Strategy's Water Quality Initiative in 2013 through fiscal year 2018, the Iowa legislature has budgeted nearly $55 million, for an annual average of $9 million. Since 2012, overall annual state funding for water quality has averaged $41 million, lower than ten years earlier from 2007 through 2009. These amounts stand in contrast to the minimum of $77 million in annual expenses estimated to meet the goals of the strategy.

The state's pathetic response to its water-quality challenges is reflected in the strategy's March 2019 annual report. The report estimates that there are 25 bioreactors in the state, treating nutrients that would otherwise flow directly through drain tiles into Iowa waterways. With each bioreactor servicing approximately 50 acres, as many as 138,000 bioreactors are needed to meet the scenarios laid out in the strategy. The March 2019 report also estimates that 760,000 acres were planted in cover crops in 2017—representing only 3.3 percent of Iowa's 23,300,000 acres planted in corn and soybeans that year. With such findings as these, the report has no choice but to conclude that early "efforts only scratch the surface of what is needed across the state to meet the non-point source nutrient reduction. Progress has occurred, but not at the scale that would impact statewide water quality measures. . . . Statewide improvements affected by conservation practices will require a much greater degree of implementation than has occurred so far."

7. To turn matters around, Iowa, along with the federal government, will need to use subsidies to reduce nutrient pollution from agricultural sources. Thus far, the Iowa Nutrient Reduction Strategy has relied on education, a limited number of financial incentives, and the willingness of farmers to adopt practices and technologies that will reduce the flow of nutrients into Iowa's waters. Quite simply, this has not been enough. In the case of a public good such as water quality, in which benefits accrue to everyone, even those who do not contribute, self-interest works to discourage farmers from participation. As a public good, the actions of Farmer Jones to plant cover crops, for example, will make little difference if no other farmers do so. On the other hand, if other farmers do plant cover crops, thereby improving overall water quality, Farmer Jones has no incentive to plant a cover crop because Jones can simply enjoy the public good provided by others.

One way to overcome self-interest, of course, is to pay farmers to plant cover crops, install bioreactors, and employ other practices that reduce nutrient pollution. Indeed, this is being accomplished under Iowa's current nutrient reduction strategy. But as indicated by its 2019 report, the money used to subsidize good water-quality practices is not enough. One current opportunity for increasing the subsidizing of good water-quality practices could come through funding the Natural Resources and Outdoor Recreation Trust, passed by voters in 2010, by adding three-eighths of a penny to the state sales tax. At the beginning of 2020, Republican Governor Kim Reynolds proposed funding the trust with an increase in the sales tax in conjunction with a decrease in the state income tax. Another option, based on the polluter pays principle, is that farmers should no longer be exempt from paying sales tax on fertilizer purchases and that these tax revenues should fund water quality. The former proposal hurts low-income Iowans, who pay a higher proportion of their income in sales taxes than higher-income households. The latter proposal hits farmers at a time of low commodity prices. Whether through these or some other funding source, obtaining action by Iowa agriculture to reduce nutrients will require subsidization.

8. In addition to subsidies, Iowa will need regulations to reduce nutrient pollution. Aldo Leopold was suspicious of relying on subsidies for farmers, primarily because they did not induce a conservation ethic. Comparing American to European farmers, he found the former lacking the latter's "sense of husbandry." Consequently, "when we conclude that we must bait the farmer with subsidies to induce him to raise a forest, or with gate receipts to induce him to raise game, we are merely admitting that the pleasures of husbandry-in-the-wild are as yet unknown both to the farmer and to ourselves." Subsidies are not enough, therefore. The experience with the Conservation Reserve Program and the decline in participation when corn and soybean prices rise, discussed in chapter 3, are examples of this.

Leopold argued for a change in ethic, but how will that happen? Iowa is betting that this will happen through a model that includes outreach and education, which will affect "farmer knowledge and attitude," which will then lead to changes in land use that will reduce nutrient pollution. But how long can we wait for farmers to turn more directly to a "sense of husbandry," not just for their crops and herds but also for their acres?

Change will require coercing collaboration, a process in which the state and the federal governments work together to expect, if not require, farmers and others to work together to protect the environment. In other words, Iowa agriculture needs more than subsidies and more than gentle persuasion—it needs regulations. The stick that accompanies the carrot provided by subsidies should be hard enough to gain attention but soft enough to encourage collaboration. The Des Moines Water Works lawsuit, for all its virtues in challenging agriculture's exemption from the Clean Water Act, was confrontational. It got people's attention, but a lot of that attention was negative.

At the state level, Iowa or its counties can require farmers to adopt one or more of the practices identified in the Iowa Nutrient Reduction Strategy. An example of this is Minnesota's Buffer Law, which requires farmers to establish 50-foot-wide perennial vegetative buffer strips along rivers, streams, and lakes as well as 16.5-foot buffers along ditches. The purpose is to filter out phosphorus, nitrogen, and sediment. Minnesota's Buffer Law was first adopted by the legislature in 2015 and then revised in 2016 and 2017. The law applies to lands in which agriculture predominates, many of which are in the southern and western parts of the state. As of September 2019, there was 98 to 99 percent compliance with the law, although there were still "thousands of parcels" that remained out of compliance. An Environmental Working Group study found that in five selected Iowa counties, only .12 percent of corn or soybean cropland would need to be converted to grass to comply with a 50-foot buffer requirement. In September 2019, a majority of elected members to Iowa's soil and water conservation districts recommended that Iowa adopt a similar 30-foot buffer. Unfortunately, in December 2019, the state's governor-appointed Soil Conservation and Water Quality Committee rejected this proposal, arguing against mandates in favor of voluntary conservation.

But nutrient pollution is a regional and a national problem and therefore requires a multistate solution. As noted in chapter 3, the federal government's remedy, the Mississippi River/Gulf of Mexico Watershed Nutrient Task Force (aka the Hypoxia Task Force), has done little more than encourage states to address the problem without providing any level of accountability that would stimulate meaningful action. This is clearly seen in the Hypoxia Task Force's 2017 report to Congress. While the 2025 (20 percent reduction in nutrients) and 2035 (45 percent reduction in nutrients) goals are affirmed, the task force announced that it is developing, "for the first time," a "Measurement Framework" whereby state and aggregate progress toward meeting these goals can be measured. Shouldn't this have been done a long time ago?

In contrast, the Chesapeake Bay Total Maximum Daily Load, launched in 2010 under an executive order by President Obama to restore and protect the bay, established not only a fixed measure of nutrient reduction in Chesapeake Bay but created a detailed process by which this goal is to be met. States must submit plans to the Environmental Protection Agency designed to meet short-term measurable goals that will lead to achievement of a long-term goal of having a full set of nutrient and sediment reduction actions in place by 2025. Accountability is achieved through Watershed Implementation Plans, two-year milestones, EPA measurement of progress, and federal actions if jurisdictions do not perform. The Chesapeake plan employs specific short-term goals, measurement, and accountability, all of which the Hypoxia Task Force and, in turn, the Iowa Nutrient Reduction Strategy lack.

9. Iowa must give local governments more control over concentrated animal feeding operations. Local governments have very limited powers over the siting of CAFOs: state law precludes local governments from regulating them. This means that families seeking to enjoy country living in Iowa must face the threat of having a CAFO located in their neighborhood. For a state that professes to be concerned about the decline of its rural areas, this seems like a very odd thing to do. Moreover, recent research on river systems in western Iowa indicates that increased concentration of animal feeding operations contributes to increased nutrient flow into rivers and streams via an increase in manure. Health issues aside, the state should decide whether it prefers people to pigs—generally, people prefer not to live around pigs.

10. In the face of climate change, Iowa must once again begin

to plan for adaptation while doing its best to achieve mitigation. As of this writing, Iowa has not engaged in any further statewide climate change analysis or planning — either measuring impacts or proposing strategies — since 2008 to 2010, when the two reports discussed in chapter 3 were issued under Governor Chet Culver's administration. Since then, the state has chosen to ignore climate change even though the evidence for increased precipitation, flooding, drought, and intensive heat waves is abundant. Specifically, the latest projections from the 2018 *Fourth National Climate Assessment* call for a decline in Midwest farm commodity productivity back to the level of the 1980s. What is Iowa doing to prepare for these challenges, and what is it doing to prevent them from taking place? It certainly seems like it is time again to look at this issue from a statewide perspective.

As noted in chapter 3, agriculture in Iowa plays an outsize role in generating greenhouse gases, resulting in the state's producing these gases at a per capita rate that is twice the national average. Iowa has a greenhouse gas problem, and yet there is little to no discussion about this or about how to reduce greenhouse gas emissions. Iowa needs to develop and enhance efforts to employ its agricultural niche to improve manure management and promote conservation tillage so that fewer greenhouse gases enter the atmosphere.

Beyond these practices, recent research shows that diet has a major impact on climate change, and to significantly reduce greenhouse gases humans will need to switch from a meat-based to a flexitarian plantcentric diet. The production of meat accounts for three-quarters of food-based greenhouse gases because of the comparative inefficiency of growing crops to feed animals, digestive fermentation from livestock, and manure-induced emissions. Since at least the publication of Frances Moore Lappé's book *Diet for a Small Planet* in 1971, environmentalists have advocated for a dietary shift to fruits, vegetables, nuts, and legumes. With increasing evidence about the effect of diet on climate change, such a switch now seems more imperative. This has clear implications for

Iowa and its emphasis on meat-based food systems, either through the raising of cattle and hogs or through the growing of crops to feed the animals that people eat. As the world hopefully moves more forcefully to address climate change, meat-based food systems and therefore Iowa's place in today's agriculture should be and will be challenged. Iowa must seriously consider this as well as other changes related to increased heat and precipitation as it moves forward in the twenty-first century.

### Iowa Should Become a State That Welcomes Diversity

Iowa has been a predominantly white state, not by nature but by design. But this is changing, and if the state wishes to address chronic population loss or stagnation in all but a few counties, it needs to recognize that its future is as a state of diversity, not homogeneity.

11. Iowa must learn to embrace diversity. From 2000 to 2010, Iowa's white population grew by 1 percent. At the same time, its African American, Asian American, and Hispanic American populations grew by 44, 45, and 84 percent, respectively. The white population is barely holding its own, while through births and in-migration African Americans, Asian Americans, and Hispanic Americans are the groups attracted to the state. The state should acknowledge the fact that people of color represent its future.

When Iowa was predominantly white, through all of the twentieth century, its share of the nation's population declined at a rate faster than that of any other state — by 65 percent. In part this is because one-third of Iowa counties stopped growing after 1900 while other states, farther west and south, had just begun to grow. Nevertheless, it means that Iowa is a population growth laggard and that if it wishes to grow, it needs to look to population groups that are not white. Iowa's lack of growth also means that it is an aging state — it requires younger people to do the jobs needed by the state's older residents. Clearly, then, it is in Iowa's interest to promote population growth by welcoming diversity.

To this end, Iowa needs to learn not only to accept diversity but to cultivate and embrace it. One example of a community that has done this is West Liberty, about fifteen miles east of Iowa City. West Liberty, whose 2017 population was estimated to be 3,755, is Iowa's first community to become majority Hispanic American, at 52 percent of the town's population. Since the 1930s, Latin Americans have been drawn to the town's meatpacking plant—originally Louis Rich but now West Liberty Foods. As its Hispanic population grew, the West Liberty Community School District elected in 1997 to begin a dual-language K–12 program—the first one in the state. The voluntary program provides the opportunity for English and Spanish speakers to learn in each language with some class periods in English and others in Spanish. Marshalltown and Sioux City have also adopted dual-language programs.

Dual-language programs enable students to learn and appreciate each other's language and culture. By doing so, they transform a challenge—the influx of nonnative speakers into a homogeneous community—into an opportunity that enriches both cultures. The programs also contribute to a community's image as a thriving, diverse, and progressive town. With a population that has increased by nearly two-thirds since 1970, West Liberty stands in contrast to many Iowa towns. In 2018, *U.S. News and World Report* named West Liberty High School the best high school in Iowa. And the websites of the city of West Liberty and its economic development arm, WeLead, both affirm the community's diversity as an important asset.

In the wake of the Mt. Pleasant raid in 2018, residents of West Liberty, like other communities with Hispanic American populations, fear they will be next: "We feel like this is going to hit West Liberty sooner or later." Yes, West Liberty has embraced diversity, but its efforts are inhibited by the federal government's immigration policies as well as by the attitude of those Iowans who support greater restrictions on immigration. If Iowa wishes to be attractive to immigrants and therefore to population growth, it needs to do a better job of ensuring that people from other nations are made to feel safe and welcome. This is why the police chiefs from Storm Lake and Marshalltown, both cities with significant Hispanic populations, opposed a 2018 Iowa legislative bill aimed at the sanctuary cities that, allegedly, do not cooperate with federal immigration officials. The two chiefs wrote: "Most significant, the proposed bill would diminish the trust that keeps our cities safe in the first place. We depend on residents, including immigrants, to come to us when they see something suspicious or potentially criminal. If they hear of a looming 'crackdown' that could affect their families and friends, they are less likely to come to us to report and prevent actual crimes." For Iowa to be a safe and welcoming place to the immigrants who wish to move there, it needs to ease their fears, not compound them.

12. Iowa must forcefully reject racism and promote equality. Despite civil rights gains over its history, clear signs of racism and inequality remain in the state. One perhaps positive sign that Iowa is beginning to move in the right direction is the decline in the number of people who voted for Steve King in the 2018 congressional election. In the 2016 election, King's opponent won only one county, Story, home of urban Ames and Iowa State University, and only 39 percent of ballots cast. In 2018, J. D. Scholten ran an aggressive campaign and won six counties and 47 percent of the vote. Even in Sioux County, which has given King his largest margins, his opponent's share of the vote grew from 16 to 25 percent between 2016 and 2018.

On the other hand, the state's African Americans continue to be mired in a second-class status, just as they were found to be seventy years ago in the studies completed in Waterloo, Davenport, and Burlington cited in chapter 4. Compared to whites, African Americans continue to struggle. According to Colin Gordon's 2019 state-by-state comparison of the ratios between white and black outcomes for various social and economic variables, Iowa repeatedly falls in the bottom half of all states — that is, the ratio of white-to-black outcomes favors whites more so in Iowa than in most if not nearly all other states.

For eighth grade math scores, for example, Iowa's white-to-black ratio is 17th from the bottom of all fifty states. For out-of-school suspensions, Iowa's white-to-black ratio is 6th from last. For the share of individuals over age twenty-five who have a college degree, Iowa's white-to-black ratio is 22nd from last. For prime-age adults (ages twenty-five to fifty-four), a much higher percentage of whites are employed than African Americans — the 2017 white-to-black ratio between the two groups places Iowa 2nd from the bottom. If we compare rates of unemployment, Iowa's ratio of white-to-black unemployment is 7th from the bottom. When we compare the white-to-black ratio of homeownership, Iowa is also 7th from the bottom. Iowa's ratio of white-to-black median income is 6th from the bottom. Its ratio of white-to-black poverty is 5th from the bottom. The state's ratio of white-to-black infant mortality is 11th from the bottom. Iowa's ratio of white-to-black incarceration is 3rd from the bottom. Iowa's record in equality for African Americans is nothing short of dismal.

While Iowa has many attributes that contributed to its 2018 Best States ranking, it continues to face many challenges related to sustainability—economic inequality, environmental degradation, lack of readiness for climate change, and racial and ethnic inequality—that place the state at a much lower ranking. Once again, therefore, Iowa appears to be at a crossroads. In what direction does it wish to move? Does it really wish to be the best state that some claim it is? If so, it must wholeheartedly evolve from a white state to a state with a more diverse population and to a state that invests in its environment and its people. If Iowa does this, its citizens will be more likely to thrive, it will become a healthier and more attractive place to live, and it will make a more positive contribution to the rest of the world.

While researching and writing this book, I consulted a wide array of print and online sources, including newspapers, books, journals, videos, and websites of state, federal, commercial, and nonprofit organizations, and had numerous discussions with colleagues. The websites of these national organizations were particularly informative: U.S. Department of Agriculture, U.S. Department of the Interior, U.S. Environmental Protection Agency, U.S. Energy Information Administration, and the National Research Council. Websites of these Iowa state organizations were also very helpful: State Data Center of Iowa, Iowa State University's Iowa Community Indicators Program, Iowa State University Extension and Outreach, Iowa Department of Agriculture and Land Stewardship, and Iowa Department of Natural Resources. Publications and other resources from the nonprofit, nonpartisan Iowa Policy Project were especially helpful, as were articles in the *Des Moines Register*, *New York Times*, and *Washington Post*.

Much of the information in this book is a synthesis of data from the aforementioned sources as well as more specialized sources. The following chapter-by-chapter citations refer to more specific topics that I discuss in this book.

### Introduction: Iowa Communities at a Crossroads

While this book is not meant to be a comprehensive history of Iowa, in it I seek to build upon and add to the three major general histories of Iowa written in the second half of the twentieth century: Leland L. Sage, *A History of Iowa* (Ames: Iowa State University Press, 1974); Joseph F. Wall, *Iowa: A Bicentennial History* (New York: W. W. Norton, 1978); and Dorothy Schwieder, *Iowa: The Middle Land* (Ames: Iowa State University Press, 1996). The sustainability focus that I outlined at the beginning of this book is broad but not well represented in any of these books, certainly not in an integrated fashion. Sage's book is primarily a political history of the state. Wall's book, published in a series of books on the states for the bicentennial of American independence, is a general history that focuses little on agriculture's impact on the environment or on social justice and diversity in the twentieth century. Schwieder's book mentions the Farm Crisis but does not cover it in great detail, nor does it do much to cover social justice and diversity in the twentieth century.

Much has happened in Iowa's economic, environmental, and social equity history since these books were written. Not surprisingly, none of these books examines climate change and the consequences it will have for Iowa. Given Iowa's increasing diversity since these books were written and the social justice issues that accompany that diversity, the emergence of climate change, the decline in the fortunes of the middle class that began at the time of the Farm Crisis, and the increasingly apparent effects of production agriculture on the environment, it is clear that Iowa's history needs to be updated.

Scott Campbell's "Green Cities, Growing Cities, Just Cities: Urban Planning and the Contradictions of Sustainable Development," *Journal of the American Planning Association* 62 (1996): 296–312, sets out the three *E*'s of sustainability—environment, equity, and economic development—in a way that reflects the tensions and contradictions among each. Campbell recognizes that urban planners and society as a whole need to balance these three often contradictory goals: a clean environment, a strong economy, and social equity.

William Cronon's *Nature's Metropolis: Chicago and the Great West* (New York: W. W. Norton, 1991) places Chicago and Iowa within their regional context of the Midwest, most significantly Illinois, Iowa, and Wisconsin, states that all figure in the tallgrass prairie. Cronon maintains that to understand the growth and development of Chicago in the nineteenth century, you have to understand its relation to Iowa. But the same can be said of Iowa: to understand its history and development, you must understand its connection to Chicago. This is revealed not only in the railroad and trade connections between the two but also, as I discuss in chapter 4, the demographic changes in Iowa over the last several decades as African Americans have moved there from Chicago.

Iowa's status, along with the status of the upper tallgrass prairie region, is reflected in the most recent statistics from the U.S. Department of Agriculture, which can be found at the USDA's National Agricultural Statistics Service Iowa Field Office Top Ten Rankings website. Agricultural land values can be found in the USDA's "Land Values

2018 Summary." Agriculture's share of the Iowa economy is reported in Stephanie Mercier, "Employing Agriculture: How the Midwest Farm and Food Sector Relies on Immigrant Labor," Chicago Council on Global Affairs, December 9, 2014.

## 1. Agriculture, Manufacturing, and Iowa's Middle Class

Iowa's railroad development, beginning in the 1850s, is chronicled in H. Roger Grant, ed., *Iowa Railroads: The Essays of Frank P. Donovan, Jr.* (Iowa City: University of Iowa Press, 2000). Also see H. Roger Grant and Don L. Hofsommer, *Iowa's Railroads: An Album* (Bloomington: Indiana University Press, 2009), and Don L. Hofsommer, *The Hook and Eye: A History of the Iowa Central Railway* (Minneapolis: University of Minnesota Press, 2005). Iowa's track mileage at the end of the nineteenth century is found online in Rand McNally's 1897 *Miles of Railroads U.S., 1839–1894*, David Rumsey Historical Map Collection.

Iowa State University's Center for Industrial Research and Service provides an overview of manufacturing's importance in the Iowa economy in its 2018 publication "Manufacturing in Iowa." Information on specific contributions of the meat-processing and farm implement manufacturing sectors is available from the State Data Center of Iowa. Wilson J. Warren presents an overview of industrialization in the rural Midwest, including Iowa, in "Beyond the Rust Belt: The Neglected History of the Rural Midwest's Industrialization after World War II," in J. L. Anderson, ed., *The Rural Midwest since World War II* (DeKalb: Northern Illinois University Press, 2014).

The close connection between farming and manufacturing in Iowa is reflected in a number of articles and books, including Brian Page and Richard Walker, "From Settlement to Fordism: The Agro-Industrial Revolution in the American Midwest," *Economic Geography* 67 (1991): 281–315; David Peters, "Income Trends for Iowa Farms and Farm Families 2003–2015," Iowa State University Extension and Outreach, December 2016; Deborah Fink, *Open Country, Iowa: Rural Women, Tradition, and Change* (Albany: State University of New York Press, 1986), and *Cutting into the Meatpacking Line: Workers and Change in the Rural Midwest* (Chapel Hill: University of North Carolina Press, 1998); Daniel Nelson, *Farm and Factory: Workers in the Midwest, 1880–1990* (Bloomington: Indiana University Press, 1995); and Keach Johnson, "Iowa's Industrial Roots, 1890–1910," *Annals of Iowa* 44 (1978): 163–190.

Wilson J. Warren's *Tied to the Great Packing Machine: The Midwest and Meatpacking* (Iowa City: University of Iowa Press, 2007) outlines the birth and transformation of meatpacking in Iowa and the Midwest. Other publications that examine meatpacking in Iowa include H. H. McCarty and C. W. Thompson, *Meat Packing in Iowa*, College of Commerce, State University of Iowa, 1933; Eric Barr, "The History of T.M. Sinclair and Company, Meatpacking Plant," Louis Berger Group, n.d.; Margaret Walsh, *The Rise of the Midwestern Meat Packing Industry* (Lexington: University Press of Kentucky, 1982); Molly Myers Naumann and Brian Schultes, *An Intensive Level Architectural and Historical Survey of the John Morrell and Company Meat Packing Plant, Ottumwa, Iowa* (Ottumwa: City of Ottumwa, 1991); and Rebecca Conard, "Bringin' Home the Bacon: The Rath Packing Company in Waterloo, 1891–1985" (Iowa City: Tallgrass Historians, 2010).

Storm Lake's evolution as a meatpacking community is described in Mark A. Grey, "Storm Lake, Iowa, and the Meatpacking Revolution: Historical and Ethnographic Perspectives on a Community in Transition," in Shelton Stromquist and Marvin Bergman, eds., *Unionizing the Jungles: Labor and Community in the Twentieth-Century Meatpacking Industry* (Iowa City: University of Iowa Press, 1997). Columbus Junction is briefly profiled in Osha Gray Davidson's *Broken Heartland: The Rise of America's Rural Ghetto* (1990; Iowa City: University of Iowa Press, 1996). The closing of meatpacking and other plants in Iowa during the 1980s is described in Mickey Lauria and Peter S. Fisher, *Plant Closings in Iowa: Causes, Consequences, and Legislative Options*, Institute of Urban and Regional Research, University of Iowa, 1983.

The advent of Iowa Beef Processors and other disruptive meat processing firms in the 1960s is described in a variety of places, including Deborah Fink, *Cutting into the Meatpacking Line: Workers and Change in the Rural Midwest* (Chapel Hill: University of North Carolina Press, 1998), which outlines the history of meatpacking in Perry; Wilson J. Warren, *Tied to the Great Packing Machine: The Midwest and Meatpacking* (Iowa City: University of Iowa Press, 2007); and Alan Barkema and Michael L. Cook, "The Changing U.S. Pork Industry: A Dilemma for Public Policy," *Economic Review* 78 (1993): 49–65.

Recruitment of Hispanics and other ethnic groups by Iowa Beef Packers et al. to work in Iowa and other midwestern meatpacking communities is discussed in William Kandel and Emilio A. Parrado,

"Restructuring of the US Meat Processing Industry and New Hispanic Migrant Destinations," *Population and Development Review* 31 (2005): 447–471; Michael J. Broadway, "Hogtowns and Rural Development," *Rural Development Perspectives* 9 (1994): 40–46; and Faranak Miraftab, *Global Heartland: Displaced Labor, Transnational Lives, and Local Placemaking* (Bloomington: Indiana University Press, 2016).

The story of Rath Packing's history and demise in Waterloo is told in Rebecca Conard, "Bringin' Home the Bacon: The Rath Packing Company in Waterloo, 1891–1985" (Iowa City: Tallgrass Historians, 2010), and John Portz, *The Politics of Plant Closings* (Lawrence: University Press of Kansas, 1990). The history of Dubuque's meatpacking sector and Dubuque Packing is reported in Ralph Scharnau, "Workers, Unions, and Workplaces in Dubuque, 1830–1990," *Annals of Iowa* 52 (1993): 50–78. Dubuque Packing's efforts to remain viable and its contentious relation with its union are reported in United Food and Commercial Workers International Union, AFL-CIO, Local No. 150-A, Petitioner, v. National Labor Relations Board, Respondent, Dubuque Packing Company, Inc. Intervenor, 1 F. 3d 24 (D.C. cir. 1993). Ottumwa's dependence upon the John Morrell meatpacking company and that company's eventual demise in the city are described in Wilson J. Warren, *Struggling with "Iowa's Pride": Labor Relations, Unionism, and Politics in the Rural Midwest since 1877* (Iowa City: University of Iowa Press, 2000).

Mason City's experience with union organizing in the meatpacking industry is described in Bruce Fehn, "Ruin or Renewal: The United Packinghouse Workers of America and the 1948 Meatpacking Strike in Iowa," *Annals of Iowa* 56 (1997): 349–378. Recent information on Mason City's north end can be found in Sylvia Bochner et al., *Mason City's North End Healthy Neighborhood Plan*, Iowa Initiative for Sustainable Communities, University of Iowa, 2018. Information on current conditions in Mason City and Ottumwa can be found in David Swenson and Liesl Eathington, "Economic and Social Indicators for Iowa's Micropolitan Counties and Cities," Department of Economics, Iowa State University, 2017.

Wayne G. Broehl, Jr., in *John Deere's Company: A History of Deere and Company and Its Times* (New York: Doubleday, 1984) tells the story of John Deere's history in the Quad Cities and in Iowa. The Hart-Parr contribution to the history of Oliver Tractors and Charles City is described in Mark R. Finlay, "System and Sales in the Heartland: A Manufacturing and Marketing History of the Hart-Parr Company, 1901–1929," *Annals of Iowa* 57 (1998): 337–373, and Robert N. Pripps and Andrew Morland, *Oliver Tractors: History of Oliver, Hart-Parr, Cockshutt and Cletrac Tractors Model Development, Variations, Specifications* (Osceola, Wisc.: Motorbooks International, 1994).

The history of labor relations in the Iowa-Illinois farm implement industry right after World War II is covered not only in Wayne G. Broehl, Jr., *John Deere's Company: A History of Deere and Company and Its Times* (New York: Doubleday, 1984), but also in Matthew M. Mettler, "A Workers' Cold War in the Quad Cities: The Fate of Labor Militancy in the Farm Equipment Industry, 1949–1955," *Annals of Iowa* 68 (2009): 359–394; Shelton Stromquist, *Solidarity and Survival: An Oral History of Iowa Labor in the Twentieth Century* (Iowa City: University of Iowa Press, 1993); and Kraig Kircher and Milton Derber, "The Quad Cities," in Milton Derber, ed., *Labor in Illinois: The Affluent Years, 1945–1980* (Urbana: University of Illinois Press, 1989).

Key works on the Iowa Farm Crisis include Gilbert C. Fite, "The 1980s Farm Crisis," *Montana: The Magazine of Western History* 36 (1986): 69–71, and *American Farmers: The New Minority* (Bloomington: Indiana University Press, 1981); Kenneth L. Peoples et al., *Anatomy of an American Agricultural Credit Crisis* (Lanham, Md.: Rowman and Littlefield, 1992); Bruce L. Gardner, *American Agriculture in the Twentieth Century: How It Flourished and What It Cost* (Cambridge, Mass.: Harvard University Press, 2002); Barry J. Barnett, "The U.S. Farm Financial Crisis of the 1980s," *Agricultural History* 74 (2000): 366–380; Kathryn Marie Dudley, *Debt and Dispossession: Farm Loss in America's Heartland* (Chicago: University of Chicago Press, 2000); Neil E. Harl, *The Farm Debt Crisis of the 1980s* (Ames: Iowa State University Press, 1990); David Swenson, "A Decade of Adjustment: Economic, Social, and Political Forces Influencing Iowa Government Policy in the 1980s," Institute of Public Affairs, University of Iowa, 1988; Mark Friedberger, *Shake-Out: Iowa Farm Families in the 1980s* (Lexington: University Press of Kentucky, 1989); Paul C. Rosenblatt, *Farming Is in Our Blood: Farm Families in Economic Crisis* (Ames: Iowa State University Press, 1990); Iowa Public Television's 2013 documentary *The Farm Crisis*; and Jim Schwab, *Raising Less Corn and More Hell: Midwestern Farmers Speak Out* (Urbana: University of Illinois Press, 1988). Of these, the most useful for the general reader are probably the Iowa Public Television documentary, which is available online, and anthropologist Kathryn Marie Dudley's *Debt and Dispossession: Farm Loss in America's Heartland* (Chicago: University of Chicago Press, 2000), based on extensive interviews and solid interpretation, which brings the reader into one community, albeit in Minnesota, experiencing the Farm Crisis. The Bob and Theresa Sullivan quote is from the Iowa Public Television documentary.

The impact of U.S. agricultural policy on the Iowa Farm Crisis is addressed in Michael Pollan, *The Omnivore's Dilemma: A Natural History of Four Meals* (New York: Penguin Press, 2006); Barry J. Barnett, "The U.S. Farm Financial Crisis of the 1980s," *Agricultural History* 74 (2000): 366–380; and William S. Eubanks II, "A Rotten System: Subsidizing Environmental Degradation and Poor Public Health with Our Nation's Tax Dollars," *Stanford Environmental Law Journal* 28 (2009): 213–310. Earl Butz's famous (or infamous) quote about growing big or getting out of farming is recorded in Curtis E. Beus and Riley E. Dunlap, "Conventional versus Alternative Agriculture: The Paradigmatic Roots of the Debate," *Rural Sociology* 55 (1990): 590–616. Information on the growth of large farms in Iowa and the Midwest is found in the 2017 U.S. Census of Agriculture and James M. Macdonald, Penni Korb, and Robert A. Hoppe, "Farm Size and the Organization of U.S. Crop Farming," Economic Research Service, U.S. Department of Agriculture, August 2013. Income trends among Iowa farmers are reported in David Peters, "Income Trends for Iowa Farms and Farm Families 2003–2015," Iowa State University Extension and Outreach, December 2016.

The 2018 and 2019 challenges for Iowa farmers posed by the trade war with China and extreme weather are reported in many places, including Mitch Smith, "Frustration Mounts among Farmers as China Trade Talks Break Down," *New York Times*, May 10, 2019; Mitch Smith, Jack Healy, and Timothy Williams, "'It's Probably Over for Us': Record Flooding Pummels Midwest When Farmers Can Least Afford It," *New York Times*, March 18, 2019; and Scott Irwin and Todd Hubbs, "Another Look at Late Planting of the 2019 Corn Crop," *farmdoc daily*, June 12, 2019.

The impact of the Farm Crisis on the farm machinery industry is reported in Ralph Scharnau, "Workers, Unions, and Workplaces in Dubuque, 1830–1990," *Annals of Iowa* 52 (1993): 50–78, and Mark Friedberger, *Shake-Out: Iowa Farm Families in the 1980s* (Lexington: University Press of Kentucky, 1989). The impact on International Harvester and other farm machinery firms, as well as on the Moline–Rock Island area and Iowa, is described in Wayne G. Broehl, Jr., *John Deere's Company: A History of Deere and Company and Its Times* (New York: Doubleday, 1984); Barbara Marsh, *A Corporate Tragedy: The Agony of International Harvester Company* (New York: Doubleday, 1985); Jeff R. Crump, "What Cannot Be Seen Will Not Be Heard: The Production of Landscape in Moline, Illinois," *Eucumene* 6 (1999): 295–317; Mark R. Finlay, "System and Sales in the Heartland: A Manufacturing and Marketing History of the Hart-Parr Company, 1901–1929," *Annals of Iowa* 57 (1998): 337–373; and Jeff R. Crump and Christopher D. Merrett, "Scales of Struggle: Economic Restructuring in the U.S. Midwest," *Annals of the Association of American Geographers* 88 (1998): 496–515.

The discussion of the impact of automation and productivity gains on employment in farm machinery manufacturing is based on numerous sources, including Michael J. Hicks and Srikant Devaraj, "The Myth and the Reality of Manufacturing in America," Center for Business and Economic Research, Ball State University, 2015, 2017; Fred Stahl, "Manufacturing Change at the John Deere Harvester Works: Report on the Visit of the Ad Hoc Lean Aircraft Initiative Team, June 7, 1994," https://dspace.mit.edu/handle/1721.1/1652; Wayne G. Broehl, Jr., *John Deere's Company: A History of Deere and Company and Its Times* (New York: Doubleday, 1984); John Deere Des Moines Works factory tour video (showing robotic manufacturing), https://www.youtube .com/watch?v=55EN9PZkrHY, September 2019; Austin Weber, "Deere Invests in Waterloo Plant," *Assembly*, March 7, 2012; Pat Kinney, "Deere Has Added 1,100 Union Jobs in Waterloo since 2009," *Waterloo Courier*, April 11, 2012; Kevin Hardy, "Robots, Artificial Intelligence and Automation Are Reshaping Iowa's Workforce: Is Your Job at Risk?," *Des Moines Register*, July 10, 2017; and Ralph Scharnau, "Workers, Unions, and Workplaces in Dubuque, 1830–1990," *Annals of Iowa* 52 (1993): 50–78. The history of UAW-Deere cooperative contracts tied to productivity gains, agreements that began after a six-month strike in 1987, is outlined in Chris Trimble, "Continuous Process Improvement at Deere and Company," Tuck School of Business, Dartmouth College, 2008.

Information on the effect of the 1980s on wages in Iowa, as well as trends in income inequality in the state and nationally, is found in the work of University of Iowa history professor Colin Gordon. See his "Wages: Iowa Needs a Raise," Iowa Policy Project, July 2018; "The Rich

Get Richer: Top Incomes in Iowa, 1917–2011," Iowa Policy Project, February 2014; and the digital project *Growing Apart: A Political History of American Inequality*, Institute for Policy Studies, https://inequality .org/research/growing-apart-political-history-american-inequality/, 2013. Income inequality data for Iowa and other states can be found in Mark W. Frank, "U.S. State-Level Income Inequality Data," http://www .shsu.edu/eco_mwf/inequality.html. For additional information on income inequality across the states, see Tim Henderson, "In Most States, the Middle Class Is Now Growing—but Slowly," *Stateline*, Pew Charitable Trusts, April 12, 2018. Dierk Herzer analyzes the impact of unionization on income inequality in "Unions and Income Inequality: A Panel Cointegration and Causality Analysis for the United States," *Economic Development Quarterly* 30 (2016): 267–274.

For unionization trends in Iowa and the effect of state legislation on public employee unions, see Barry T. Hirsch, David A. Macpherson, and Wayne G. Vroman, "Estimates of Union Density by State," *Monthly Labor Review* 124 (2001): 51–55, updated annually at http:// www.unionstats.com/; "Attacks on Collective Bargaining: Hidden Costs, Untold Consequences for Iowans," Iowa Policy Project, February 2017; Iowa Code, 2017, chapter 20, https://www.legis.iowa.gov/docs /ico/chapter/20.pdf; Jason Noble and Brianne Pfannenstiel, "Here Are the 5 Key Changes in Iowa's Collective Bargaining Bill," *Des Moines Register*, February 8, 2017; Iowa Legislature, House File 291, signed by Governor Terry Branstad, February 17, 2017; Senator Jason Schultz, "The Schultz Perspective," *Missouri Valley Times News*, February 24, 2017; and Brianne Pfannenstiel, "Branstad Signs Bills Limiting Workers' Compensation, Blocking Minimum Wage Hikes," *Des Moines Register*, March 30, 2017.

Information on the effect of the Farm Crisis and population loss as well as Walmart on downtowns in small-town Iowa is based on Osha Gray Davidson, *Broken Heartland: The Rise of America's Rural Ghetto* (1990; Iowa City: University of Iowa Press, 1996); Georgeanne M. Artz and Kenneth E. Stone, "Revisiting WalMart's Impact on Iowa Small-Town Retail: 25 Years Later," *Economic Development Quarterly* 26 (2012): 298–310; and my personal observations. The consequences of school consolidation for small towns in Iowa are portrayed in the *Des Moines Register*'s 2015 documentary *Lost Schools*.

Recent U.S. Census Bureau population data for both cities and counties are reported by Iowa State University via its Iowa Community Indicators Program website: "Annual Estimates of the Total Population for Cities" and "Annual Estimates of the Total Population for Counties." Information on micropolitan cities in Iowa can be found in David Swenson and Liesl Eathington, "Economic and Social Indicators for Iowa's Micropolitan Counties and Cities," Department of Economics, Iowa State University, 2017.

The stories of industrial decline in Ft. Madison, Burlington, Clinton, and Newton are reported in a variety of sources. On Ft. Madison, see Lynn Smith, "Walter A. Sheaffer," in David Hudson, Marvin Bergman, and Loren Horton, eds., *The Biographical Dictionary of Iowa* (Iowa City: University of Iowa Press, 2008), and "Sheaffer Pen Factory in Fort Madison to Close in Spring," *Mason City Globe Gazette*, January 4, 2008. On Burlington, see "Burlington Shops Stand Tall in Tough Times," https://www.ble-t.org/pr/news/headline.asp?id=5315, December 23, 2002, and Rex Troute, "BNSF Shops Remain Vacant," *Burlington Hawk Eye*, February 28, 2016.

On Clinton, including the Clinton Corn Processing strike, refer to Deborah Morse-Kahn and Joe Trnka, *Clinton, Iowa: Railroad Town* (Ames: Iowa Department of Transportation, 2003), and Adrienne M. Birecree, "Strike and Decertification at Clinton Corn Products," in Charles Craypo and Bruce Nissen, eds., *Grand Designs: The Impact of Corporate Strategies on Workers, Unions, and Communities* (Ithaca, N.Y.: ILR Press, Cornell University, 1993).

Information on Newton and the impact of the Maytag closure can be found at Louis Uchitelle, "Is There (Middle Class) Life after Maytag?," *New York Times*, August 26, 2007. Data on manufacturing worker earnings before and after the Maytag closing in Newton were obtained from the U.S. Bureau of Economic Analysis, "State and Local Personal Income," via an e-mail that David Swenson of Iowa State University sent me.

Mason City's dilemma regarding the Prestage pork-processing plant is described in Donnelle Eller, "Mason City Pork Plant Snags $15M in State Incentives," *Des Moines Register*, March 29, 2016, and Adam Belz, "Trouble in River City: Turning Away a $240 Million Hog Plant, Mason City Looks Ahead," *Minneapolis Star Tribune*, June 20, 2016. For an overview of public opinion on the Mason City hog plant project, see the May 3, 2016, Mason City City Council nearly seven-hour public hearing on that city's website.

## 2. Corn, Hogs, and Water

The tallgrass prairie ecosystem and its functions within the natural environment have been well described in a variety of works that include Cornelia F. Mutel, *The Emerald Horizon: The History of Nature in Iowa* (Iowa City: University of Iowa Press, 2008); Daryl D. Smith, "Iowa Prairie: Original Extent and Loss, Preservation and Recovery Attempts," *Journal of the Iowa Academy of Science* 105 (1998): 94–108; John B. Newhall, *A Glimpse of Iowa in 1846* (Burlington, Iowa: W. D. Skillman, 1846); Bohumil Shimek, "The Prairies," *Bulletin of the State University of Iowa New Series 35, Contributions from the Laboratories of Natural History* 6 (1911): 169–240; Margaret Fuller, *Summer on the Lakes, in 1843* (Boston: C. C. Little and J. Brown, 1844), excerpt reprinted in John T. Price, ed., *The Tallgrass Prairie Reader* (Iowa City: University of Iowa Press, 2014); "Iowa Prairies," Iowa Association of Naturalists, https://www.iowanaturalists.org/wp-content/uploads/2018/07/IAN203.pdf, September 2001; R. Michael Miller, "Prairie Underground," in Stephen Packard and Cornelia F. Mutel, eds., *The Tallgrass Restoration Handbook: For Prairies, Savannas, and Woodlands* (Washington, D.C.: Island Press, 1997); William E. McClain and Sherrie L. Elzinga, "The Occurrence of Prairie and Forest Fires in Illinois and Other Midwestern States, 1679 to 1854," *Erigenia* 13 (1994): 79–90; R. C. Anderson, "The Historic Role of Fire in the North American Grassland," in S. L. Collins and L. L. Wallace, eds., *Fire in North American Tallgrass Prairies* (Norman: University of Oklahoma Press, 1990); Lloyd C. Hulbert, "Causes of Fire Effects in Tallgrass Prairie," *Ecology* 69 (1988): 46–58; William K. Stevens, "Home on the Range (or What's Left of It)," *New York Times*, October 19, 1993; and Alan K. Knapp et al., "The Keystone Role of Bison in North American Tallgrass Prairie," *BioScience* 49 (1999): 39–50.

Soon after settlement of Iowa by Anglo-Americans began in the 1830s, Iowa's prairie-induced soil fertility was recognized by the federal government in David D. Owen, John Locke, and E. Phillips, *Report of a Geological Exploration of Part of Iowa, Wisconsin, and Illinois: Made under Instructions from the Secretary of the Treasury of the United States, in the Autumn of the Year 1839* (Washington, D.C.: Government Printing Office, 1844).

The adaptation of European and eastern American agriculture to the prairie and its consequences for the prairie are described in the following works: Allan G. Bogue, *From Prairie to Corn Belt: Farming on the*

*Illinois and Iowa Prairies in the Nineteenth Century,* 2nd ed. (Lanham, Md.: Ivan Dee, Rowman and Littlefield, 2011); Ian Frazier, "John Deere Was a Real Person, His Invention Changed the Country," *smithsonianmag.com,* November 2013; Wayne G. Broehl, Jr., *John Deere's Company: A History of Deere and Company and Its Times* (New York: Doubleday, 1984); William J. Haddock, *A Reminiscence: The Prairies of Iowa and Other Notes* (Iowa City: Printed for Private Circulation, 1901); Cornelia F. Mutel, *The Emerald Horizon: The History of Nature in Iowa* (Iowa City: University of Iowa Press, 2008); and Laura L. Jackson, "Restoring Prairie Processes to Farmlands," in Dana L. Jackson and Laura L. Jackson, eds., *The Farm as Natural Habitat: Reconnecting Food Systems with Ecosystems* (Washington, D.C.: Island Press, 2002).

The peculiarities of wet prairies and wet prairie farming, primarily in north central Iowa, are described in these works: Katherine Louise Andersen, "Historical Alterations of Surface Hydrology in Iowa's Small Agricultural Watersheds," master's thesis, Iowa State University, 2000; Leslie Hewes, "The Northern Wet Prairie of the United States: Nature, Sources of Information, and Extent," *Annals of the Association of American Geographers* 41 (1951): 307–323; Leslie Hewes and Phillip E. Frandson, "Occupying the Wet Prairie: The Role of Artificial Drainage in Story County, Iowa," *Annals of the Association of American Geographers* 42 (1952): 24–50; and Bradley A. Miller, William G. Crumpton, and Arnold G. van der Valk, "Spatial Distribution of Historical Wetland Classes on the Des Moines Lobe," *Wetlands* 29 (2009): 1146–1152.

Prairie potholes and the prairie pothole region are described by John Madson, *Where the Sky Began: Land of the Tallgrass Prairie* (1982; Iowa City: University of Iowa Press, 1995); Rex R. Johnson, Fred T. Oslund, and Dan R. Hertel, "The Past, Present, and Future of Prairie Potholes in the United States," *Journal of Soil and Water Conservation* 63 (2008): 84–87; and T. E. Dahl, "Status and Trends of Prairie Wetlands in the United States 1997 to 2009," Fish and Wildlife Service, U.S. Department of the Interior, 2014.

The employment of drainage ditches and drain tiles to dry the wet prairies in Iowa and the Midwest and their consequences are covered in Bradley A. Miller, William G. Crumpton, and Arnold G. van der Valk, "Spatial Distribution of Historical Wetland Classes on the Des Moines Lobe," *Wetlands* 29 (2009): 1146–1152; T. E. Dahl, "Wetlands Losses in the United States, 1780's to 1980's," Fish and Wildlife Service, U.S.

Department of the Interior, 1990; Allan G. Bogue, *From Prairie to Corn Belt: Farming on the Illinois and Iowa Prairies in the Nineteenth Century*, 2nd ed. (Lanham, Md.: Ivan Dee, Rowman and Littlefield, 2011); Mary R. McCorvie and Christopher L. Lant, "Drainage District Formation and the Loss of Midwestern Wetlands, 1850–1930," *Agricultural History* 67 (1993): 13–39; Samuel J. Imlay and Eric D. Carter, "Drainage on the Grand Prairie: The Birth of a Hydraulic Society on the Midwestern Frontier," *Journal of Historical Geography* 38 (2012): 109–122; Mark B. David, Laurie E. Drinkwater, and Gregory F. McIsaac, "Sources of Nitrate Yields in the Mississippi River Basin," *Journal of Environmental Quality* 39 (2010): 1657–1667; Michael Burkart, "The Hydrologic Footprint of Annual Crops," in Cornelia F. Mutel, ed., *A Watershed Year: Anatomy of the Iowa Floods of 2008* (Iowa City: University of Iowa Press, 2010); Gary R. Sands, "How Agricultural Drainage Works," University of Minnesota Extension, 2008; "Facts about Drainage and Drainage Districts," Iowa Drainage District Association, n.d.; Katherine Louise Andersen, "Historical Alterations of Surface Hydrology in Iowa's Small Agricultural Watersheds," master's thesis, Iowa State University, 2000; Ralph E. Heimlich and Linda L. Langner, "Swampbusting: Wetland Conversion and Farm Programs," Economic Research Service, U.S. Department of Agriculture, August 1986; John Madson, *Where the Sky Began: Land of the Tallgrass Prairie* (1982; Iowa City: University of Iowa Press, 1995); and James J. Dinsmore, *A Country So Full of Game: The Story of Wildlife in Iowa* (Iowa City: University of Iowa Press, 1994). The story of Plover, Curlew, and Mallard is told in H. Roger Grant, ed., *Iowa Railroads: The Essays of Frank P. Donovan, Jr.* (Iowa City: University of Iowa Press, 2000).

Beyond the advent of the steel moldboard plow and water drainage, other technological innovations that affected the development of agriculture in Iowa and the tallgrass prairie region are reviewed in Guy A. Lee, "The Historical Significance of the Chicago Grain Elevator System," *Agricultural History* 11 (1937): 16–32; William Cronon, *Nature's Metropolis: Chicago and the Great West* (New York: W. W. Norton, 1991); Allan G. Bogue, *From Prairie to Corn Belt: Farming on the Illinois and Iowa Prairies in the Nineteenth Century*, 2nd ed. (Lanham, Md.: Ivan Dee, Rowman and Littlefield, 2011), and "Changes in Mechanical and Plant Technology: The Corn Belt, 1910–1940," *Journal of Economic History* 43 (1983): 1–25; Bruce L. Gardner, *American Agriculture in the*

168     BIBLIOGRAPHIC ESSAY

*Twentieth Century: How It Flourished and What It Cost* (Cambridge, Mass.: Harvard University Press, 2002); and Michael Carolan, "Number of Commodities Produced for Sale on at Least 1 Percent of All Farms for Selected Years, 1920–2002," Leopold Center for Sustainable Agriculture, Iowa State University, 2002.

Technological changes in agriculture after 1940, particularly regarding the development of chemical fertilizers, are well described in J. L. Anderson, *Industrializing the Corn Belt: Agriculture, Technology, and Environment, 1945–1972* (DeKalb: Northern Illinois University Press, 2009). Holly Miller's quote is from a transcription of an interview that can be found at "Postwar Fertilizer Boom" on the Wessels Living History Farms website.

The introduction of concentrated animal feeding operations to hog farming and its consequences are described in a number of works, including J. L. Anderson, *Industrializing the Corn Belt: Agriculture, Technology, and Environment, 1945–1972* (DeKalb: Northern Illinois University Press, 2009); 2017 U.S. Census of Agriculture; Mark Honeyman and Michael Duffy, "Iowa's Changing Swine Industry," *Animal Industry Report*, https://lib.dr.iastate.edu/ans_air/, 2006; and *Literature Review of Contaminants in Livestock and Poultry Manure and Implications for Water Quality*, U.S. Environmental Protection Agency, July 2013. Early CAFO adopter Carl Frederick is quoted in Anderson's book.

Data on manure spills and leakages are assessed in "Work Plan Agreement 9/11/2013 between the Iowa Department of Natural Resources and the Environmental Protection Agency Region 7," Iowa Department of Natural Resources, August 1, 2015; Matthew Patane, "Iowa Manure Spills Jump 65% in 2013," *Des Moines Register*, February 4, 2014; Manure Discharge Chart, Iowa Department of Natural Resources, 2019; JoAnn Burkholder et al., "Impacts of Waste from Concentrated Animal Feeding Operations on Water Quality," *Environmental Health Perspectives* 115 (2007): 308–312; Christopher S. Jones et al., "Livestock Manure Driving Stream Nitrate," *Ambio* 48 (2019): 1143–1153; James Merchant and David Osterberg, "The Explosion of CAFOs in Iowa and Its Impact on Water Quality and Public Health," Iowa Policy Project, January 2018, which includes the quotes from the 2017 Iowa law that stipulates the requirements for determining that a specific CAFO was the cause of an individual's ill health; "Concentrated Animal Feeding Operations: EPA Needs More Information and a Clearly Defined

Strategy to Protect Air and Water Quality," U.S. Government Accountability Office, September 24, 2008; "Combating Antibiotic Resistance: A Policy Roadmap to Reduce Use of Medically Important Antibiotics in Livestock," Expert Commission on Addressing the Contribution of Livestock to the Antibiotic Resistance Crisis, 2017; John A. Kilpatrick, "Animal Operations and Residential Property Values," *Appraisal Journal* (Winter 2015): 41–50; and Jan L. Flora et al., "Hog CAFOs and Sustainability: The Impact on Local Development and Water Quality in Iowa," Iowa Policy Project, October 2007.

Less than successful efforts by local governments in Iowa to regulate concentrated animal feeding operations are analyzed in Nadia S. Adawi, "State Preemption of Local Control over Intensive Livestock Operations," *Environmental Law Reporter* 44 (2014): 10506–10523; Christopher A. Novak, "Agriculture's New Environmental Battleground: The Preemption of County Livestock Regulations," *Drake Journal of Agricultural Law* 5 (2000): 429–469; and Dave Murphy, "Iowa Governor 2010: Who Will Be the Worst Environmental Governor of the 21st Century?," *Huffington Post*, October 29, 2010, which includes the quote from Governor Terry Branstad on local control of CAFOs in Iowa.

Iowa's Master Matrix for siting CAFOs and its apparent effects on rural environments are described in Teresa Galluzzo and David Osterberg, "Permitting Pigs: Fixing Faults in Iowa's CAFO Approval Process," Iowa Policy Project, November 2008; Mitchell Schmidt, "Hog Farm Proposal by West Branch Man Draws Criticism," *Iowa City Press-Citizen*, June 16, 2014; "Master Matrix," and "Iowa's Section 303(d) Impaired Waters Listings," Iowa Department of Natural Resources; "State Panel Denies Petition to Strengthen Environmental Protections," Iowa Citizens for Community Improvement, 2017; Iowa Legislature, Senate File 447, signed by Governor Terry Branstad, March 29, 2017; and these articles by Donnelle Eller: "Iowa's Hog Confinement Loopholes Causing a Stink," *Des Moines Register*, June 11, 2016, which includes the quote from North English retiree Gary Netser; "Iowa Uses Satellites to Uncover 5,000 Previously Undetected Animal Confinements," *Des Moines Register*, September 15, 2017; and "Iowa Could Support 45,700 Livestock Confinements, but Should It?," *Des Moines Register*, March 8, 2018, which includes the quote and observation from Luke Haffner and hog farmer Trent Thiele.

The effects of erosion and sedimentation on water quality in Iowa and beyond are discussed in U.S. Environmental Protection Agency, *Water Quality Conditions in the United States: A Profile from the 2000 National Water Quality Inventory*, 2002, and "Agricultural Nonpoint Source Fact Sheet," 2005; Adam J. Heathcote, Christopher T. Filstrup, and John A. Downing, "Watershed Sediment Losses to Lakes Accelerating Despite Agricultural Soil Conservation Efforts," *PLoS ONE* 8 (2013): e53554; Art Cullen, *Storm Lake* (New York: Penguin Random House, 2018); Kent Hytrek, "After 15 Years, Dredging of Storm Lake Ends," *Sioux City Journal*, December 24, 2017; "Soil Erosion on Cropland 2007," Natural Resources Inventory, Natural Resources Conservation Service, U.S. Department of Agriculture, April 2010; Laura Miller, "Cost of Soil Erosion in Iowa, Not a Pretty Picture," *Leopold Letter* 27 (2015): 1, 4; Catherine DeLong, Richard Cruse, and John Wiener, "The Soil Degradation Paradox: Compromising Our Resources When We Need Them Most," *Sustainability* 7 (2015): 866–879; and Rick Cruse and Hillary Olson, "Soil Erosion: How Much Is Tolerable?," in Rachel Unger, ed., *Getting into Soil and Water: 2010* (Ames: Iowa Water Center, Iowa State University, 2010).

The rise of soybeans as an important commodity after World War II and their effect on land use in Iowa are described in several works. The decline in perennial forage crops and the increase in row cropping through soybeans are discussed in Julia Olmstead and E. Charles Brummer, "Benefits and Barriers to Perennial Forage Crops in Iowa Corn and Soybean Rotations," *Renewable Agriculture and Food Systems* 23 (2007): 97–107, and Dana L. Dinnes et al., "Nitrogen Management Strategies to Reduce Nitrate Leaching in Tile-Drained Midwestern Soils," *Agronomy Journal* 94 (2002): 153–171.

The dramatic shift to soybean production and, with continued corn production, the dominance and effect of row crop agriculture on water quality in Iowa and the Midwest are discussed in Keith Whigham, "Iowa Soybean Production History," *Integrated Crop Management*, January 21, 2002; Michael Carolan, "Number of Commodities Produced for Sale on at Least 1 Percent of All Farms for Selected Years, 1920–2002," Leopold Center for Sustainable Agriculture, Iowa State University, 2002; Laura L. Jackson, "Restoring Prairie Processes to Farmlands," in Dana L. Jackson and Laura L. Jackson, eds., *The Farm as Natural Habitat: Reconnecting Food Systems with Ecosystems* (Washington, D.C.: Island Press, 2002); J. L. Hatfield, L. D. McMullen, and C. S. Jones,

"Nitrate-Nitrogen Patterns in the Raccoon River Basin Related to Agricultural Practices," *Journal of Soil and Water Conservation* 64 (2009): 190–199; Simon Donner, "The Impact of Cropland Cover on River Nutrient Levels in the Mississippi River Basin," *Global Ecology and Biogeography* 12 (2003): 341–355; Y.-K. Zhang and K. E. Schilling, "Increasing Streamflow and Baseflow in Mississippi River since the 1940s: Effect of Land Use Change," *Journal of Hydrology* 324 (2006): 412–422; Ada Hayden, "The Value of Roadside and Small Tracts of Prairie in Iowa as Preserves," *Proceedings of the Iowa Academy of Science* 54 (1947): 28–29; and Bohumil Shimek, "The Persistence of the Prairie," *University of Iowa Studies in Natural History* 11 (1925): 3–24.

  Data and analysis of the effect of corn ethanol on Iowa corn production can be found in a variety of sources: *Monthly Energy Review*, U.S. Energy Information Administration; "Corn Production and Portion Used for Fuel Ethanol," U.S. Department of Energy, https://afdc.energy .gov/data/10339; "Ethanol Production," Iowa Corn Growers Association; "Six States Account for More Than 70% of U.S. Fuel Ethanol Production," *Today in Energy*, U.S. Energy Information Administration, August 15, 2018; Scott Irwin, "Ethanol Prices Drive Corn Prices, Right?," *farmdocdaily*, October 9, 2013; "Cash Corn and Soybean Prices," Ag Decision Maker, Iowa State University Extension and Outreach, August 2019; "Prices Received: Corn Prices Received by Month—United States," National Agricultural Statistics Service, U.S. Department of Agriculture, 2019; "Feed Grains Data: Year Book Tables," Economic Research Service, U.S. Department of Agriculture, July 12, 2019; Alan Stern, Paul C. Doraiswamy, and E. Raymond Hunt, Jr., "Changes in Crop Rotation in Iowa," *Journal of Applied Remote Sensing* 6 (2012): 063590-1; "Conservation Reserve Program—Cumulative Enrollment by Fiscal Year," Farm Service Agency, U.S. Department of Agriculture; Silvia Secchi et al., "Land Use Change in a Biofuels Hotspot: The Case of Iowa, USA," *Biomass and Bioenergy* 35 (2011): 2391–2400; Christopher K. Wright and Michael C. Wimberly, "Recent Land Use Change in the Western Corn Belt Threatens Wetlands and Grasslands," *Proceedings of the National Academy of Sciences* 110 (2013): 4134–4139; Ryan Schuessler, "The Enormous Threat to America's Last Grasslands," *Washington Post*, June 16, 2016; and Tyler J. Lark, J. Meghan Salmon, and Holly K. Gibbs, "Cropland Expansion Outpaces Agricultural and Biofuel Policies in the United States," *Environmental Research Letters* 10 (2015): 044003.

Data on fertilizer use on corn can be found at "Fertilizer Use and Price, Table 10 — Nitrogen Used on Corn, Rate per Fertilized Acre Receiving Nitrogen, Selected States, 1964–2016" and "Fertilizer Use and Price, Table 12 — Phosphate Used on Corn, Rate per Fertilized Acre Receiving Phosphate, Selected States, 1964–2016," Economic Research Service, U.S. Department of Agriculture.

Information on nitrate as nitrogen is found in the Khan Academy video *The Nitrogen Cycle*, https://www.khanacademy.org/science/high-school-biology/hs-ecology/hs-biogeochemical-cycles/v/nitrogen-cycle; "Nitrogen in Waters: Forms and Concerns," Minnesota Pollution Control Agency, June 2013; Paul J. Jasa et al., "G96-1279 Drinking Water: Nitrate-Nitrogen (Revised November 1998)," Digital Commons@University of Nebraska-Lincoln, 1996; National Research Council, *Nitrate and Nitrite in Drinking Water* (Washington, D.C.: National Academies Press, 1995); Alexis Temkin et al., "Exposure-based Assessment and Economic Valuation of Adverse Birth Outcomes and Cancer Risk Due to Nitrate in United States Drinking Water," *Environmental Research* 176 (2019): 108442; and Kate Payne, "Study Estimates Thousands of Cancer Cases Are Linked to Nitrates in Drinking Water," Iowa Public Radio, June 14, 2019.

Sources of information on fertilizer infiltration in Iowa's waterways are numerous and include the following: J. L. Hatfield, L. D. McMullen, and C. S. Jones, "Nitrate-Nitrogen Patterns in the Raccoon River Basin Related to Agricultural Practices," *Journal of Soil and Water Conservation* 64 (2009): 190–199; Bill Stowe, executive director, Des Moines Water Works, "Feeding the World: Challenges for Water Quality and Quantity," address at the University of Iowa Public Policy Center Forkenbrock Lecture Series, April 9, 2015; "2013 Survey of Iowa Groundwater," Iowa Geological and Water Survey, Iowa Department of Natural Resources, May 2, 2015; Donald B. McDonald and Roger C. Splinter, "Long-Term Trends in Nitrate Concentration in Iowa Water Supplies," *Journal of the American Water Works Association* 74 (1982): 437–440; Donnelle Eller, "High Nitrate Levels Plague 60 Iowa Cities, Data Show," *Des Moines Register*, July 7, 2015; "Estimated Nitrate Concentrations in Groundwater Used for Drinking," U.S. Environmental Protection Agency; "Nitrate-Nitrogen in Iowa Rivers," Iowa Water Fact Sheet 2001-5, Geological Survey Bureau, Iowa Department of Natural Resources, 2001; "Dictionary of Water Terms," U.S. Geological Survey; Y.-K. Zhang and K. E. Schilling, "Effects of Land Cover on Water Table, Soil Moisture,

Evapotranspiration, and Ground Water Recharge: A Field Observation and Analysis," *Journal of Hydrology* 319 (2006): 328–338; Dana L. Dinnes et al., "Nitrogen Management Strategies to Reduce Nitrate Leaching in Tile-Drained Midwestern Soils," *Agronomy Journal* 94 (2002): 153–171; Richard G. Allen et al., "Crop Evapotranspiration: Guidelines for Computing Crop Water Requirements, FAO Irrigation and Drainage Paper 56," Food and Agricultural Organization of the United Nations, Rome, 1998; Keith E. Schilling, "Historical Perspectives on Water Quantity and Quality in Iowa," paper presented at Feeding the World: Challenges for Water Quality and Quantity, Iowa City, April 9, 2015; Y.-K. Zhang and K. E. Schilling, "Increasing Streamflow and Baseflow in Mississippi River since the 1940s: Effect of Land Use Change," *Journal of Hydrology* 324 (2006): 412–422; Keith E. Schilling, "Relation of Baseflow to Row Crop Intensity in Iowa," *Agriculture, Ecosystems and Environment* 105 (2005): 433–438; Keith E. Schilling and Robert D. Libra, "Increased Baseflow in Iowa over the Second Half of the 20th Century," *Journal of the American Water Resources Association* 39 (2003): 851–860; and Keith E. Schilling, Zhongwei Li, and You-Kuan Zhang, "Groundwater–Surface Water Interaction in the Riparian Zone of an Incised Channel, Walnut Creek, Iowa," *Journal of Hydrology* 327 (2006): 140–150.

## 3. Challenging Iowa Agriculture

The science and lead-up to the Des Moines Water Works lawsuit are covered in a number of sources, including K. F. Schilling and C. F. Wolter, *Water Quality Improvement Plan for Raccoon River, Iowa*, Water Improvement Section, Iowa Department of Natural Resources, 2008; J. L. Hatfield, L. D. McMullen, and C. S. Jones, "Nitrate-Nitrogen Patterns in the Raccoon River Basin Related to Agricultural Practices," *Journal of Soil and Water Conservation* 64 (2009): 190–199; "Fact Sheet," updated December 10, 2015, and "Historic Nitrate Levels in Des Moines Water Works' Source Water," May 13, 2013, Des Moines Water Works; *Nitrogen in Agricultural Systems: Implications for Conservation Policy*, Economic Research Service, U.S. Department of Agriculture, 2011; Timothy Meinch, "Water Works Requests Damages in Federal Suit," *Des Moines Register*, March 16, 2015; "Water Works: Nitrate Removal Has Cost $1.5 Million since December," *Des Moines Register*, July 27, 2015; and "Clean Water Act Litigation FAQ," *Des Moines Water Works Blog*, May 5, 2015.

The Des Moines Water Works lawsuit can be found at Board of Water Works Trustees of the City of Des Moines v. Sac County Board of Supervisors et al., 2015. Legal arguments enveloping the lawsuit are found in a number of sources: "Editorial: 14 Facts to Weigh in Water Works Lawsuit," *Des Moines Register*, April 14, 2015; J. B. Ruhl, "Farms, Their Environmental Harms, and Environmental Law," *Ecology Law Quarterly* 27 (2000): 263–350; National Research Council, *Mississippi River Water Quality and the Clean Water Act: Progress, Challenges, and Opportunities* (Washington, D.C.: National Academies Press, 2008); Donnelle Eller, "Iowans Support Water Lawsuit, but Split on Who Should Pay," *Des Moines Register*, February 27, 2016; Phyllis Coulter, "Illinois Drainage Group Sets Up Legal Defense Fund, Eyes Iowa Suit," *Illinois Farmer Today*, February 4, 2016; Jonathan Coppess, "Thinking about the Des Moines Water Works Lawsuit and the History of Drainage," *Policy Matters*, September 30, 2015; and Eldon L. McAfee, "Dismissed Des Moines Water Works Lawsuit Explained," *National Hog Farmer*, April 17, 2017. For a more recent legal effort to compel the Department of Natural Resources to take action in cleaning up the Raccoon River, see Iowa Citizens for Community Improvement and Food and Water Watch v. Iowa Department of Natural Resources, Petition for Injunctive and Declaratory Relief, filed in the Iowa District Court for Polk County, March 27, 2019.

The campaign against the Des Moines Water Works lawsuit is discussed in a variety of sources, including "Editorial: Ads Are Smear Campaign against Stowe," *Des Moines Register*, December 10, 2015; FarmersNotLawyers.com video *Iowa Partnership for Clean Water "War,"* https://vimeo.com/133076211, 2016; David Johnson, "Farm Bureau Chokes Iowans' Voices," *Des Moines Register*, March 13, 2016; Clay Masters, "Should Farmers or City Pay to Clean the Water? Iowa May Decide," *MPRNews*, May 18, 2016; Tom Cullen, "Ag Business Group Mum on Donors to Legal Defense Fund," *Storm Lake Times*, April 20, 2016, and "Heard at the Nineteenth Hole," *Storm Lake Times*, July 20, 2016; and William Petroski, "Branstad: 'Des Moines Has Declared War on Rural Iowa,'" *Des Moines Register*, January 13, 2015.

The relationship of chemical fertilizers to eutrophication and the Gulf of Mexico Dead Zone is reported in a variety of places: Richard B. Alexander et al., "Differences in Phosphorus and Nitrogen Delivery to the Gulf of Mexico from the Mississippi River Basin," *Environmental*

*Science and Technology* 42 (2008): 822–830; Keith E. Schilling and Robert D. Libra, "The Relationship of Nitrate Concentrations in Streams to Row Crop Land Use in Iowa," *Journal of Environmental Quality* 29 (2000): 1846–1851; "Nutrient Pollution: EPA Needs to Work with States to Develop Strategies for Monitoring the Impact of State Activities on the Gulf of Mexico Hypoxic Zone," Office of Inspector General, U.S. Environmental Protection Agency, September 3, 2014; Stuart Schmitz, "Harmful Algal Blooms: Status of Surveillance in Iowa," presentation to the Iowa Water Resources Coordinating Council, February 17, 2016; and Michael F. Chislock et al., "Eutrophication: Causes, Consequences, and Controls in Aquatic Ecosystems," *Nature Education Knowledge* 4 (2013): 10.

The varying size of the Gulf Dead Zone, as well as government efforts to reduce it, is discussed in "Gulf of Mexico 'Dead Zone' Is the Largest Ever Measured," National Oceanic and Atmospheric Administration, August 2, 2017, as well as the following Environmental Protection Agency publications: *Action Plan for Reducing, Mitigating, and Controlling Hypoxia in the Northern Gulf of Mexico*, Mississippi River/Gulf of Mexico Watershed Nutrient Task Force, January 2001; *Hypoxia in the Northern Gulf of Mexico: An Update by the EPA Science Advisory Board*, December 2007; *Gulf Hypoxia Action Plan 2008*, Mississippi River/Gulf of Mexico Watershed Nutrient Task Force, 2008; and *Mississippi River/ Gulf of Mexico Watershed Nutrient Task Force 2015 Report to Congress*, 2015. See also the following Louisiana Universities Marine Consortium works: *About Hypoxia*; "Summer 2018 'Dead Zone' in the Gulf of Mexico Is Smaller Than Average," July 31, 2018, and press release, August 1, 2019.

The state of Iowa's primary official response to the Gulf Dead Zone is the Iowa Nutrient Reduction Strategy, documented at Iowa Department of Agriculture and Land Stewardship, Iowa Department of Natural Resources, and Iowa State University College of Agriculture and Life Sciences, 2013, 2014, 2016, and 2017. To evaluate the success of nutrient reduction programs in Iowa, Illinois, and Indiana in promoting the use of cover crops, the Environmental Working Group has conducted two surveys of cover crop practice in Iowa. The most recent one is Soren Rundquist, "Cover Crops: Reducing Farm Runoff While Saving Soil," May 17, 2019.

A selection of news stories and opinions regarding Iowa's slow pace toward implementing its nutrient reduction strategy can be found at

David Osterberg and Aaron Kline, "A Threat Unmet: Why Iowa's Nutrient Strategy Falls Short against Water Pollution," Iowa Policy Project, July 2014; Tony Leys, "Branstad Vetoes Millions for REAP, Other Programs," *Des Moines Register*, May 31, 2014; Jason Noble and Brianne Pfannenstiel, "'Biggest and Boldest' Water Quality Plan Gets Mixed Reception," *Des Moines Register*, January 5, 2016; William Petroski and Brianne Pfannenstiel, "Who Won? Who Lost? Iowa Legislature Heads Home," *Des Moines Register*, April 29, 2016; "IA-Gov: Sales Tax Hike for Conservation May Become Fault Line in 2018," *Bleeding Heartland*, September 15, 2016; James Q. Lynch, "Iowa Water Quality Legislation Headed to Gov. Reynolds," *Cedar Rapids Gazette*, January 23, 2018; "A Flawed Water Quality Bill Falls Far Short," *Cedar Rapids Gazette*, January 26, 2018; Brianne Pfannenstiel, "After Years-Long Debate, Water Quality Legislation Is Headed to the Governor," *Des Moines Register*, January 24, 2018; and Art Cullen, "Throwing Money Around," *Storm Lake Times*, January 26, 2018.

Regarding climate change and the contributions of various greenhouse gases, each year the Iowa Department of Natural Resources reports the amount of greenhouse gases produced by various activities in Iowa. These estimates can be found at *2017 Iowa Statewide Greenhouse Gas Emissions Inventory Report*, Iowa Department of Natural Resources, December 27, 2018. In 2008 and 2010, state-appointed panels completed two important studies of climate change in Iowa. One focused on Iowa's generation of greenhouse gases and the policies required to reduce them: *Final Report*, Iowa Climate Change Advisory Council, December 23, 2008. The other examined the effects of climate change on Iowa: *Climate Change Impacts on Iowa, 2010*, Iowa Climate Change Impacts Committee, January 1, 2011. As noted, these studies have not been followed up with comparable reports that update both information on climate change and policies that Iowa should consider in responding to climate change.

Other sources consulted on climate change and agriculture, especially in Iowa, are Cornelia F. Mutel, *A Sugar Creek Chronicle: Observing Climate Change from a Midwestern Woodland* (Iowa City: University of Iowa Press, 2016); Eric A. Davidson, "The Contribution of Manure and Fertilizer Nitrogen to Atmospheric Nitrous Oxide since 1860," *Nature Geoscience* 2 (2009): 659–662; Eric A. Davidson et al., "Excess Nitrogen in the U.S. Environment: Trends, Risks, and Solutions," *Issues in*

*Ecology*, report number 15 (Winter 2012); and the following from the U.S. Environmental Protection Agency: Nitrous Oxide Emissions and Methane Emissions websites and *Inventory of U.S. Greenhouse Gas Emissions and Sinks: 1990–2017*, April 11, 2019.

Resources available on carbon sequestration in soils include National Academies of Sciences, Engineering, and Medicine, *Negative Emissions Technologies and Reliable Sequestration: A Research Agenda* (Washington, D.C.: National Academies Press, 2019); K. Paustian et al., "Agricultural Soils as a Sink to Mitigate $CO_2$ Emissions," *Soil Use and Management* 13 (1997): 230–244; Zhen Yu et al., "Long-Term Terrestrial Carbon Dynamics in the Midwestern United States during 1850–2015: Roles of Land Use and Cover Change and Agricultural Management," *Global Change Biology* 24 (2018): 2673–2690; "4 per 1000" initiative website; Ronald Amundson and Léopold Biardeau, "Opinion: Soil Carbon Sequestration Is an Elusive Climate Mitigation Tool," *PNAS*, November 13, 2018; James Temple, "Carbon Farming Is the Hot (and Overhyped) Tool to Fight Climate Change," *MIT Technology Review*, June 21, 2019; and Ryan Schuessler, "The Enormous Threat to America's Last Grasslands," *Washington Post*, June 16, 2016.

Reports on agricultural residue as energy feedstock are examined in *Final Report*, Iowa Climate Change Advisory Council, December 23, 2008, but are more skeptically viewed a decade later in Lee R. Lynd, "The Grand Challenge of Cellulosic Biofuels," *Nature Biotechnology* 35 (2017): 912–915.

Iowa's energy profile, including its leadership in the employment of wind energy, is summarized at the U.S. Energy Information Administration's Iowa State Profile and Energy Estimates website. For additional information on the potential for various renewable energy sources, see Anthony Lopez et al., "U.S. Renewable Energy Technical Potentials: A GIS-Based Analysis," National Renewable Energy Laboratory, July 2012.

There are several significant sources of information on the likely extent and effects of climate change, especially in the Midwest. These include *Fourth National Climate Assessment*, vol. 1: *Climate Science Special Report*, and vol. 2: *Impacts, Risks, and Adaptation in the United States* (Washington, D.C.: U.S. Global Change Research Program, 2017, 2018). Of particular relevance to Iowa in volume 2 is chapter 21, covering the Midwest, by Jim Angel et al. Information on likely consequences for

Iowa is reported in R. Frankson et al., "Iowa State Climate Summary," *NOAA Technical Report NESDIS 149-IA*, 2017, as well as the annual climate statements issued since 2011 by climate experts at Iowa colleges and universities — see Gene Takle et al., "Iowa Climate Statement 2019: Dangerous Heat Events Will Be More Frequent and Severe," https://iowaenvironmentalfocus.org/iowa-climate-statement/, 2019. For a summary of the impact of 2019 rainfall on farming, including the quote from Iowa farmer Aaron Heley Lehman, see John Schwartz, "A Wet Year Causes Farm Woes Far Beyond the Floodplains," *New York Times*, November 21, 2019. For information on Iowa counties designated for assistance, see "Iowa Severe Storms and Flooding (DR-4421)," Federal Emergency Management Agency, 2019.

For a more fully global perspective on climate change, consult Robert Henson, *The Thinking Person's Guide to Climate Change*, 2nd ed. (Boston: American Meteorological Society, 2019), and beyond that the various reports of the Intergovernmental Panel on Climate Change, which is the United Nations body for evaluating the science related to climate change. Of special importance to Iowa is the IPCC's 2019 report *Climate Change and Land*.

Research on Iowa and midwestern flooding and heat events attributable to climate change is reported in Iman Mallakpour and Gabriele Villarini, "The Changing Nature of Flooding across the Central United States," *Nature Climate Change* 5 (2015): 250–254, and Harry J. Hillaker, "The Drought of 2012 in Iowa," https://www.iowaagriculture.gov/climatology/weatherSummaries/2012/DroughtIowa2012Revised.pdf, n.d. The connection between increased flooding related to climate change and the Gulf Dead Zone is explored in Nancy N. Rabalais et al., "Global Change and Eutrophication of Coastal Waters," *ICES Journal of Marine Science* 66 (2009): 1528–1537. The consequences of increased flooding for toxins in the water are examined in Dana Kolpin and Keri Hornbuckle, "What's in Your Floodwaters?," in Cornelia F. Mutel, ed., *A Watershed Year: Anatomy of the Iowa Floods of 2008* (Iowa City: University of Iowa Press, 2010).

## 4. Why Is Iowa So White?

Data on how Iowa's whiteness compares to other states can be most conveniently found in *Governing* magazine's "State Population by Race, Ethnicity Data." For current and recent data on Iowa's nonwhite population groups—African Americans, Hispanic Americans, Native Americans, and Asian Americans—consult the various reports for these groups issued by the State Data Center of Iowa. A very useful guide to population data for each of these groups from 1790 to 1990 for each state is found at Campbell Gibson and Kay Jung, "Historical Census Statistics on Population Totals by Race, 1790 to 1990, and by Hispanic Origin, 1970 to 1990, for the United States, Regions, Divisions, and States," Population Division, U.S. Census Bureau, 2002.

Key resources for the history of Native Americans in Iowa include Martha Royce Blaine, *The Ioway Indians* (Norman: University of Oklahoma Press, 1995); Thomas F. Schilz and Jodye L. D. Schilz, "Beads, Bangles, and Buffalo Robes: The Rise and Fall of the Indian Fur Trade along the Missouri and Des Moines Rivers, 1700–1820," *Annals of Iowa* 49 (1987): 5–25; Lance M. Foster, *The Indians of Iowa* (Iowa City: University of Iowa Press, 2009); Michael D. Green, "'We Dance in Opposite Directions': Mesquakie (Fox) Separatism from the Sac and Fox Tribe," *Ethnohistory* 30 (1983): 129–140; William T. Hagan, *The Sac and Fox Indians* (Norman: University of Oklahoma Press, 1958); and Eric Steven Zimmer, "Red Earth Nation: Environment and Sovereignty in Modern Meskwaki History," Ph.D. dissertation, University of Iowa, 2016. Zimmer's dissertation covers the entire history of the Meskwaki in Iowa, including their return to the Tama area after being forced to relocate to Kansas. He focuses primarily on the relationship between the Meskwaki and the environment with an eye to how the Meskwaki developed and maintained sovereignty over their land.

The story of the Meskwaki and the Sauk in Illinois and Iowa where the Rock River joins the Mississippi, as well as in the Dubuque area, is told well by Kerry A. Trask in *Black Hawk: The Battle for the Heart of America* (New York: Henry Holt, 2006). Trask describes the Sauk and Meskwaki communities and the disastrous treaties that were put upon them, followed by Black Hawk's attempt to return to Illinois from Iowa and the ill-fated war that ensued. The subtitle *Battle for the Heart of America* describes the importance of the struggle between the Sauk and the U.S. government for control of the Midwest, including the Sauk villages in Illinois and in all of Iowa as well. Another recent history of Black Hawk—Patrick J. Jung's *The Black Hawk War of 1832* (Norman: University of Oklahoma Press, 2007)—focuses on the military history of the war as well as the failure of Black Hawk's belief that other Indians as well as the British would join him in fighting the white settlers.

In this chapter, I relied on several key works about African Americans in nineteenth-century Iowa: Robert R. Dykstra, *Bright Radical Star: Black Freedom and White Supremacy on the Hawkeye Frontier* (Cambridge, Mass.: Harvard University Press, 1993); Leslie A. Schwalm, *Emancipation's Diaspora: Race and Reconstruction in the Upper Midwest* (Chapel Hill: University of North Carolina Press, 2009); and Leola Nelson Bergmann, *The Negro in Iowa* (Iowa City: State Historical Society of Iowa, 1969). Dykstra's book describes Iowa's civil rights contradictions—the black codes of the antebellum period and the voting rights act of 1868 inspired by Ulysses Grant's description of Iowa as "the bright Radical star." It includes the quote from Dubuque's Ed Langworthy about African Americans moving from the slave state of Missouri to Iowa. Schwalm's book tells the story of emancipation for African Americans escaping to Iowa, Minnesota, and Wisconsin during the Civil War and the lives they built in the period of Reconstruction. Her book broadens our understanding of Reconstruction to include the Midwest as well as the South. Alexander Clark's contributions to the early desegregation of schools in Iowa are reported in Iowa Public Television's 2012 documentary *Alexander Clark and the First Successful Desegregation Case in the United States*. The film includes testimony from legal scholar Paul Finkelman regarding the case's pioneering legacy to civil rights history.

Bergmann's slim volume on African Americans in Iowa helps tell their story after Reconstruction until World War II, including the shift in the black population away from smaller communities to the state's urban centers. Her book can be read alongside James W. Loewen's *Sundown Towns: A Hidden Dimension of American Racism* (New York: New Press, 2005), although as noted it is not clear that Loewen's thesis applies to Iowa as much as it apparently does to Illinois.

The story of African Americans in one small Iowa community, Newton, is told in Dwain Conrad Coleman's master's thesis, "Still in the Fight: The Struggle for Community in the Upper Midwest for African American Civil War Veterans," Iowa State University, 2016. As noted in the text, it is still not clear why the African American population in Newton declined in the early decades of the twentieth century.

Rural African Americans also thrived, for a short while, in the coal-mining town of Buxton, whose story is told in Dorothy Schwieder, Joseph Hraba, and Elmer Schwieder, *Buxton: A Black Utopia in the Heartland* (Iowa City: University of Iowa Press, 2003), and in Richard M. Breaux, "'We Were All Mixed Together': Race, Schooling, and the Legacy of Black Teachers in Buxton, 1900–1920," *Annals of Iowa* 65 (2006): 301–328.

The story of the settlement of African Americans in early twentieth-century Waterloo is told in Robert Neymeyer, "May Harmony Prevail: The Early History of Black Waterloo," *Palimpsest* 61 (1980): 80–91.

After World War II, the era of Iowa's civil rights movement is told in a variety of works documenting racial discrimination in Iowa cities. These include League for Social Justice, *Citizen 2nd Class: Negro Segregation and Discrimination in Davenport* (Davenport, Iowa: Greyhound Press, 1951); George William McDaniel, "Catholic Action in Davenport: St. Ambrose College and the League for Social Justice," *Annals of Iowa* 55 (1996): 239–272; Katrina M. Sanders, "The Burlington Self-Survey in Human Relations: Interracial Efforts for Constructive Community Change, 1949–1951," *Annals of Iowa* 60 (2001): 244–269; Louis Bultena and Harold Reasby, "Negro-White Relations in the Waterloo Metropolitan Area," unpublished paper, 1955, Iowa State Teachers College, United Packinghouse Workers of America Papers, State Historical Society of Wisconsin, Mss. 118, Box 347, Folder 13, Negro-White Relations, 2–5; Robert Benjamin Stone, "The Legislative Struggle for Civil Rights in Iowa: 1947–1965," master's thesis, Iowa State University, 1990; Robert E. Goostree, "The Iowa Civil Rights Statute: A Problem of Enforcement," *Iowa Law Review* 37 (1951): 242–248; Noah Lawrence, "Since It Is My Right, I Would Like to Have It: Edna Griffin and the Katz Drug Store Desegregation Movement," *Annals of Iowa* 67 (2008): 298–330; and Bruce Fehn, "'The Only Hope We Had': United Packinghouse Workers Local 46 and the Struggle for Racial Equality in Waterloo, Iowa, 1948–1960," *Annals of Iowa* 54 (1995): 185–216. Also see the interview with Ralph Helstein in Shelton Stromquist, *Solidarity and Survival: An Oral History of Iowa Labor in the Twentieth Century* (Iowa City: University of Iowa Press, 1993).

The consequences of urban renewal and interstate highway construction for the African American Center Street neighborhood in Des Moines and the brief experience of the Black Panthers in that city are told in Bill Silag, Susan Koch-Bridgford, and Hal Chase, eds., *Outside

*In: African-American History in Iowa, 1838–2000* (Iowa City: State Historical Society of Iowa, 2001); *Negro Business and Information Directory*,
Negro Chamber of Commerce, Des Moines, 1940, available at University of Iowa Libraries Digital Library (this documents the number and
variety of businesses in the Center Street area prior to urban renewal
and the interstate highway); Gaynelle Narcisse, *They Took Our Piece
of the Pie!: Center Street Revisited* (Des Moines: Iowa Bystander Co.,
1996); and Bruce Fehn and Robert Jefferson, "North Side Revolutionar-
ies in the Civil Rights Struggle: The African American Community in
Des Moines and the Black Panther Party for Self-Defense, 1948–1970,"
*Annals of Iowa* 69 (2010): 51–81, which includes the quote from Hobart
DePatten about urban renewal's impact on Center Street.

The immigration of African Americans from Chicago into other
parts of the Midwest, including Iowa, is profiled and evaluated in
Alden Loury, "Chicago's Story of Population Loss Is Becoming an Exclusive about Black Population Loss," *Metropolitan Planning Council
News*, May 30, 2017; Danya E. Keene, Mark B. Padilla, and Arline T.
Geronimus, "Leaving Chicago for Iowa's 'Fields of Opportunity': Com-
munity Dispossession, Rootlessness, and the Quest for Somewhere to
'Be OK,'" *Human Organization* 69 (2010): 275–284; and Mikel Livings-
ton and Steven Porter, "The Truth about the Great Chicago Migration
Myth," *Lafayette Journal and Courier*, October 18 and 20, 2014. Chica-
go's role as the Promised Land for African Americans immigrating
into the Midwest is described in Nicholas Lemann's *The Promised
Land: The Great Black Migration and How It Changed America* (New
York: Alfred A. Knopf, 1991).

Reports on racial conditions and inequities in Iowa City, Des Moines,
and the state of Iowa, with primary reference to the criminal justice
system, are found in "Racial Equity in Iowa City and Johnson County,"
Coalition for Racial Justice, July 23, 2013; "Johnson County Select Juvenile Justice System Planning Data, 2016," Iowa Department of Human
Rights, June 2017; "Recommendations and Action Plan for Reducing
Disproportionate Minority Contacts in Iowa's Juvenile Justice System," Community and Strategic Planning Project Advisory Committee, November 2014; *State-by-State Data*, the Sentencing Project, 2018;
Charly Haley, "Iowa Near Top for Jailing Blacks," *Des Moines Register*,
June 16, 2016; *The War on Marijuana in Black and White: Billions of Dollars Wasted on Racially Biased Arrests*, American Civil Liberties Union,

June 2013; Kathy A. Bolten, "Blacks Hit Hard by Iowa's Mandatory Sentences," *Des Moines Register*, April 4, 2016; Sarah Fineran, "2017 Public Safety Advisory Board Annual Report," December 1, 2017; *Every 25 Seconds: The Human Toll of Criminalizing Drug Use in the United States*, Human Rights Watch, American Civil Liberties Union, October 2016; and Jason Clayworth, "Iowa Could Soon Be Alone in the Nation with Felon Voting Ban—and Become a Bigger Target for Ban's Opponents," *Des Moines Register*, November 26, 2019.

Iowa's disproportionate rates of juvenile detention and issues with the school-to-prison pipeline are reported in Mackenzie Ryan, "Schools Rethink Discipline," *Des Moines Register*, November 27, 2016; *Revealing New Truths about Our Nation's Schools*, Office for Civil Rights, U.S. Department of Education, March 2012; and Daniel Losen et al., "Are We Closing the School Discipline Gap?," UCLA Civil Rights Project, February 23, 2015, table 7.

Racial differences in Polk County are thoroughly reported in *One Economy, Building Opportunity for All: The State of Black Polk County*, Directors Council, Des Moines, April 2017. Colin Gordon's "Race in the Heartland: Equity, Opportunity, and Public Policy in the Midwest," Iowa Policy Project, October 2019, includes statewide comparisons of blacks and whites that show a variety of consistently poor outcomes for blacks in Iowa relative to other states. The Nadine Petty quote appeared in Wylliam Smith, "Smith: The Reality of Being Black in Iowa," *Daily Iowan*, May 2, 2018.

Research on the Hispanic American experience in Iowa as well as in the Midwest is found in the following works: Omar Valerio-Jiménez, "Racializing Mexican Immigrants in Iowa's Early Mexican Communities," *Annals of Iowa* 75 (2016): 1–46; Migration Is Beautiful website, Iowa Women's Archives, University of Iowa Libraries, 2016; Faranak Miraftab, *Global Heartland: Displaced Labor, Transnational Lives, and Local Placemaking* (Bloomington: Indiana University Press, 2016); Jorge Durand, Douglas S. Massey, and Emilio A. Parrado, "The New Era of Mexican Migration to the United States," *Journal of American History* 86 (1999): 518–536; Marta María Maldonado, "Not Just Laborers: Latina/o Claims of Belonging in the U.S. Heartland," in Omar Valerio- Jiménez, Santiago Vaquera-Vásquez, and Claire F. Fox, eds., *The Latina/o Midwest Reader* (Urbana: University of Illinois Press, 2017), which includes the quote from the Perry Hispanic American; and Marta María Maldonado,

"Latino Incorporation and Racialized Border Politics in the Heartland: Interior Enforcement and Policeability in an English-Only State," *American Behavioral Scientist* 58 (2014): 1927–1945. Outcomes for Hispanic Americans in Iowa can be found in *Race for Results: 2017 Policy Report*, Annie E. Casey Foundation.

The major immigration raids in Marshalltown, Postville, and Mt. Pleasant are reported in the following publications: Jan L. Flora, Claudia M. Prado-Meza, and Hannah Lewis, "After the Raid Is Over: Marshalltown, Iowa and the Consequences of Worksite Enforcement Raids," American Immigration Council, January 25, 2011; Cassie L. Peterson, "An Iowa Immigration Raid Leads to Unprecedented Criminal Consequences: Why ICE Should Rethink the Postville Model," *Iowa Law Review* 95 (2009): 323–346; Mark A. Grey, Michele Devlin, and Aaron Goldsmith, *Postville, U.S.A.: Surviving Diversity in Small-Town America* (Boston: Gemma, 2009); Cindy Juby and Laura E. Kaplan, "Postville: The Effects of an Immigration Raid," *Families in Society: The Journal of Contemporary Social Services* 92 (2011): 147–153; Alison Gowans, "Iowa's Hometown to the World: Postville Immigration Raid Leaves Lingering Fears, New Hopes," *Cedar Rapids Gazette*, March 26, 2017; Nicole L. Novak, Arline T. Geronimus, and Aresha M. Martinez-Cardoso, "Change in Birth Outcomes among Infants Born to Latina Mothers after a Major Immigration Raid," *International Journal of Epidemiology* 46 (2017): 839–849; Kristen Bialik, "ICE Arrests Went Up in 2017, with Biggest Increases in Florida, Northern Texas, Oklahoma," *FACT TANK*, Pew Research Center, February 8, 2018; Alan Gomez, "ICE Arresting More Non-Criminal Undocumented Immigrants," *USA Today*, May 17, 2018; and Trip Gabriel, "An ICE Raid Leaves an Iowa Town Divided along Faith Lines," *New York Times*, July 3, 2018.

The Trump coalition in Iowa and the politics of immigration in a state dependent on immigrant labor are discussed in Harry Enten and Perry Bacon, Jr., "Trump's Hardline Immigration Stance Got Him to the White House," *FiveThirtyEight*, September 12, 2017; Jennifer Jacobs, "Iowa Poll: Nearly Half Want to Round Up Immigrants," *Des Moines Register*, September 2, 2015; Natasha Korecki and Quint Forgey, "Trump's New Rallying Cry: Mollie Tibbetts," *Politico*, August 22, 2018; Office of the Governor of Iowa, "Gov. Reynolds Issues Statement on Mollie Tibbetts," August 21, 2018; and Donnelle Eller and Kevin Hardy, "Mollie Tibbetts' Death Put a Spotlight on Undocumented Immigrants:

But Can Iowa's Economy Thrive without Them?," *Des Moines Register*, August 24, 2018. The interview with dairy farmer Darin Dykstra is in the online edition of this article.

The more recent history of Asian Americans, particularly refugees, in Iowa is told in part in Matthew R. Walsh, *The Good Governor: Robert Ray and the Indochinese Refugees of Iowa* (Jefferson, N.C.: McFarland, 2017); Sanjita Pradhan, "State of Asian Americans and Pacific Islanders in Iowa, 2015," Office of Asian and Pacific Islander Affairs, Iowa Department of Human Rights, September 2015; Natalie Krebs, "Refugees Help Bridge Healthcare Gap in Their Communities," Iowa Public Radio, October 24, 2019; Lee Rood, "Burma to Iowa," *Des Moines Register*, five-part series, June 7–15, 2015; and Clare McCarthy, "Response to Refugees in Iowa Has Changed in 40 Years," *IowaWatch.org*, August 5, 2015. Finally, Trump administration efforts to reduce the number of refugees are reported in David Nakamura, Maria Sacchetti, and Seung Min Kim, "Trump Administration Slashes Refugee Limit for the Third Consecutive Year to a Historic Low of 18,000," *Washington Post*, September 26, 2019.

### 5. The Best State in America?

The *U.S. News and World Report* story "Iowa Is the Best State in the US, Says 2018 Best States Report" appeared on February 27, 2018. The actual searchable rankings can be located at an archived link: https://web .archive.org/web/20180228223328/https://www.usnews.com/new/best -states/rankings.

Three recent research articles by University of Iowa scientists on Iowa's contribution to the Gulf Dead Zone can be found at Christopher S. Jones et al., "Iowa Stream Nitrate and the Gulf of Mexico," *PLoS ONE* 13 (2018): e0195930; Christopher S. Jones and Keith E. Schilling, "Iowa Statewide Stream Nitrate Loading: 2017–2018 Update," *Journal of the Iowa Academy of Science* 126 (2019): 6–12; and Christopher S. Jones et al., "Livestock Manure Driving Stream Nitrate," *Ambio* 48 (2019): 1143–1153.

For a review of recent flooding in Iowa, see A. Arenas Amado et al., "Three Decades of Floods in Iowa," IIHR — Hydroscience and Engineering, University of Iowa, 2018, as well as "Disaster Declarations for States and Counties," Federal Emergency Management Agency, 2018. Iowa's ranking as a top state for flooding in recent years is reported in Rob Moore, "Trump Announced a $12 Billion Resilience Competition??,"

Natural Resources Defense Council, November 21, 2017. For one of the few examples of recent statewide climate change planning, see "Iowa's Bridge and Highway Climate Change and Extreme Weather Vulnerability Assessment Pilot," Iowa State University Institute for Transportation, March 2015.

For a recent assessment of how Iowa income growth compares to other states, see Tim Henderson, "In Most States, the Middle Class Is Now Growing — but Slowly," *Stateline*, Pew Charitable Trusts, April 12, 2018. Data on public support for higher education in Iowa can be found at Brandon Borkovec, "Tuition Rising — Is Anyone Surprised?," *Iowa Policy Points*, April 3, 2018, Iowa Policy Project. Information on state minimum wage levels can be found at "State Minimum Wages: 2018 Minimum Wage by State," National Conference of State Legislatures, July 1, 2018. For information on the twenty-one states raising their minimum wages by January 1, 2020, see Yannet Lathrop, "Raises from Coast to Coast in 2020," National Employment Law Project, December 23, 2019.

For how Des Moines became a more attractive place to live and work, see Colin Woodard, "How America's Dullest City Got Cool," *Politico*, January 21, 2016.

Aldo Leopold's classic essay "The Land Ethic" is found in his *A Sand County Almanac*, 2nd ed. (New York: Oxford University Press, 1968).

For recent reports on Iowa's water-quality funding, see "Water Quality Initiative," Budget Unit Brief — FY 2019, Legislative Services Agency, November 15, 2018; David Osterberg and Natalie Veldhouse, "Lip Service: Iowa's Inadequate Commitment to Clean Water," Iowa Policy Project, April 2019; *Iowa Nutrient Reduction Strategy Annual Progress Report*, Iowa Department of Agriculture and Land Stewardship, Iowa Department of Natural Resources, and Iowa State University College of Agriculture and Life Sciences, March 2019; and "Iowa Water Quality Initiative: 2018 Legislative Report," Iowa Department of Agriculture and Land Stewardship, 2018.

For ideas on how to pay for improved water quality, see David Osterberg, Peter Fisher, and Natalie Veldhouse, "Choosing the Right Stream: How Iowa Can Keep Clean Water Priorities and Funding Equity Together," Iowa Policy Project, July 2019.

The most recent U.S. Environmental Protection Agency report to Congress on the Gulf Dead Zone is *Mississippi River/Gulf of Mexico Water-*

*shed Nutrient Task Force 2017 Report to Congress*, 2017. The Chesapeake Bay experience with numeric standards is described in Jamison E. Colburn, "Coercing Collaboration: The Chesapeake Bay Experience," *William and Mary Environmental Law and Policy Review* 40 (2016): 677–743, and the executive summary portion of *Chesapeake Bay Total Maximum Daily Load for Nitrogen, Phosphorus, and Sediment*, U.S. Environmental Protection Agency, December 29, 2010.

For a review of food systems and climate change, see Marco Springmann et al., "Options for Keeping the Food System within Environmental Limits," *Nature* 562 (2018): 519–525. For information on Iowa's sluggish population growth in the twentieth century, see John Besl, "A Short Retrospective on 20th Century U.S. Population Change," *Indiana Business Review* (Spring 2001): 11–12, and Frank Hobbs and Nicole Stoops, *Demographic Trends in the 20th Century*, U.S. Census Bureau, 2002.

Finally, Iowa's dismal record of providing opportunity for African Americans is documented in Colin Gordon's "Race in the Heartland: Equity, Opportunity, and Public Policy in the Midwest," Iowa Policy Project, October 2019.

Warren, Wilson, 4

Washington, 29

water quality: in Board of Water
Works Trustees of the City
of Des Moines v. Sac County
Board of Supervisors et al.,
64–68, 76–77, 148; Clean Water
Act and, 49, 52, 65–67, 148;
drainage and, 64–68, 70, 73–74,
145; drinking water, 59, 63–68,
134; Gulf of Mexico, 61, 63, 65,
68–73, 76, 84, 134–135, 139, 143–
145, 148–149; Iowa Nutrient
Reduction Strategy for, 72–77,
79, 145–146, 148–149; nitrate
influencing, 45, 48–49, 57–61,
63–68, 70, 72–77, 80, 134; phosphorus influencing, 57–58,
61, 68, 70–72, 74, 77, 80, 148;
Republican Party and, 67,
75–77; sedimentation and, 54;
sustainability and, 143–151

Waterloo: African American
population of, 89, 107, 109–110,
112–114, 153; farm implement
manufacturing in, 15, 17, 21–23,
44; meatpacking in, 6–8, 10–11,
122, 130; population loss, 29

Webb, Archie, 102

Webster City, 89, 142

West Burlington, 31

West Liberty, 30, 152–153

wetlands, 40–42, 73, 88

wheat, 5, 38, 43

Whig Party, 96, 98–99, 101

white Iowans: diversity and, 89–
90, 131–132, 151; Native Americans and, 91, 94–97, 106, 115,
131; settlers, 1, 5, 35–44, 91, 94–
96

white supremacy, 98–101, 106

Whiterock Conservancy, 87–88

Wilson, Thomas, 104

wind energy, 81, 86–87, 136

Winnebago, 91–92

Wisconsin, 98, 107, 111, 116

Woodbury County, 90–91

World War II: civil rights after,
111–120

Worth County, 51

Yankton Sioux, 91

*The Biographical
Dictionary of Iowa*
edited by David Hudson,
Marvin Bergman, and
Loren Horton

*A Bountiful Harvest:
The Midwestern Farm
Photographs of Pete Wettach,
1925–1965*
by Leslie A. Loveless

*Buxton: A Black Utopia
in the Heartland*
by Dorothy Schwieder, Joseph,
Hraba, and Elmer Schwieder

*A Country So Full of Game:
The Story of Wildlife in Iowa*
by James J. Dinsmore

*Ecological Restoration
in the Midwest: Past, Present,
and Future*
edited by Christian Lenhart and
Peter C. Smiley, Jr.

*The Ecology and Management
of Prairies in the Central
United States*
by Chris Helzer

*The Emerald Horizon:
The History of Nature in Iowa*
by Cornelia F. Mutel

*Enchanted by Prairie*
photographs by Bill Witt,
essay by Osha Gray Davidson

*Exploring Buried Buxton:
Archaeology of an Abandoned
Iowa Coal Mining Town with a
Large Black Population*
by David Gradwohl
and Nancy M. Osborn

*Fragile Giants: A Natural
History of the Loess Hills*
by Cornelia F. Mutel

*Frontier Forts of Iowa: Indians,
Traders, and Soldiers, 1682–1862*
edited by William E. Whittaker

*Grand Excursions on the
Upper Mississippi River:
Places, Landscapes, and
Regional Identity after 1854*
edited by Curtis C. Roseman
and Elizabeth M. Roseman

*An Illustrated Guide to Iowa
Prairie Plants*
by Paul Christiansen
and Mark Müller

*The Indians of Iowa*
by Lance M. Foster

*An Iowa Album:*
*A Photographic History,*
*1860–1920*
By Mary Bennett

*Iowa Railroads: The Essays*
*of Frank P. Donovan, Jr.*
edited by H. Roger Grant

*Iowa's Archaeological Past*
by Lynn M. Alex

*Iowa's Geological Past:*
*Three Billion Years of Change*
by Wayne I. Anderson

*Landforms of Iowa*
by Jean C. Prior

*Nothing to Do but Stay:*
*My Pioneer Mother*
By Carrie Young

*Of Men and Marshes*
by Paul L. Errington

*Of Wilderness and Wolves*
by Paul L. Errington

*Okoboji Wetlands:*
*A Lesson in Natural History*
by Michael J. Lannoo

*Out Home*
by John Madson

*A Practical Guide to*
*Prairie Reconstruction*
by Carl Kurtz

*Stories from under the Sky*
by John Madson

*A Sugar Creek Chronicle:*
*Observing Climate Change*
*from a Midwestern Woodland*
by Cornelia F. Mutel

*Sunday Afternoon on the Porch:*
*Reflections of a Small Town in*
*Iowa, 1939–1942*
photographs by Everett W. Kuntz,
text by Jim Heynen

*The Tallgrass Prairie Reader*
edited by John T. Price

*Twelve Millennia: Archaeology of*
*the Upper Mississippi River Valley*
by James Theler and Robert
Boszhardt

*Up on the River: People and*
*Wildlife of the Upper Mississippi*
by John Madson

*A Watershed Year: Anatomy of*
*the Iowa Floods of 2008*
edited by Cornelia Mutel

*Where the Sky Began:*
*Land of the Tallgrass Prairie*
by John Madson